Proceedings
Conference on Training Clinical Child Psychologists

Meeting at the Holiday Inn
Hilton Head Island, South Carolina

May 15-18, 1985

June M. Tuma
Editor

Routledge
Taylor & Francis Group
NEW YORK AND LONDON

First Published by
Lawrence Erlbaum Associates, Inc., Publishers
10 Industrial Avenue
Mahwah, New Jersey 07430

Transferred to Digital Printing 2009 by Routledge
270 Madison Avenue, New York, NY 10016
27 Church Road, Hove, East Sussex BN3 2FA

Conference
Supported by a grant from the
Section on Clinical Child Psychology

and

Planning Meetings
Supported by a grant from the
Ester Katz Rosen Fund of the American Psychological Foundation
and the
Section on Clinical Child Psychology

Orders should be placed with the editor
Department of Psychology, Louisiana State University
Baton Rouge, Louisiana 70803

Publisher's Note
The publisher has gone to great lengths to ensure the quality of this reprint but points out that some imperfections in the original may be apparent.

Preface

The Conference on the Training of Clinical Child Psychologists was held at Hilton Head Island, South Carolina, from May 15 to May 18, 1985. It was made possible by a grant from the Section on Clinical Child Psychology (Section 1, Division 12) with some supporting funds from The Society of Pediatric Psychology (Section 5, Division 12).

Forty-nine people participated in the conference. In addition, there were a number of other psychologists, who from 1977, have had input into the planning of the conference and who supported the plans for holding such a conference. The Participants are listed in Appendix A and their demographical characteristics are presented in Appendix B.

As will be noted in the pages to follow, a number of individuals served on the original conference planning committee (Alan Barclay, co-chair, Theodore Blau, Alan O. Ross, June M. Tuma, co-chair, and Diane Willis). This committee was ably assisted by Jan Woodring and Gary VanderBos of the American Psychological Association to map out the formal structure of the conference and also to submit a funding proposal to the National Institute of Mental Health. The APA staff were also instrumental in securing funding from the Ester Katz Rosen Fund of the American Psychological Foundation for planning meetings.

The second training committee of the Section on Clinical Child Psychology (Jean Elbert, James H. Johnson, Annette LaGreca, Thomas Ollendick, Carolyn Schroeder, and June Tuma, chair) was formed by action of the president-elect (Diane Willis) in 1982. Although the original charge to that committee (to formulate training guidelines for clinical child psychologists) had nothing to do with a conference, this committee reaffirmed the need for a conference and persuaded the executive committee of the Section to fund the conference in conjunction with participant-funding for personal and travel expenses.

The training committee played a key role in the planning of the Hilton Head Conference. Thus, the training committee became the Conference Committee; James Johnson secured the site, Jean Elbert obtained travel information for the participants and all members of the committee established dialogues with persons presenting position papers. In addition, these people chaired the various plenary sessions.

It must be noted here that almost half of the conference participants had an official role in the conference. Because funds were not available to bring in support personnel (including observers and non-participant recorders), the participants were assigned service as discussion leaders and reporters for the small group sessions. Their sense of dedication and cooperation made the conference move smoothly. They are listed in Appendix C.

Thanks are due the Conference Planning Committee for reviewing the draft of the Conference Proceedings and for their help with the editing of manuscripts.

June M. Tuma
Conference Coordinator

Prologue

The Conference on the Training of Clinical Child Psychologists met at Hilton Head Island, South Carolina, from May 15 through May 18, 1985. The conference hoped to identify, examine, and assess the major influences, directions, goals, and actions of consequence to clinical child psychology and to clinical child psychologists. The 49 conferees represented a broad spectrum of background, experience, interests, roles, and responsibilities. With this range of individuals, many issues gained breath and depth during the process.

The goals of the Conference were threefold: (a) to stimulate discourse meaningful to clinical child psychologists as well as the total psychological community; (b) to clarify major issues and alternative actions; (c) to formulate and implement feasible proposals for strengthening the professional preparation of clinical child psychologists.

The Conference was not meant to perfect any finite training blueprint; rather, the goal was to explore those issues which pertain to the major goal of training competent psychologists to work with children, youth, and families. To that purpose, the *Proceedings*, reported here, are intended to be a set of suggestions that will stimulate continuing dialogue; no specific and precise guidelines for clinical child psychology training are possible here.

As stated in the goals printed here, this Conference should be considered a first step in realizing a goal of bringing together all those psychologists who deliver services to children, youth, and families to explore boundary issues; inherent in all specialties working with children, youth, and families are both similarities and differences. Those are the issues that emerge as important to promote a spirit of cooperation among all those with expertise to further the cause of helping our future generations.

June M. Tuma
Conference Coordinator

Table of Contents

The Hilton Head Conference on Training Clinical Child Psychologists: History and Background

June M. Tuma[1]
Louisiana State University

Beginning in February 1977, at an executive committee meeting of the Society of Pediatric Psychology, opinions concerning the need for a conference on training psychologists who serve children were voiced. Eventually, Section 1, Division 37, and other segments of APA were involved. Several meetings were held during the annual meetings of APA, Allan Barclay and I presented the conference proposal to the APA Education and Training Board, and, eventually, the conference was approved for sponsorship by the American Psychological Association. The American Psychological Foundation supported several planning meetings of the first conference committee which was composed of Alan Barclay and June Tuma, co-chairs, Ted Blau, Alan Ross and Diane Willis.

This committee wrote a proposal for a conference which was routed to the Board of Professional Affairs, the Board of Social and Ethical Responsibility for Psychology, the Board of Scientific Affairs, and, finally, to the APA Board of Directors for their action in the fall of 1978. This draft was also routed to interested parties in the psychological community for their reaction.

With a projected conference date in 1981, the proposal (Tuma & VanderBos, 1979) was expanded to include reactions from others and was forwarded to NIMH for funding consideration in January, 1980, but did not receive favorable vote due to the reviewers' opinion that a conference should address *all* psychologists working with children (the proposal is presented in abbreviated form in Tuma, 1982). The committee decided not to further pursue federal funding because of the committee's view that specialty requirements in clinical child psychology should be addressed before pursuing a larger scale conference. Instead, the committee decided to pursue private funding and/or participant funding for a conference to be held in the summer of 1983. Announcements of the conference were published and a number of position papers were received. However, private funding was also impossible and, for a time, it appeared that the conference would not be held. What the promoters of the conference lacked was funds for publication and distribution of proceedings and for follow-up. Without funds for the proceedings, the conference seemed to be an ineffectual exercise.

There was, however, a rebirth of interest in the conference in June of 1983 during an Emerald Isle meeting of the training committee of Section 1, appointed by Diane Willis, President of Section 1 (Section 1, 1983a). The training committee (composed of Jean C. Elbert, James H. Johnson, Thomas H. Ollendick, Carolyn Schroeder, and June M. Tuma, as chair) dispensed with the training committee charge to make recommendations for training in assessment, intervention, and consultation at Emerald Isle (Elbert, 1983; Johnson, 1983a, 1983b; Ollendick, 1983; Section 1, 1983b; Tuma, 1983). In addition to rather specific recommendations in those areas, the committee recommended to Section 1 that a training conference was the only way to make impact on training in clinical child psychology and asked that Section 1 consider sponsorship of such a conference (Section 1, 1983b, 1984a). The executive committee of Section 1, meeting at APA's annual meeting in the fall of 1983, approved the conference, and at the midyear meeting of 1984, allocated money for publication and distribution of conference proceedings (Section 1, 1984a, 1984b). Plans were then made to hold the conference in May, 1985, at Hilton Head Island. Finalization of the program and specific funds were allocated at the executive committee meeting of Section 1 in January, 1985 (Section 1, 1985) (for a more detailed history of the conference, see Appendix D).

Goals of the Conference

Goals of the conference were still very similar to those proposed originally (Johnson & Tuma, 1983; Tuma, 1982, 1984). The impetus for the conference stemmed from the fact that there are presently far too few psychologists who are adequately trained to meet the mental health needs of children and adolescents (Tuma, 1982). Thus, the internal and external stresses leading to the conference were (1) demand for services and (2) manpower deficits.

Demand for Services to Children. The 1977 United States Census data indicate that children under 18

[1]Conference Coordinator

comprise roughly 30% of the total population. Approximately 15% of those are in need of mental health services (Denham, 1979). In spite of the needs of this population for mental health services, only about 10% of American children and adolescents are served by the present mental health system (ADAMHA, 1978). Some of the more prominent factors accounting for this underservice are related to service availability and methods of service delivery. However, basic to the underservice is also a severe manpower shortage of appropriately trained psychologists.

Manpower Needs in Psychology. Few psychological service providers are primarily devoted to serving this population (VanderBos, Nelson, Stapp, Coates, & Batchelor, 1979). Based on data from the first survey of all licensed and/or certified heath service providers in psychology (Mills, Wellner, & VanderBos, 1979), VanderBos et al. (1979) estimated that almost 19,000 psychologists were licensed/certified, relevantly trained, and actively providing mental health services. However, the survey revealed that less than 1% of the health service provider psychologists spent a majority of their time (over 75%) providing services to children. In addition, this report further indicated that at least half of all licensed psychologists practitioners provide virtually no services to children. About 5,000 doctoral level psychologists provide *some* services to children as part of their clinical practice (Denham, 1979), and this appears to equal 1,000 full time equivalents. The current supply of fully trained psychologists (meaning they have completed an organized program in clinical child psychology with a specialized child-oriented internship), has been estimated at less than 500. The comparison of the known need for services to child populations show the need for an estimated 5,000 additional fully-trained, doctoral-level clinical child psychologists by 1989 (VanderBos, et al., 1979).

American Psychology Training Programs. How are American psychology training programs increasing the manpower to serve these children in need? It has been pointed out that mental health professionals in the child area require special skills that go beyond adult work (Wohlford, 1979) and that clinical child psychology should be recognized as a specialty in its own right (Wenar, 1979; Wohlford, 1979). Recognition as a specialty area would help to insure that training psychologists to work with children would be more specific to the skills and knowledge required for particular demands of service. In addition, the new NIMH emphasis on priority-focused training specifies that training programs must demonstrate curriculum, practicum, internship, research, and student identification pertinent to the priority area (Denham, 1979).

Currently, in the absence of specialty recognition for clinical child psychology and the consequent special training, many embarrassing and unethical situations abound in the psychological community. With the demand for clinical child psychologists outstripping the supply, it is not uncommon to find that psychologists trained to work only with adults (absence of an exposure to training with children) obtain jobs in settings where they work primarily with children (Wohlford, 1979).

When we, the committee, started to lay plans for the conference in 1977, we had no data concerning the kinds of training programs in clinical child psychology, how many we had, nor how psychologists practising clinical child psychology were trained. A great deal of information has been gathered since our initial assessment for the need for the conference.

Educational Backgrounds of Clinical Child Psychologists. Data obtained from a survey of Section 1 members revealed that only 25% of the respondents indicated that their graduate programs offered specialization in clinical child psychology (Tuma & Pratt, 1982). Respondents also indicated that most of these programs offered optional child concentrations within a general clinical psychology training program or in conjunction with another area of psychology. Only a few of the programs offered a degree or track program in clinical child psychology (10% and 15%, respectively). There were only about 12 programs identified as providing training in clinical child psychology in the late 1960's and about 30 in the late 1970's plus about 30 "informal programs". These data (e.g., Mannarino & Fischer, 1982) point to a possible preponderance of reliance on informal educational pursuits. Roberts (1982) also notes that the few clinical child psychology training programs available today most commonly developed specialty courses and experiences within a general clinical psychology training program.

Unfortunately, the survey of clinical child psychology training programs (Mannarino & Fischer, 1982) reveals some serious confusion about training content, and, indeed, definitions of clinical child psychology. Many graduate departments of psychology that claimed to offer formal or informal courses of instruction in clinical child psychology were deficient in their offerings from the standpoint of offering coursework or experiences to prepare students to work with children competently. The survey team concluded that this confusion in the academic community surrounded knowledge of the necessary and sufficient elements for clinical child psychology training.

Rate of Production. Some idea of the rate of production of doctoral clinical child psychologists can also be advanced from the data collected by Mannarino and Fischer (1982). The formal and informal program respondents reported production rates of 88 and 93, respectively, in an average year. At this rate, the production of doctoral clinical child psychologists falls short of the projected need of 5,000 clinical child psychologists by 1989 (VanderBos et al., 1979) by about two-thirds.

A cause for even greater concern, however, is the fact that the psychologists trained as *clinical child psychologists* by these programs vary greatly in the breadth and depth of training opportunities and, consequently, some will not be adequately trained to deliver services to children and their families because of the non-existence of criteria for training in this area.

Graduate training programs and internship setting have traditionally focused their efforts in the adult area and have failed to provide adequate training for working with children. Although previous training conferences in clinical psychology made some statements regarding training for specialty practice to children, none addressed the issue to any great extent. With the recent change in NIMH funding priority areas (ADHMA, 1978), the picture has changed somewhat, but most of the additional programs developed in response to the NIMH mandate involve clinical child training offered on an informal basis which is highly individualized without benefit of a well defined program structure (Mannarino & Fischer, 1982).

With the obvious need for more well trained psychologists to work with children and the apparent movement toward providing more training opportunities for specialty or subspecialty training, a major question relates to what specifically should be the nature of clinical child psychology training. The conference was seen as a vehicle to address this need by bringing together a wide variety of psychologists who have roles in formulating decisions about such training.

Recent Developments

The conference participants in 1985 had some other additional information available to them, that would not have been available to an earlier conference. Information has been gathered and some steps toward making psychology as a whole more responsive to the needs of children have already been taken. For example, the early papers prepared for the proposed conference were published in a special training issue of the *Journal of Clinical Child Psychology* (Brady & Friedrich, 1982; Goldman, 1982; Johnson & Robbins, 1982; Mannarino & Fischer, 1982; Roberts, 1982; Tuma, 1982; Tuma & Pratt, 1982). In addition, with the urging of Division 37 (Division of Children, Youth, and Families), Section 1 (Section on Clinical Child Psychology) and Section 5 (Society of Pediatric Psychology) of Division 12, and other related divisions, APA supported the Interdivisional Coalition for Children, Youth, and Families, which functioned for many years. By now, the Coalition has been phased out of existence since its most ambitious goal was realized: Creation of a person in APA's central office who monitors all issues concerning children. Also, a Task Force on Training (Erickson, Roberts, & Tuma) was created by Division 37. This Task Force prepared a document (and was subsequently endorsed by Division 37) of recommendations regarding minimal training requirements that should be required of persons planning to work with children, youth, and families (Erickson, Roberts, & Tuma, 1983; Roberts, Erickson, & Tuma, 1985) (see Appendix E).

In addition, in 1983, the *Journal of Clinical Child Psychology* initiated plans for publication of a new section designed as a forum for the expression of views regarding clinical child training (Johnson & Tuma, 1983; Section 1, 1983a). Then, finally, in 1982, because of the continuing support and need for a conference, under the presidency of Diane Willis, Section 1 established a National Training Committee who were charged with the task of considering those issues relevant to special training in clinical child psychology and developing guidelines for training programs. This committee made some specific suggestions for training (Elbert, 1983; Johnson, 1983a, 1983b; Ollendick, 1983; Section 1, 1983b; Tuma, 1983) but also reaffirmed the desirability of holding a conference.

Issues for the Conference

Several specific issues were posed for the conference.

1. **Specialty Training in Clinical Child Psychology.** Should there be specialty training in clinical child psychology? Isn't the generically trained clinical (adult) psychologist sufficiently trained to provide services to children? Some suggest that effort should be directed toward furthering guidelines of *all* clinical psychology training programs to become truly general programs by adequately training clinical students to work with children as well as adults. Thus, the concept of generic training might be broadened to include relevant training in the child *and* adult areas. This position would require specification of required child courses, practica, and other training experiences that should be included as a required part of *general clinical training.*

2. **Boundary Issues.** How does the clinical child

psychologist differ from other child professionals (e.g., school psychologists, pediatric psychologists, applied developmental psychologists, etc.)? Are there distinct areas of specialization or should all of these be subsumed under the more general heading of clinical child psychology? Or should clinical child psychology be subsumed under one of those headings? Assuming that there are differences, a major question concerns how, and to what degree, do (or should) these areas differ in terms of training and in terms of the nature and range of clinical services provided?

3. **Curriculum Issues.** To what extent should clinical child psychologists be trained in basic psychology (developmental, learning, physiological, social, cognition, etc.) and which courses are most essential to their training? To what extent should research be an integral part of clinical child training? If research is important, what types of research experiences are desirable and why? What types of courses need to be included in the curriculum to foster the development of research skills?

4. **Models of Training.** Related to both research and training issues, one might ask what is the most desirable model of training for clinical child psychology? Can this training best be accomplished within the traditional scientist-practitioner model of training, within a practitioner-scientist model, or within a strict applied clinical model? Regardless of the specific model subscribed to, is specialty training best accomplished within the organizational structure of a general clinical psychology program or within a strict specialty program which has a structure and requirements apart from the general clinical program. Or can specialty training be best carried out when presented within the context of general developmental psychology training or when combined and well integrated with related areas, such as school psychology?

Other issues identified were the levels of training (academic, internship, postdoctoral/continuing education), issues related to quality control and the role of NIMH and APA in training clinical child psychologists. These issues are obviously only a small sampling to be considered by any conference. We all know that even though specific issues are delineated prior to the conference, the needs of the participants and the process of the deliberations alter the course of what a priori may appear to be important and what acutally is. As we went into the conference, we were cognizant that, as with all conferences, the possibility existed that more issues might be raised than would be answered.

Implementation

One last issue concerns the implementation of the conference recommendations. What do we hope to come from this conference? We have some idea of what impact conferences have had in the past from Lloyd and Newbrough (1965) in their presentation of the history of conferences on graduate education in psychology. In their view, conferences are held not only to formulate actions to carry out. Only Boulder and Northwestern conferences clearly accomplished this. There have been a number of other conferences: Palo Alto, Miami, Chicago, Vail (clinical), Greyston (counseling), and Thayer (school). There have also been some more specific conferences: those recent ones include those that concentrated on medical psychology and aging and the 1972 Menninger conference on postdoctoral training. Lloyd and Newbrough view all subsequent conferences as assessing and monitoring an ongoing process which began with the initial conference. Thus, effectiveness of each subsequent conference is judged differently. They state

> . . . a conference should be viewed as a response to forces at work both within and without the profession. It serves the function of mediating agent for these forces; its effect results from the interaction of these forces in the conference process. A response to forces internal to the profession is the need to survey the current climate of opinion within psychology. This seems to be present at all conferences and in part represents a monitoring function. It may also reflect a need for the reaffirmation of the identity or unity of psychology, which finds its specialities becoming increasingly diverse. In this way a conference can be a device for accomodation which provides a means for disparate elements to come together, have a shared experience in the professional ferment, and go away with strengthened ties to the profession. This may include concerns to change emphases in the existing system and to pull diverging elements back.
>
> The other set of forces at a conference are those from outside the profession . . . Conference are stimulated by and are a response to changes in society.
>
> . . . a conference should be seen as a mediating instrument in the process of a profession's development. It gathers its identity from the forces, internal and external, that it mediates. Its effect on the profession is dependent upon the interplay of these forces. (p.14)

We can see that the Hilton Head Conference on the Training of Clinical Child Psychologists has been stimulated from within by the concern with the present status of training programs, manpower shortages, as well as the inadequate manner in which conferences in the past have dealt with issues relevant to training clinical child psychologists. From without, the impetus comes from the pressing demand for services to children in need as well as the recent NIMH funding priorities of clinical child psychology training.

If this conference is indeed a mediating instrument in the process of a profession's development, what will this conference serve to mediate? At best, we can hope for constructive changes in training programs for clinical child psychologists; at least, we can hope that the consciousness-raising aspects will make *all* psychologists more sensitive to the multitude of issues important to serving children, youth, and families.

References

ADAMHA. (1978). *Manpower Policy Analysis Task Report.* Rockville, MD: U.S. Department of Health Education and Welfare.

Brady, C.A., & Friedrich, W.N. (1982). Levels of intervention: A model for training in play therapy. *Journal of Clinical Child Psychology, 11,* 39-43.

Denham, W.H. (1979, August). NIMH policy in relation to training for service delivery to children and youth: Implications for psychology education. In Barclay, A. (Chair), *Clinical child psychology: Mapping a future,* Symposium presented at the annual meeting of the American Psychological Association, New York.

Elbert, J.C. (1983). Report of the subcommittee on assessment issues. *Journal of Clinical Child Psychology, 12,* 373-374.

Erickson, M.T., Roberts, M.C., & Tuma, J.M. (1983). Guidelines for training psychologists to work with children, youth, and families. In J.M. Tuma (Ed.) (1985), *Proceedings: Conference on the training of clinical child psychologists.* Baton Rouge, LA: Section on Clinical Child Psychology.

Goldman, J. (1982). Clinical child psychology training and credentialing. *Journal of Clinical Child Psychology, 11,* 8-12.

Johnson, J.H. (1983a). Report of the subcommittee on child treatment. *Journal of Clinical Child Psychology, 12,* 373.

Johnson, J.H. (1983b). Preliminary report of the Section 1 clinical child training questionnaire. *Journal of Clinical Child Psychology, 12,* 372-373.

Johnson, J.H., & Robbins, R.L. (1982). On the need for clinical child psychology training within the context of general clinical training programs. *Journal of Clinical Child Psychology, 11,* 27-34.

Johnson, J.H., & Tuma, J.M. (1983). Editorial: Training in clinical child psychology: A brief overview of selected issues, *Journal of Clinical Child Psychology, 12,* 365-368.

Lloyd, D.N., & Newbrough, J.R. (1965). Previous conferences on graduate education in psychology: A summary and review. In American Psychological Association, *Preconference materials: Prepared for the conference on the professional preparation of clinical psychologists.* Washington, D.C.: Author.

Mannarino, A.P., & Fischer, C. (1982). Survey of graduate training in clinical child psychology, *Journal of Clinical Child Psychology, 11,* 22-26.

Mills, D.H., Wellner, A.J., & VanderBos, G.R. (1979). The National Register survey: The first comprehensive study of all licensed/certified psychologists. In C.A. Kiesler, N.A. Cummings, & G.R. VanderBos (Eds.), *Psychology and National Health Insurance.* Washington, D.C.: American Psychological Association.

Ollendick, T.H. (1983). Report of the subcommittee on continuing education. *Journal of Clinical Child Psychology, 12,* 374.

Roberts, M.C. (1982). Clinical child psychology programs: Where and what are they? *Journal of Clinical Child Psychology, 11,* 13-21.

Roberts, M.C., Erickson, M.T., & Tuma, J.M. (1985). Addressing the needs: Guidelines for training psychologists to work with children, youth, and families. *Journal of Clinical Child Psychology, 14,* 70-79.

Section 1. (1983a). Minutes of the meeting of the executive committee, February 25 and 26, 1983. *Journal of Clinical Child Psychology, 12,* 314-217.

Section 1. (1983b). Minutes of the meeting of the executive committee, August 25, 1983. *Journal of Clinical Child Psychology, 12,* 369-374.

Section 1. (1984a). Minutes of the meeting of the executive committee, February 4 and 5, 1984. *Journal of Clinical Child Psychology, 13,* 103-107.

Section 1. (1984b). Minutes of the meeting of the executive committee, August 26 and 27, 1984. *Journal of Clinical Child Psychology, 13,* 326-329.

Section 1. (1985). Minutes of the executive committee, January 26 and 27, 1984. *Journal of Clinical Child Psychology, 14,* 264-267.

Tuma, J.M. (1982). Proposal for a national conference on professional preparation of clinical child psychologists. *Journal of Clinical Child Psychology, 11,* 3-7.

Tuma, J.M. (1983). Report of the Section 1 committee on training clinical child psychologists. *Journal of Clinical Child Psychology, 12,* 372-374.

Tuma, J.M. (1984). National Conference on the Training of Clinical Child Psychologists. *Journal of Clinical Child Psychology, 14,* 223-234.

Tuma, J.M., & Pratt, J.M. (1982). Clinical child psychology practice and training: A survey. *Journal of Clinical Child Psychology, 11,* 27-34.

Tuma, J.M., & VanderBos, G.R. (1979). *Proposal for a conference on the professional preparation of clinical child psychologists.* Grant submitted to the National Institute of Mental Health.

VanderBos, G.R., Nelson, S., Stapp, J., Olmedo, E., Coates, D., & Batchelor, W. (1979). *APA input to NIMH regarding planning for mental health personnel development.* Washington, D.C.: American Psychological Association.

Wenar, C. (1979, November 29). *Personal communication,* Ohio State University.

Wohlford, P. (1979). Clinical child psychology: The emerging specialty. *The Clinical Psychologist, 12,* 25-26.

The Issues

Conference Issues: Introduction

June M. Tuma
Louisiana State University

The purpose of plenary sessions at a training conference, such as the present one, is to provide background and stimulus materials in the form of position papers for the conferees. Usually, conferences have a format which incorporates a division of the conferees into small groups to permit them to consider the materials presented at plenary sessions and to establish a direction for reaching consensus on training issues. The small groups are then enabled to formulate resolutions to the conference as a whole.

The first plenary meeting was designed to bring to the attention of the conferees material that would reflect the status quo of training in clinical child psychology as well as some of the contextueal issues surrounding the conference. To that end, several presentations were assembled.

First, a brief history of the conference planning and the issues before the conference were presented by the conference coordinator, June Tuma. Then, Don Routh presented a review of clinical child psychology training to the present. He also presented an analysis of the rate of production of eminent clinical child psychologists by different universities by looking at the biographical listings of members of the Section on Clinical Child Psychology. He then came to some conclusions about the manner in which our programs have trained clinical child psychologists and offered some suggestions for students deciding on a strategy for training.

Anticipating the major thrust of this conference (establishing training guidelines for clinical child psychologists), Michael Roberts discussed the guidelines (see Appendix E) recently developed by Division 37 for minimal training of psychologists working with children, youth, and families. He and his committee (Marilyn Erickson and June Tuma) reasoned that this document may save some work for this conference; that is, it presents the *basic* ingredients of clinical child psychology training (as well as for other psychologists working with this population). This conference, then, may take the propositions of this document, select those that it deems important for this specialty group of psychologists, add to it, delete from it, and so forth.

Patricia Aletky reflected on the issues internal to organized psychology that have particular relevance to the conference issues. The complicated history of specialty regulation was elucidated and the point was made that political and economic pressures impinge on training issues.

Stanley Schneider presented some history of NIMH involvement in training and also provided some provocative statements concerning the importance of life-span developmental conceptualizations and orientation for those working with children, youth, and families. He also outlined a model program that would incorporate such an *ethos* in its training mission.

Lest conferees lose sight of the overall dimensions and magnitude of a *successful* conference, Alan Ross presented a short history of conferences on training in clinical psychology, their mission, their shortcomings, and their successes. Most importantly, he tried to give this conference a formula for success: assertive and active implementation of conference recommendations.

And, finally, in this section are presented synopses of the three concurrent small group discussions. Honore Hughes served as reporter for the academic level of training, and, thus, presented a synopsis of the deliberations of this group. Similarly, Anthony Mannarino and Thomas Ollendick presented their analyses of discussions of the groups designated to consider internship and postdoctoral/continuing education levels of training. (The format of presenting the synopses of the three concurrent small group discussions following the position papers will be followed throughout these *Proceedings.)*

The Training of Clinical Child Psychologists

June M. Tuma
Louisiana State University

Welcome to the Hilton Head Conference on the Training of Clinical Child Psychologist! I say this with some enthusiasm because this conference has been a long time coming. Even though the initial idea of holding a conference was posed in 1977, for awhile, it looked as if we would not be able to hold the conference at all.

As is usually the case, the reason it appeared that we should scrap the whole idea was because of funding. As Stan Schneider will tell you later this morning, some issues are more serious than funding, but when you are trying to hold a conference, it assumes unbelievably important proportions. However, perhaps because of a generous endowment of tenacity, it soon appeared to me that we, the Conference Committee and supporters, were looking for "permission" to hold the conference. The conceptualization that money was such permission and those who controlled the money were dictating to us what was or what was not important to do in regard to a conference soon took hold. I was suprised to see that so many of you, the same people in this audience, held the same view. We *did* feel that a training conference was more important and necessary for a variety of reasons. We persisted. We dreamed. We worked hard. We became creative. We were discouraged. However, along with the vacillation of our assessment of the feasibility of such a conference as time went on, one thing did not change: that was that the conference was needed at this time. The seeds of the idea of the specific Hilton Head Conference were sown at an Emerald Isle Training Committee Meeting of Section 1 in June of 1983. These seeds were able to sprout into announcements of the actuality of the conference later that year under the Section 1 President, Diane J. Willis. We owe Dr. Willis a vote of appreciation for giving us the encouragement and support to finalize the plans for this conference.

Let me back up a bit and give you some history. It all began in Oklahoma City at a meeting of the Society of Pediatric Psychology, where I was a Member-at-Large, also serving as chair of the Training Committee. During the report on training, the Executive Committee decided that it would be timely to hold a conference on training to determine the overlap and differences between such sub-speciality areas as pediatric psychology, clinical child psychology, school psychology, developmental psychology, and so on. This was the stimulus, originally. There were also issues identified concerning how training should proceed to develop a psychologist to serve children in various age groups and settings. As in any discussion of who serves whom and in what manner is he/she prepared, the discussion centered on the seemingly thousands of people serving children in the absence of any identifiably appropriate training. Also highlighted were the societal concerns of underservice to children in addition to perhaps substandard service because of the profession's lack of clear definition of the required training. So you can see that early on, the issues were clear to us, those of us who were child clinicians.

Reviewing the gravity of the issues at that Oklahoma meeting, we immediately telephoned the President of Section 1, Paul Wolhford, to determine if we could meet with the Executive Committee of Section 1 to discuss our collaboration on a project that would culminate in a training conference. We also decided to include the new Division 37 (Division on Children, Youth and Families) in this venture. There was consideration of including other segments of APA, those particularly that were composed of developmental psychologists and school psychologists, because the amount of overlap of function and training have to be tremendous. We envisioned getting together all psychologists who were concerned with children at any level and perhaps come up with a definition of role, function, and required training that would encompass *all* psychologists who work with children. Alan Ross later told me, when we were working together on the first conference planning committee, that eventually, we would only have an area that is called *child psychology*. That is, we would drop the *clinical* in front of *child psychology,* and implied in this is that all areas of child psychology would do likewise.

However, as we began to work out some preliminary ideas about what it would take to get together so many psychologists who have different training backgrounds and different role definitions, we quickly realized that our own house was not in order — we could not *really* define the roles and training of clinical child psychologists. How, then, could we possibly address boundary issues with pediatric psychology, with developmental psychology, with school psychology? The first order of business appeared to be to have a small conference that defined mainly those issues: What we are, what we do, how we are trained now, what kind of courses and other experiences prepare us to do what we do, and the *big* question of do we want to do it differently? That is, do we want to pursue specialty training? And *if* we do, we'd better know the implications for other professional considerations, such as how such specialized training would limit us in other ways in our professional careers. What implications would it have on certification and licensure? How would proper training be monitored? How would limitation of practice within specialty areas be enforced? This is only a small sampling of the issues that are introduced by the simple consideration of specialty training.

Once we define ourselves, the boundary issues become exceedingly important. What do clinical child psychologists do that is any different from what school psychologists do, from what applied developmental psychologists do, from what pediatric psychologists do? What things do all of these psychologists do that are the same? Who *should* do them? Who should not? These are very important issues from ethical, social, and economic points of view. However, the questions appear to be impossible to answer without clear definitions of role functions of all child-oriented professional psychologist groups.

Because our thinking was so clear about the difficulty of addressing the boundary issues without clear definitions from all involved groups, it was especially disheartening when the NIMH grant was not funded because of a particularly pointed reservation of the review panel that we were not making it a *boundary issue conference,* including to equal degree school psychologists, developmental psychologists, etc. This is what happened. After the original Conference Committee, Allan Barclay, Theodore Blau, Diane Willis, Alan Ross, and I, took the proposal for the conference to the Education and Training Board, the Board of Professional Affairs, the Board of Social and Ethical Responsibility for Psychology, the Board of Scientific Affairs, and, finally, to the Board of Directors of the American Psychological Association. The American Psychological Foundation funded the committee to meet several times a year to prepare a grant to submit to NIMH for funding. This was accomplished in 1980 with the aforementioned result. During this planning time there were calls for papers for the conference, open meetings, a symposium during the APA annual meetings, and a lively correspondence among interested parties. A special issue on Training in Clinical Child Psychology was published as my first issue as editor of the *Journal of Clinical Child Psychology.* Donald K. Routh, as editor of the *Journal of Pediatric Psychology,* also later published a special issue on training pediatric psychologists. But the conference was not to be, it seemed.

What I have observed between then and now is a continuing interest in resolving the issues about training clinical child psychologists. In spite of our inability to get funding for this conference, such that the participants would be supported in their roles, we are here at Hilton Head to consider the issues that are just as crucial today as they were in 1980. It is a credit to each of you and your supporting universities that you are here today to contribute to the resolution of a number of problems in the training of clinical child psychologists.

Training Clinical Child Psychologists[1]

Donald K. Routh
University of Miami

At present there is no consensus on standards for training clinical child psychologists (as distinct from training clinical psychologists in general). This presents a dilemma for the student who wants to become a child clinician. How can such a student select the best school to attend? The lack of consensus also makes it difficult for faculty and clinical supervisors who are attempting to provide relevant graduate, internship, or postdoctoral training. This chapter reviews the literature on clinical child training and presents some new data on the current members of the Section on Clinical Child Psychology, where they were trained, and on the long term relative quality of some graduate training programs.

As regular readers of *Advances in Clinical Child Psychology* are well aware, the field of clinical psychology originated with attempts to help children. This child emphasis was found in the early university psychology department clinics at Pennsylvania and elsewhere and also (of course) in the child guidance centers set up by the Commonwealth Fund. However, during World War II and the postwar years, the military, the Veterans Administration, and the National Institute of Mental Health transformed the field of clinical psychology into an adult-oriented profession. It was therefore necessary for those clinical pychologists who still worked primarily with children to reframe their field as the "sub-specialty" of clinical child psychology. One impetus to this development was a book written by Alan O. Ross (1959) on *The Practice of Clinical Child Psychology.* Ross felt that four steps were necessary before this field could be thought to have re-gained its professional maturity, so to speak. The first of these was simply recognition that a specialty of clinical child psychology existed. This was provided at least in part by the organization in 1962 of the Section on Clinical Child Psychology as "Section 1" of the APA Division of Clinical Psychology, and the fact that this Section has so far survived all threats to its existence over the last two decades. It is interesting that Section 1 has not (like many other offshoots of Division 12) gone on to become a separate division. It has not been replaced or (as will be seen) even diminished in size by the formation of the relatively new APA Division of Child, Youth, and Family Services (Division 37). Yet the larger field of psychology has not necessarily recognized clinical child psychology as a specialty. At the present time there is even considerable active discussion as to just what the nature of a *specialty* in psychology is, and how it should be defined. For example, are clinical, counseling, and school psychology really separate specialties, or do they have more in common as fields providing human services than they have distinctive features? Needless to say, these broader issues will have to be resolved before the issue of *subspecialties* can be properly addressed.

A second step that the field of clinical child psychology would have to take, according to Ross (1959), was the establishment of a scientific journal. The *Journal of Clinical Child Psychology* published by the Section since 1971 has developed into a respected peer-refereed professional journal. It has been joined by other publications such as the *Journal of Abnormal Child Psychology* (begun in 1973) and the present annual series, *Advances in Clinical Child Psychology* (begun in 1977). The lead issue of the journal *Child Development* in 1984 heralded the emergence of "developmental psychopathology" as a separate area of research, a scientific event that has no doubt gladdened the heart of every child clinician. Textbooks and handbooks of clinical child psychology and child psychopathology are published in abundance, and courses in behavior disorders of childhood appear to have become a staple even of the undergraduate curriculum in psychology.

A third step on Ross's list was setting up professional meetings. The Section on Clinical Child Psychology has presented an invited symposium at the meetings of the American Psychological Association each year for most of its history, and as of 1985 its time allotment for such symposia is to be doubled (at least on a trial basis). APA Division 37 (Division of Child, Youth, and Family Services) provides an additional annual forum for the presentation of research papers and symposia.

[1]Chapter to appear in B.B. Lahey & A.E. Kazdin (Eds.), *Advances in Clinical Child Psychology*. Vol. 8. New York: Plenum, 1985.

The final step toward the maturity of the specialty outlined by Ross was setting up standards for training. This is the step that has so far not been taken successfully. At this point the American Psychological Association accredits doctoral training programs only in clinical, counseling, school, and organizational-industrial psychology, and approves internships only for clinical and counseling psychology. The American Board of Professional Psychology (ABPP) has awarded its diplomas only in clinical, counseling, school, and organizational-industrial psychology, although recent plans have been made to offer diplomas also in psychoanalysis and in clinical neuropsychology. There was an attempt beginning in the early 1960s by a group of senior psychologists within the American Asssociation of Psychiatric Clinics for Children to set up standards for predoctoral internship training in clinical child psychology. At one point 14 clinics had been approved under these standards (Cass, Cain, & Waite, 1970). However, I have been unable to find any more recent references to this organization's accreditation efforts. From the beginning it seemed to me rather odd for such a "psychiatric" association to be evaluating standards for training psychologists, and perhaps this was the reason the AAPCC accreditation system failed to take hold.

Intense discussions have taken place lately on training in professional psychology in general (American Psychological Association, 1980). The question concerns what training is needed for all psychologists who provide human services rather than training for particular specialties (not to mention sub-specialties). The Criteria for Accreditation of Doctoral Training Programs and Internships in Professional Psychology recommended by the above committee were approved by the APA Council of Representatives and have subsequently been widely adopted by state licensure boards and by the National Register of Health Service Providers in Psychology. These criteria specify that training in professional psychology is to be doctoral training at least three academic years in length. It must include instruction in such areas as scientific and professional ethics and standards, research design and methodology, statistics, psychological measurement, and history and systems. Professional training must also include coursework in the following substantive content areas: biological bases of behavior, cognitive-affective bases of behavior, social bases of behavior, and individual behavior. In addition, the Criteria specify that professional psychologists must be trained in areas such as psychodiagnosis, psychological assessment, intervention procedures, consultation, program evaluation, and so on. Professional training programs must require a formal internship. State licensure boards and the National Register require an additional, postdoctoral year of supervised experience as well. These generic guidelines are obviously important in training in clinical child psychology insofar as it views itself as a specialty area within the broad domain of professional psychology.

Recent Literature on Training in Clinical Child Psychology

One might suppose that clinical child psychologists would emerge solely from graduate training programs in clinical psychology, but this is not the case. Information summarized by Routh (1977) on doctoral level members of the Section on Clinical Child Psychology as of 1975 indicated that only 67% of these individuals were trained in clinical psychology, with a substantial minority having backgrounds in educational, developmental, counseling, or school psychology. Indeed, a number of the members of Section 1 continued to identify their main field as school or developmental psychology, seeing clinical child psychology as a subspecialty of these. It was pointed out that substantial numbers of Section 1 members were in private practice or worked in medical, educational, child guidance, or community mental health settings and suggested that trainees receive practicum work in such places. It was also noted that Section 1 members frequently belonged to the APA divisions concerned with developmental, personality, and social psychology, implying the likely importance of these areas in the training of clinical child psychologists. Routh (1977) noted that the universities training the most Section 1 members were often not those known for having specialized programs in the clinical child area; rather, they tended to be institutions such as New York University, the University of Michigan, and others better known for producing large numbers of clinical psychology graduates in general. No attempt was made to assess the quality of graduate training programs in clinical child psychology; the article simply listed the number of graduates of each of the larger programs who were members of Section 1.

A survey of Section 1 members by Tuma and Pratt (1982) confirmed one implication of the above study, that few of the members of the Section had received formal specialty training in clinical child psychology during their graduate training. Indeed, they ranked post-doctoral fellowship training in clinical child psychology as the most valuable level of experience they had received. The interpretation of this survey is, however, somewhat clouded by its low response rate (40%).

Roberts (1982) attempted to describe, in some depth, a number of different graduate training programs in clinical child psychology. He identified four different training patterns or models. The most common pattern involved general clinical psychology training with later specialization in the clinical child area, as seen in the programs at the University of Alabama and at Purdue University. A second training pattern involved a doctoral program specifically in clinical child psychology, such as the programs at the University of Denver and the University of Washington (for a detailed account of the program at the University of Washington, see Perry, 1978). The third model called for clinical child training within a developmental psychology program, an example being Ohio State University. And the fourth training pattern involved clinical child psychology training within a school psychology doctoral program, as seen in the combined school/clinical child program at the University of Virginia.

Mannarino and Fischer (1982) attempted to survey all of the graduate training programs in clinical child psychology. They found a dramatic increase in the number of such programs over previous surveys (i.e., 36 "formal programs" in clinical child psychology and 29 "informal programs" in the field). They speculated that perhaps the increased number of departments willing to claim the availability of such specialty training might be related to the emphasis of the National Institute of Mental Health [during the Carter administration] on children and youth as an underserved population. This points up a problem in any such attempt to survey graduate training programs. In the absence of consensus about training standards, and with no confirmation of the information via site visit or collateral sources of facts, one cannot be confident that meaningful data are being provided by respondents. At this point, practically any department can claim, without fear of successful contradiction, that it offers training in clinical child psychology.

A notable recent trend is for organizations concerned with clinical child psychology to arrive at their own criteria for training programs. In 1983, for example, there appeared the Report of the Task Force on Training of the Division of Child, Youth, and Family Services [Division 37] of the APA. This document was concerned with the *minimal* levels of training necessary for professional psychologists working with children, youth, and families rather than with specialty training. Nevertheless, the Task Force report is of interest here in that a specialist should certainly meet minimal training levels. Included among the topics considered essential for adequate training by the Task Force were the following: developmental psychology, child psychopathology, developmental disabilities, child assessment, child psychotherapy, parent and family therapy, research methods in child psychology, and ethics and legal issues related to children and families. It is unclear at present how this Report will actually be implemented. The most ambitious effort along these lines is a proposal for a National Conference on Professional Preparation of Clinical Child Psychologists (Tuma, 1982). A first draft of this proposal was prepared in 1977 by June M. Tuma, in consultation with Allan Barclay and others, and was approved by the APA Education and Training Board, the Board of Professional Affairs, the Board of Social and Ethical Responsibility for Psychology, the Board of Scientific Affairs, and (in the fall of 1978) by the APA Board of Directors. The proposal was then written up as a grant application for possible funding by the National Institute of Mental Health but did not receive a favorable vote. Reportedly, the NIMH review committee feared that the proposed conference would focus too much on "elitist" issues of credentialing and excluding unqualified persons from the field. There are still plans to hold such a National Conference (Johnson & Tuma, 1983), but probably with funds provided largely by the participants.

A Look at Present Members of the Section on Clinical Child Psychology

The previous report by the author concerning the 1975 membership of Section 1 (Routh, 1977) seemed to generate at least some information with implications for training in the field, as reported above. Using the APA Biographical Directory also produces data on a higher percentage of the membership than is generally possible from a mail survey. It was therefore thought that it might be worthwhile to update the study with a similar analysis of the current membership of Section 1, but with some additional attention to the issue of the quality as well as quantity of training in clinical child psychology offered by the differnt graduate programs.

One reader of a preliminary draft of this chapter objected to the implicit identification of the field of clinical child psychology with Section 1 of Division 12 and stated that as important as this group is to the field, it is not isomorphic with it. One has to agree with this caveat. In the author's own experience, practicing clinical child psychologists are the most likely to belong to Section 1, whereas academics and researchers are less so. Nevertheless, there is no organization that is more respresentative of the field, to the author's knowledge.

Method

The official 1983 membership list of the Section on Clinical Child Psychology was obtained from the secretary of the organization. Of the 830 members (and 115 student affiliates) listed there, 719 of the members were found to have both a doctoral degree and an elaborated listing in the 1981 *Biographical*

Directory of American Psychological Association (the most recent one published). The information routinely noted included the field of psychology in which the doctoral degree was obtained, the university granting the degree, the current major field within psychology, and whether clinical child psychology was listed as either major field or specialty area, the divisional memberships or fellowship status within APA, the work setting(s) of the individual, and professional credentials such as ABPP or ABPH status and state licensure (the Directory did not list certification as a school psychologist, as had the one used in the previous study). In addition, the list of members was compared with the 1983 membership roster of the Society of Pediatric Psychology (Section 5 of Division 12, APA) and with the 1983 edition of the *National Register of Health Service Providers in Psychology*. Also, information was obtained on fellow status in Division 37, APA from the 1984 *APA Membership Register* (Division 37 had not yet named its first fellows by the time the 1981 directory was published).

Results

The fact that there are 830 members of Section 1 in 1983 constitutes an increase from the 738 members of the Section eight years previously. There was a corresponding increase from 549 to 719 members with doctoral degrees and elaborated listings in the directory (who were the subjects of further analysis).

Table 1 shows the fields in psychology in which the Section members obtained their doctoral degrees, and the change in these percentages from the 1975 data. As this Table indicates, about 6% of the 1983 members were originally trained in clinical psychology (which is a relative decrease from the 67% so trained in the 1975 sample). As in the previous study, no other type of graduate training in psychology was close to the frequency of clinical. Developmental and school psychology were the next most common, with educational and counseling psychology close behind. As compared to the 1975 data, the present members of Section 1 were relatively more likely to have been trained in developmental or school psychology with a lesser increase in the percentage of those trained in counseling psychology and a decrease in other areas.

Table 1. *Field of Psychology in Which Clinical Child Psychologists Obtained their Doctoral Degrees*

Field	Number	Percent	Change from 1975 (%)
Clinical	434	60	−7
Developmental	55	8	+3
School	55	8	+3
Educational	49	7	−1
Counseling	46	6	+1
Experimental	15	2	0
General	14	2	−1
Other or none listed	51	7	−2

Table 2 shows the area given as the current major field by 1983 Section 1 members. Clinical psychology was again generally the first choice as the professional identification listed by these psychologists, but there was a relative decrease of 9% in this choice compared to the 1975 data. The major area of increase in this Table was in the "other" category (up 9% from 1975), which included 15 individuals who listed "clinical child psychology" as their major field and another 25 who listed "pediatric psychology" as their major field. It is not possible to be sure whether this is a real change in the preferences of individuals, since these particular choices were not allowed by the directory compiler in 1975. In any case, the increase in preferences for developmental or school psychology as these individual's current major field seems to be meaningful though small.

Table 2. *Area Listed as Current Major Field by Clinical Child Psychologists*

Area	Number	Percent	Change from 1975 (%)
Clinical	520	72	−9
Developmental	43	6	+1
School	41	6	+1
Counseling	15	2	−1
Community	11	2	+1
Educational	9	1	−1
Other	79	11	+9
None listed	1	0	−2

Table 3 shows the professional credentials held

Table 3. *Professional Credentials of Clinical Child Psychologists*

Type of Credential	Number	Percent	Change from 1975 (%)
State Licensure	644	90	+14
National Register	437	61	
Diplomate, ABPP or ABPH	144	20	−3
Subclass of Diplomas			
Clinical	(119)		
Counseling	(3)		
School	(22)		
Clinical Hypnosis	(2)		

by Section 1 members. There is certainly a decided tendency of these psychologists to obtain state licensure, with the percentage doing so up from 76% in the 1975 sample to 90% in the present one. The National Register has emerged into prominence since the previous study, and it is of interest that well over half of these Section 1 members are already listed there. As Table 3 also shows, however, now only about one in five Section 1 members are ABPP or ABPH diplomates (versus one in four in 1975). The biggest change in this respect, however, is that in 1975 only a single ABPP diplomate in school psychology belonged to Section 1, whereas by 1983, 22 of them did.

Table 4 indicates the current professional activities and work settings of Section 1 members. The numbers sum to more than 100% because individuals often listed more than one work setting. The most frequent activity listed was private practice, as was true for the 1975 sample, but the frequency of listing this activity has gone up by a full 10%. The frequency of work activities involving a university psychology department, a medical school, or a non-university medical setting have all gone up, especially the work in a medical school setting. On the other hand, listings of all other kinds of work settings have declined a bit, including the child guidance center, community mental health center, and school system. The "other" category that went up 7% includes more individuals working in schools of professional psychology ($n = 11$) and university departments of child development and family studies ($n = 8$).

Table 4. *Professional Activities listed by Clinical Child Psychologists*

Activity or Setting	Number	Percent	Change from 1975 (%)
Private Practice	324	45	+10
University Pyschology Dept.	193	27	+4
University Medical School	163	23	+8
Medical (other than university)	85	12	+2
Child Guidance Center	61	8	−1
School or School System	53	7	−1
Commmunity Mental Health Center	47	7	−2
University Education Dept.	32	4	−1
Residential Treatment Center	24	3	−1
State Government	18	3	0
Private or Government Research	10	1	−1
Other	60	8	+7

Table 5 indicates the most frequent organizational affiliations of Section 1 members within APA, including APA divisions founded since 1975. Only half of the present Section 1 members belong to the Division of Clinical Psychology, a decrease of 12% since 1975. A third of them belong to the Society of Pediatric Psychology, also a decrease since 1975. Almost a third belong to the new Division of Child, Youth, and Family Services. As before, about one in five Section 1 members belong to the Division of Psychotherapy. Their membership in all other APA divisions has decreased, including those concerned with school psychology; developmental, personality, and social psychology; with state affairs; consulting psychology; and the psychological study of social issues.

Table 5. *Membership in APA Divisions and Societies by Clinical Child Psychologists*

Organization	Number	Percent	Change from 1975 (%)
Div. of Clinical Psychology	358	50	−12
Soc. of Pediatric Psychology	237	33	−9
Div. of Child, Youth & Families	229	32	
Div. of Psychotherapy	158	22	0
Div. of School Psychology	98	14	−3
Div. of Developmental Psychol.	76	11	−4
Soc. for Psych. Stud. Soc. Iss.	56	8	−2
Div. of State Psychol. Affairs	52	7	−8
Div. of Consulting Psychology	45	6	−4
Div. of Personality & Soc. Psy.	33	5	−6

Table 6 lists the graduate schools that conferred doctoral degrees to 10 or more persons who later became Section 1 members. Note that unlike the

Table 6. *Graduate Schools with Largest Number of Doctoral Degrees Granted to Persons now Members of the Section on Clinical Child Psychology*

University	Number
New York University#	23
Columbia University#	22
Ohio State University	22
University of Michigan#	19
University of Pittsburgh#	19
University of Minnesota	17
University of Texas at Austin#	17
Pennsylvania State University#	15
University of Chicago#	14
University of Iowa#	14
University of Kansas	14
Purdue University	14
Boston University#	12
Case Western Reserve University#	11
Michigan State University	11
University of North Carolina at Chapel Hill	11
Rutgers University	11
Catholic University of America	10
Harvard University#	10
University of Illinois#	10
University of Oklahoma	10
Syracuse University	10
Temple University	10

#—Produced an average or larger porportion of peer-recognized clinical child psychologists among graduates who were members of Section 1. See text for further explanation.

corresponding Table in the Routh (1977) paper, this one considered doctoral degrees in any area of psychology, not just in clinical. Nevertheless, as in the previous study, the institutions listed tend to be urban or large state universities in the northeastern and midwestern parts of the country. The only exceptions to this rule are state universities in the south, namely the University of North Carolina at Chapel Hill and the University of Texas.

The final data to be reported involved an attempt to identify a subgroup of Section 1 members who had been clearly recognized for excellence by their professional peers. This group was defined as consisting of individuals who either had an ABPP or ABPH diploma, were fellows of APA, had held the position of President of the Section, had served as editor of its journal, or had received its Distinguished Contribution Award. This peer-recognized group was found to contain 178 members, or 25% of the sample. In further investigation of the characteristics of this group, it was found that 70% had been trained in the field of clinical psychology (as contrasted with 60% of the sample as a whole as indicated in Table 1). Ninety-eight percent of the peer -recognized group were licensed psychologists (as compared to 90% for the sample as a whole — Table 3). Thirty-eight percent of the peer-recognized group were affiliated with university psychology departments (as contrasted with 27% of the sample as a whole — Table 4). Eighty percent of the peer-recognized group (vs. 50% of the overall sample) belonged to the Division of Clinical Psychology. Indeed the individuals in peer-recognized group were somewhat more likely that the sample as a whole to belong to each of the APA divisions listed in Table 5, though equally likely to belong to the Society of Pediatric Psychology.

The graduate schools listed in Table 6 ranged from 10 to 47% of the proportion of their graduates who were in Section 1 who were members of the peer-recognized group. If this percentage was at least 25% (the percentage of the whole sample who had received some form of peer recognition for excellence) an asterisk was placed beside the name of the university in Table 6. About half of the universities listed merited this distinction.

Discussion

The present data confirm not only the survival but the growth of the Section on Clinical Child Psychology (despite the formation of a new APA division many thought would replace it). Why has this happened? It must be that many Section members see clinical child psychology as a subspecialty of clinical rather than as a completely independent field. I recall how fiercely the late Herbert E. Rie opposed the formation of the new Division 37 because he thought it might destroy Section 1 and with it its members' hard won identity as *clinical* child psychologists. His fears turned out to be groundless.

In a way the growth of Section 1 has rendered it less purely clinical. For example, currently it has more developmental and school psychologists than before among its members (see Table 1). Yet the percentage of Section 1 members working in the schools or teaching in university schools of education has decreased (Table 4). Perhaps the developmental and school psychologists coming into Section 1 (including the 21 who are ABPP diplomates in school psychology) are people who have moved into teaching in medical school settings or into private practice activities, more compatible with an identifaction with the clinical field. The increase in private practice activities and the growth in numbers of licensed psychologists in the Section are certainly among the strongest trends found by the present study (see Tables 3 and 4).

A third trend in the data that decreases comment is the decreasing tendency of Section 1 members to belong to other APA divisions and organizations, even the Division of Clinical Psychology. Perhaps for many private practitioners who do both child and adult therapy, Section 1 and the Division of Psychotherapy provide sufficient organizational involvement (that division seems to the the only one that is "holding its own" in retaining members of Section 1, according to Table 5).

It remains to discuss the implications of the present study for training. The universities listed in Table 6 as training the most child clinicians are, as in the Routh (1977) study, in many cases ones that train many clinical psychologists rather than having specialized programs in the clinical child area.

In fact, many universities known for their specialized clinical child programs (for example those discussed in detail by Roberts, 1982) do not look good as far as the present data on programs' quality (Table 6) are concerned. Are some of the institutions producing relatively large numbers of specialized clinical child psychologists doing so at the expense of the quality of their training in basic psychology? In looking at Table 6, one should acknowledge the truism that in any class, half must of necessity be below average.

To add some depth to the analysis of program quality, I thought it might be worthwhile to discuss in more detail the graduates of the one university listed in Table 6 I know best, the University of Iowa (Routh, 1982), I have come to have considerable information about that local scene. Of the 14 members of Section 1 who received PhDs from the University of Iowa, six are listed as being in the "peer-recognized" group. It is interesting to note that none of these was a product of a specialized clinical child psychology training program. Their PhD degrees were granted for the most part long ago, in years ranging from 1941 to 1973. Three were graduates of the (APA approved) clinical psychology program; two were graduates of the Child Welfare Research Station (i.e., they were trained as child psychologists), and the final one received the PhD through the division of educational psychology of the College of Education. The most salient fact that emerges from a closer look at these individuals is that almost every one had a distinguished mentor, though not necessarily one identified as a child clinican. Among the mentors were: Arthur L. Benton, I.E. Farber (2 students), Kurt Lewin, and Robert R. Sears. The realization of how these particular students were trained leads one to wonder if our task forces and surveys concerned with training clinical child psychologists are not somehow on the wrong track. Does the key to the graduate education of an excellent child clinican lie in specialized coursework and practicum experiences in graduate school or in the intellectual challenge of a strong background in psychology? I realize that the two need not be in incompatible. Perhaps, however, the specialized clinical child training is best reserved for the internship or postdoctoral fellowship level as it was for this group.

There is a problem inherent in the present method of evaluating program quality by proportion of graduates receiving some form of objective peer recognition. This is that within the first five years after receiving a doctoral degree, no one receives an ABPP or ABPH diploma, becomes an APA fellow, or is named President, editor, or Distinguished Contribution awardee of Section 1. These forms of recognition take much longer than that. Thus by the time this type of information on "program quality" is available, it may be of interest primarily to the historian and say little about the nature of the present training program. In the example mentioned above, three of the five distinguished members are now retired, and one other is deceased. How long should a program be able to live on past glory, or have to suffer because of past mediocrity? I do not have a solution other than the traditional one of self-study and site visits to the question of solidly evaluating the quality of a present training program.

General Discussion

What can be concluded from this review of the literature and these new data on current Section 1 members about training clinical child psychologists? One conclusion may be simply that one needs to be patient. We cannot arrive at subspecialty training criteria until we have specialty criteria, and we cannot have those until we agree about the nature of professional psychology training in general. At least there has been considerable progress in that area. The Criteria for Accreditation of Doctoral Training Programs and Internships (American Psychological Association, 1980) are becoming widely understood and accepted throughout the field. These criteria are now used by site visitors to training programs, and by members of state boards of examiners in psychology. The National Register's standard definition of "health service provider in psychology" together with litigation and freedom-of-choice legislation are enabling many more professional psychologists to receive third party payment for their services.

Now that there is more agreement about the nature of professional pychology training, there can begin to be more productive discussions about specialty criteria in psychology. For example, in the 1984 meeting of the Board of Directors of the Division of Clinical Psychology there was discussion of whether clinical psychology should be considered a specialty or simply a generic field of human service delivery by psychologists. In this discussion it was becoming clear that much of what goes on in graduate training, including professionally oriented courses and practica, is common to clinical, counseling, and school psychology programs. Trainees in all of these areas need to know about interviewing, testing, and the general principles of pyschological treatment, for example. The Board ended up deciding, in fact voting, in favor of the proposition that there *was* a specialty of clinical psychology, but in the future no one could be considered a specialist in this sense who did not have at least a year in an organized postdoctoral training program in the specialty. Although most pychologists are ambivalent about the "medical model," it is easy to see that this discussion is converging on the way medical people are trained as a model for psychology. Medical students are trained in generic fashion, and the MDs and licenses of physicians do not limit them to one area of practice. Specialization is a voluntary process involving postdoctoral ("residency") training and board certification. Will this kind of model work for psychology training? Evidently, the leadership of the Division of Clinical Psychology thinks so. People in the field of clinical child psychology will probably have to wait some more to find out whether this or some other model is accepted by psychology before its discussions of subspecialty training criteria can move toward a firm consensus.

Meanwhile, what can one say to a prospective graduate student who is interested in going into clinical child psychology? Personally, my advice to such students is to begin with a list of APA-approved graduate training programs in clinical psychology.

This would seem to guarantee the student training meeting the criteria of the American Psychological Association (1980) and thus of internships, state licensure boards, and the National Register. (Perhaps one should not discourage such a student from accepting admission to a high quality program in developmental or school psychology as a viable alternative. Of the universities listed in Table 6, Harvard and Chicago for example have excellent track records despite the absence of any APA-approved programs on these campuses.) Then, within the APA-approved list, one can try to narrow the possibilities to schools with well known programs or visible faculty in clinical child psychology and related areas. Table 6 has its limits as a guide because (as already noted) it is based more on history than the present programs and because it lists only schools with large numbers of graduates. In any case, I think it would be safe advice to a student to get into a good clinical program even though not specialized, with the idea of picking up relevant clinical child experience at the internship or postdoctoral level. As pointed out in the introduction to this chapter, there are now many doctoral programs that purport to offer specialized training in clinical child psychology (including the joint program in developmental and clinical psychology at the University of Iowa, with which the author is associated). However, since there are no consensual criteria that a program has to meet to merit this specialty label, the prospective student should probably not use such a self-designation as a basis for judging worth, or the lack of it.

Finally, do there seem to be any implications of the present review for the forthcoming National Conference on Professional Preparation of Clinical Child Psychologists? One recommendataion might be to take Tuma and Pratt's (1982) results quite seriously and concentrate on discussions of training at the postdoctoral level rather than on the graduate school curriculum. It also might be worthwhile to follow the example of the specialties of psychoanalysis and neuropsychology and make a serious effort to set up criteria for an ABPP diploma in clinical child psychology.

References

American Psychological Association. (1980). *Accreditation handbook*. Washington, D.C.: Author.

Cass, L., Cain, A., & Waite, R. (1970). American Association of Psychiatric Clinics for Children training standards for predoctoral internship in clinical child psychology. *Professional Psychology, 1,* 170-174.

Johnson, J.H., & Tuma, J.M. (1983). Editorial . . . Training in clinical child psychology: A brief overview of selected issues. *Journal of Clinical Child Psychology, 12,* 365-368.

Mannarino, A.P., & Fischer, C. (1982). Survey of graduate training in clinical child psychology. *Journal of Clinical Child Psychology, 11,* 22-26.

Perry, M.A. (1978). Development of a clinical child psychology training program. *Professional Psychology, 9,* 677-684.

Roberts, M.C. (1982). Clinical child psychology programs: Where and what are they? *Journal of Clinical Child Psychology, 11,* 13-21.

Ross, A.O. (1959). *The practice of clinical child psychology.* New York: Grune & Stratton.

Routh, D.K. (1977). What is a clinical child psychologist? *The Clinical Psychologist, 30,* 23-25.

Routh, D.K. (1982). Intellectual progeny of Seashore and Spence: Iowa psychologists. In D.K. Routh (Ed.), *Learning speech, and the complex effects of punishment: Essays honoring George J. Wischner.* New York: Plenum.

Tuma, J.M. (1982). Proposal for a national conference on professional preparation of clinical child psychologists. *Journal of Clinical Child Psychology, 11,* 3-7.

Tuma, J.M., & Pratt, J.M. (1982). Clinical child psychology practice and training: A survey. *Journal of Clinical Child Psychology, 11,* 27-34.

Consideration on the "Guidelines for Training Psychologists to Work With Children, Youth, and Families" for the National Conference on the Training of Clinical Child Psychologists

Michael C. Roberts
The University of Alabama

Task Force on Training of Division 37

I present for consideration by the Conference the document entitled "Guidelines for Training Psychologists to Work with Children, Youth, and Families" (see Appendix E). I suggest that these minimal recommendations for training can serve as the basis for discussion and action by this Conference.

This document is one in which I had some part in preparing as a member of the Task Force on Training for the Division of Child, Youth and Family Services (Division 37 of the American Psychological Association). This Task Force was chaired by Marilyn T. Erickson, and included June M. Tuma and myself. The Task Force was appointed by then Division 37 President, Carolyn Schroeder, in 1981, with the purpose of considering issues for predoctoral, internship, and postdoctoral training for psychologists working with children, youth, and families. A draft statement was prepared for review by Division 37's Executive Committee and, with several modifications, was finally approved in August, 1983.

One particular reason for putting the *Guidelines* before this conference is that it is generally better to have something to *work from* and *react to* rather than having to confront a blank screen and then to have to fill it in with the myriad of ideas we all bring to this conference. While I certainly have some interest in the Guidelines, I personally neither expect nor intend for it to remain unaffected by our deliberations this week. It is there for us to start with.

We have provided you with the Guidelines document. [A copy of the *Guidelines* is printed in these *Proceedings* in Appendix E.] I will not review it point by point at this time. However, I do encourge your careful consideration of it. At this time, I would like to discuss some important points for our deliberations. Some of these points are represented in the Guidelines. Additionally, there is background thinking of the Division 37 Executive Committee and the Task Force from shaping this final document not in the document and which may be useful in our discussions. The specifics of the Guidelines are better outlined in the written document. They are also being published in the *Journal of Clinical Child Psychology* (Roberts, Erickson, & Tuma, 1985) for even wider dissemination.

When Carolyn Schroeder appointed us, the charge to the Task Force was not unlike the charge to this Conference: define the training experiences thought to be necessary to enhance the quality of psychological services provided to children, youth, and families. This was in reaction to frequently voiced concerns about the quality of services and about who is qualified to provide them. This was no easy task for the Task Force and it will not prove easy for this Conference.

Terminology Considerations

The Division 37 recommendations use the term *psychologists working with children, youth, and families,* which is a generic phrase attempting to encompass all professional psychologists who provide some type of services to these populations. Although Dr. Erickson, Dr. Tuma, and I personally identify with the label *clinical child psychologist,* and indeed, our first few drafts used that phrase to the exclusion of others, we recognized the problems associated with clinical child psychology being the exclusive beneficiaries of the Guidelines. These basic training recommendations should serve to define the training of all psychologists who are providing professional services to children, regardless of specialty area, label or title one uses in the provision of those services.

What we proposed in these recommendations are not *guild-like* standards that might preclude competent service provision by any psychologist. These are more a recognition that certain training experiences and coursework are necessary, but not sufficient, to be a competent psychologist working with children, youth, and families. Therefore, we developed the somewhat cumbersome term, psychologists working with children, youth, and families.

It was additionally not lost on the Task Force that our sponsoring organization, Division 37, had a broader constituency than the subgroup of psychologists who identify themselves as clinical child psychologists. These recommendations have relevance to a number of groups within the psychology profession and the document has been presented to those groups as it is now to this conference for clinical child psychology.

The Task Force viewed the training issue less as a guild issue, less as an issue targeted to or for psychologists, and more as an issue squarely in the role of advocating quality services for children. Thus, first and foremost, the Task Force was concerned more with children and their families and who will be best prepared or competent to provide services to them. We concluded that certain training experiences and exposures are necessary, and will be necessary to provide optimal services. We felt that the profession would be shortchanging children to argue that anybody with too much less can provide the types of service we all would agree should be provided. Consequently, we tried to structure the Training Guidelines to outline minimally acceptable training experiences, while at the same time being flexible in the way a person acquires the training background in order to meet both the fact and spirit of the Task Force report.

One additional issue about the labels of the professional discipline confronting the task force, and now facing this training conference, is the concern over usage of terms already extant in state licensing statutes and APA accreditation. The Guidelines avoid the issue, but this conference on *clinical* child psychology cannot get away from it so easily.

Set of Training Criteria

When you examine the *Guidelines,* you will see that the most important considerations are present on training clinical child psychologists. The fundamental academic coursework, the research components, the applied training in assessment and therapy, all broadly defined, are present. What is lacking to some extent is a clearly articulated statement about *clinical child psychology.* These Guidelines speak to the *basic* training issues of clinical child psychology. *More* can be added to this document. Specifically, guidelines can be added for internship and post-doctoral training in clinical child psychology. Statements can be formulated on the relationship of clinical child psychology to other groups *within* the rather generic phrase, psychology working with children, youth, and families, such as applied developmental psychology, school psychology, counseling psychology, or other groups. More can be added, but the basics are there in the document.

While some have argued that *current* training efforts or even those outlined in the *Guidelines* are inadequate in terms of content and numbers (e.g., assessment training, Elbert, 1984), the Task Force recognized that there are necessary limitations on how much coursework and experience can be required at the predoctoral level. Additionally, the Training Guidelines are compatible with the standards for accreditation of doctoral programs in professional psychology (American Psychological Association, 1980). The accreditation criteria are based on the notion that one is a psychologist first and a specialist second. Fundamental psychology requires a firm grounding in biological, cognitive-affective, and social bases of behavior, and individual differences as well as scientific and professional ethics and standards, research design and methodology, statistics, psychological measurement, and history and systems of psychology. With these as a basis, then, under the accreditation criteria, professional courses and experiences are added such as psychodiagnostics and assessment, intervention procedures, consultation, program evaluation, and research training for the professional psychologist, etc.

The Division 37 Task Force, in preparing the *Guidelines,* recognized that there are reasonable limitations on how much and what can be required in the predoctoral university-based specialty training program over the basic core of psychology. Some additional requirements or deletion of some requirements might improve the training product. And some of these changes are deemed essential by some people in the field. We did not challenge that issue in the *Guidelines.*

This conference will consider the APA Accreditation Criteria under which most programs function in the presentation by Patricia Aletky. The conference may want to suggest modifications which would allow improvement of subspecialty offerings in clinical child psychology. The Task Force did consider recommending that APA accreditation site visiting panels contain at least one bonafide clinical child representative when reviewing such specialty programs. However, this recommendation was dropped with the changes in labels.

A criterion of *ease of implementation* of the recommendations coming from this conference may also need to be considered so that there is not resistance from the APA governance or from training directors and psychology departments who have to implement the clinical child training. In the final draft of the *Guidelines,* the Task Force met this issue by adding the section entitled "Examples of Existing Training Programs Fulfilling the Training Recommendations" to demonstrate that the *Guidelines could* be and *are* being implemented. At this conference we need to recognize, as the Task Force was compelled to acknowledge, that we live in relation to a number of other forces and interests. A sense of a "world of our own" may come to pervade this conference after three days that we need to avoid so that what we suggest *will* come to be. In this conference, participants will want to have reasonableness and reality as goals.

Ethical Considerations

The Task Force stated that a critical concern about who can *do* psychology of this type is ultimately derived from the APA Ethical Standards, the Principle of Competence: "Psychologists recognize the boundaries of their competence. . ." (p. 2). Additionally, for those choosing to practice professional psychology for children, the Standard for Providers of Psychological Services 1.6 similarly applies: "Psychologists shall limit their practice to their demonstrated areas of professional competence." This consideration, above all others, draws some lines between those who can or cannot do clinical child psychology, for example. This line drawing by the ethics standards is not just an issue targeted to the professional, but speaks more to the issue of helping children and families. This conference will also need to have this uppermost in its collective mind.

Survey Results

In developing the training recommendations, the Task Force had a wealth of material on training, much of it from the clinical child psychology area, although certainly related groups had been and are actively concerned with training issues. The Task Force conducted surveys of programs who claimed to have specialty training programs with a variety of foci and labels. These included, for example, clinical child, applied developmental, family therapy, school, counseling, developmental psychopathology, among others.

I conducted two surveys of clinical child training programs, with one published (Roberts, 1982a) and the other presented in an APA symposium (Roberts, 1982b). These surveys and those of others (e.g., Mannarino & Fisher, 1982) were included in the Task Force deliberations and in various APA convention symposia on training topics.

When I examined the training programs (Roberts, 1982a), I found some differences in terms of bureaucratic structure and *statements* of training philosophies. However, despite these apparently superficial differences, the training patterns had much in common. For example, all the training programs purport to prepare students for work in a variety of settings. Students develop the necessary skills in assessment, treatment, and research, with children through practical experience. Students usually gain specialized knowledge through coursework in the areas of normal child development, childhood behavior disorders, treatment procedures for children and families, and experimental methods in the area. Students are typically encouraged to understand children and their behavior in the context of life-span human development. Supervised child practicum experiences in a wide variety of placements takes a major role in preparing the students for child-related predoctoral internships. Most of the programs ascribe to training for proficiency in both research and applied clinical activities. These commonalities are usually found regardless of the program and regardless of which one of the four types of training models I outlined: (a) general clinical training with additional subprogram specialization, (b) specific, specialized program training, (c) clinical training within a developmental psychology program, and (d) clinical child training in conjunction with school psychology (Roberts, 1982a). We have scheduled speakers at this conference on each of these four training models (Marilyn Erickson, Martha Perry, Richard Abidin, Felicisima Serafica). I am hopeful that these presenters will attend to the general issues of training clinical child psychologists within the models. The Task Force took as its orientation, and I think it applies equally well for this conference, to refrain from advocating participants' own models and their particular programs. For the most part, the commonalities across programs are larger than any uniqueness. And, of course, there are *many* more clinical child programs of quality than the ones on the conference agenda.

As a result of the findings of the first survey, along with other input, the Task Force concluded that it is not so much the *form* of the training, but more importantly, the *substance* of the training which should be of concern, and this assumption underlines the *Guidelines* document. This attention to the substance, not the model or training pattern, also concerns this conference. The Task Force recommendations recognize that there are diversity and commonality of existing training programs and that there are several adequate ways to achieve quality training for competent psychologists to work with children, youth, and families.

The Task Force also found that no one model of training can present evidence that a single training pattern or program type likely prepares its graduates to function more ably than any other type program. Strong assertions and chauvinism to the side, no evaluative data have been collected. If the evidence is not present to promote one training model over the others, then this conference, as the Task Force did, may find the wiser course to refrain from endorsing only one model. Indeed, the *Guidelines* focus most appropriately on what specialty curriculum is needed *within* whatever the training program.

Paul Wohlford, a former President of the Section on Clinical Child Psychology, stated a similar view that: "Service to children, youth, and families, embraces different functions in several different settings, and may involve several levels of expertise. In brief, I favor pluralistic training models and service delivery models to render the wide array of services needed by children, youth, and families." (Wohlford, 1978, p. 89)

Heresy

Although the Task Force *Guidelines* assert it to be true, and this existence of this conference assumes it, there is little real evidence to support our oft-repeated statement that *competence is tied to training for that competence.* I may be the heretic at the religious revival, but we may need to consider here whether we *really* need to be doing this or that we might be on the beach instead.

And now for another possibly heretical thought: Some people asserted to the Task Force that the profession is facing a *failure* with regard to training clinical child psychologists and other related specialties. Although not stated in the final document, I recall our thinking and others' input, that there were and are, little data to support that clinical child training is *universally* deficient or that the models and programs are *totally* inadequate. The evidence is not present to support this assertion. We may speculate about a failure, we may describe some unfortunate experiences with poor training, we may recognize the limitations of our programs in not providing all a child practitioner needs to have, and we may have to recommend changes to improve the training process and product, but the data just are not convincing that there is a failure of current training efforts. What we have now is not necessarily the best that we can get, but that if there is a need for changes, modifications can be made while retaining the strengths of existing formats and diversity (Roberts, 1980).

Having said that, however, let me momentarily reverse myself. While the data are not present about program failure, in a second survey of clinical child training programs done for the Division 37 Task Force (Roberts, 1982b) I found that for many existing programs some of the topics of training recommended in the *Guidelines* (which were then not yet finally formulated) were not even available to matriculating students, much less required of them. The responses to the survey were from programs claiming the title of "clinical child psychology training programs" (based on the list of Mannarino & Fischer, 1982, and ones added). Forty-six of the 53 programs did not have at least one of the topics even available and 31 of the 53 did not have two or more topics available. In fact, two programs did not have anything available for *seven* of the 13 topics listed on the questionnaire that eventually formed the basis of the *Guidelines*! Additionally, about one-third of the programs did not have readily apparent or coordinated and articulated specialty programs even though they proclaimed to have specialized training in clinical child psychology. Now to return to my earlier point, these survey results suggest to me, as they did to the Task Force, that something needs to be done about the *content* of the training for several programs, but not automatically or necessarily the training model. That is what is recommended in the *Training Guidelines.*

Since few clinical programs currently provide all or most of the topics listed, then we again must focus on the future. If we can relieve ourselves from an allegiance to particular models or from preconceived notions that will hinder our discussions here, then we can attend to what is really needed to *best* serve children. At this conference, we are faced with the heretical questions, is training really tied to competence and is the current training effort inadequately preparing child professionals? I have my own ambivalent thoughts on this which I will share in later discussions outside the role I have been assigned in this plenary session.

Internship

The Task Force, in formulating *Guidelines* for predoctoral training, also acknowledged that there needs to be intensive specialized training in child work at the internship level and post-doctoral levels. The present *Guidelines* document does not attend much to this since it was the minimal entry level skills or basic training from the predoctoral, university-based programs which became the primary concern to the Task Force. One caution we on the Task Force heard, and I pass it on to you, is that no assumption should be made that the university programs should do *all* the specialty training. There are many other tasks at the university level. Historically, internships were often the first clinical experience students obtained. This has now changed with many students acquiring the equivalent of internship experience at their home university prior to their internship year. Despite this trend, internships need to use caution about expecting such high levels of clinical experiences when there are other requirements to fulfill at the university level to become a well-rounded, well-trained, full-fledged psychologist. This conference will have to attend more to the interactions and reactions involving internships and university programs.

Credentialling

Finally, in a number of discussions, one idea has been repeated in a variety of ways. The Task Force and the Division 37 Executive Committee discussed credentialling or special licensing of psychologists working with children, youth, and families. (Several others have also written on this issue, e.g., Goldman, 1982). As the *Guidelines* document indicates, the training recommendations are not meant for that purpose, although a letter from the training director was recommended. Thus, the issue was avoided. And there is some sentiment for continuing to do so. Brendan Maher may have articulated most cogently the thinking of those opposed to this in his plenary address to the Training Conference on Health Psychology and it applies to clinical child psychology equally well:

> . . . high standards of competence and knowledge will create status and acceptance by other professions to a degree that *cannot* be achieved by *certification, credentialling,* or any other of the various political techniques that may be employed in the service of autonomy. (Maher, 1983, p. 43). [emphasis mine]

How we handle this aspect of specialty training will be an important later issue. However, relevant to training for the "high standards of competence and knowledge," I think you will find the *Training Guidelines* are a solid basis for attaining the product that will achieve "status and acceptance by other professions," regardless of any recommendation for certification.

Final Words

Finally, I turn to H.L. Mencken who asserted that "to every complex question there is a simple answer, and it is wrong." While this statement is itself a simple answer to a complex question, I suggest that we face an arduous task for the next few days to avoid either arriving at too simple answers or asking too complex questions than we need to frame.

My purpose in coming before this conference is twofold. First, I place before you the training recommendations of the Task Force from Division 37. Second, I wanted to outline some of the thinking that went into formulating the *Guidelines* as background for our later discussions at this Conference. I do not think the Task Force did the job intended for this conference. I do think these *Guidelines* form an excellent basis for *deliberation* and for *part* of the eventual recommendations this Conference will declare.

References

American Psychological Association. (1980). *Accreditation handbook.* Washington, DC: Author.

Elbert, J.C. (1984). Training in child diagnostic assessment. A survey of clinical psychology graduate programs. *Journal of Clinical Child Psychology, 13,* 122-133.

Goldman, J. (1982). Clinical child psychology training and credentialing. *Journal of Clinical Child Psychology, 11,* 8-12.

Maher, B. (1983). The education of health psychologists: Quality counts — numbers are dangerous. *Proceedings of the National Working Conference on Education and Training in Health Psychology,* May 23-27, 1983. In *Health Psychology, 2,* Supplement, 37-47.

Mannarino, A.P., & Fisher, C. (1982). Survey of graduate training in clinical child psychology. *Journal of Clinical Child Psychology, 11,* 22-26.

Roberts, M.C. (1980, September). Breadth of specialty training. In J.M. Tuma (Chair), *Specialty versus generic training: A case for clinical child psychology.* Symposium presented at the annual meeting of the American Psychological Association, Montreal.

Roberts, M.C. (1982a). Clinical child psychology programs: Where and what are they? *Journal of Clinical Child Psychology, 11,* 13-21.

Roberts, M.C. (1982b, August). Training of clinical child psychologists. In M.T. Erickson & M.C. Roberts (Chairs), *Training of professional child psychologists: Standards for minimal competence.* Symposium presented at the annual meeting of the American Psychological Association, Washington, DC.

Roberts, M.C., Erickson, M.T., & Tuma, J.M. (1985). Addressing the needs: Guidelines for training psychologists to work with children, youth, and families. *Journal of Clinical Child Psychology, 14,* 70-79.

Wohlford, P. (1978). A challenge to clinical psychology: Better training to serve children. *Journal of Clinical Child Psychology, 7,* 89-90.

Specialization and the Regulation of Practice in Organized Psychology[1]

Patricia J. Aletky[2]
American Psychological Association

For the past three decades, the American Psychological Association (APA) has been involved in the development, promulgation, dissemination, and continual revision of standards for the practice of psychology. The objective of these standards has been to promote quality assurance of psychological services for providers, consumers, and third-party sanctioners of such services. In addition, over the past two decades, APA has promulgated policy with regard to the regulation of psychology. Standard development may be thought of as reflecting issues internal to organized psychology, while issues relating to regulation reflect the way in which organized psychology presents itself to the outside world. On both the internal and external fronts, the issues are in a constant state of flux, reflecting the continuous process of change within professional psychology.

Current status of specialization within APA

There are two major policy documents which address the practice of psychology, each of which is the subject of current controversy: (1) *Standards for Providers of Psychological Services* (APA 1977) and (2) *Specialty Guidelines for the Delivery of Services* (APA 1981b). While there are pressures for official recognition of new specialities, such as health, forensic, or neuropsychology, the only currently recognized specialties are clinical, counseling, school, and industrial/organizational psychology.

For the past four years or so, the *Standards for Providers* ("generic standards") have been under revision. In the past year, the proposed revision, slated to be submitted for final approval, was withdrawn from the Council of Representative's agenda because of legal concerns. Recently, APA members have become increasingly concerned about legal implications of APA policy particularly, vulnerability to antitrust actions and liability for malpractice litigations. A general theme with regard to the standards has been the question of whether the standards reflect minimally acceptable levels of performance or are to be viewed as presenting ideals to which professionals should strive (i.e.. "aspirational"). As of this writing, the entire standards revision project is on hold, with no likely resolution in the next few months.

Since the revision of the *specialty guidelines* is contingent upon revision of the generic standards, the *specialty guidelines* project, too, is on hold. When the revised standards are approved, the Committee on Professional Standards will then be charged with beginning to revise the specialty guidelines, to assure that they properly explicate the generic standards. This project, when it occurs, is sure to stimulate its own level of controversy. For example, within clinical psychology, there are those who believe that clinical is not a specialty; within counseling psychology there are those who very much would like the *specialty guidelines* collapsed with clinical because they perceive little functional difference between clinical and counseling in practice. School psychologists have some rather unique concerns, for example, those relating to Master's level providers. Futhermore, industrial/organizational psychology includes those who believe their concerns are so different from those of health care providers that they should not be included in organized psychology's statements relating to clinical, counseling, and school psychology. At this point in time, it is difficult to predict the future of the *specialty guidelines,* the only APA policy document describing in detail the practice of psychology at the applied level.

While there are growing pressures among constituencies for official recognition of new specialties within psychology, APA has had a moratorium on such recognition since 1981. Currently, the Board of Professional Affairs, under which the Subcommittee on Specialization has functioned, is considering a proposal to hold a conference for discussion among all interested parties during 1986. It is hoped that out of such a conference would emerge some consensus about criteria by which new (or perhaps any) specialties within psychology could be defined. Thus, it could be many years before APA adopts any formal policy in this area. In the mean-

[1]Adapted from two presentations at the Conference Training of Clinical Child Psychologists.

[2]The views presented herein represent those of the author rather than any official position of the American Psychological Association.

time, there is nothing to stop groups outside of APA, such as the American Board of Professional Psychology (ABPP) or other, newer, credentialing bodies, from offering their own recognition to psychologists in various new specialities. Should clinical child psychologists seek official recognition as a specialty, the group should obviously seek representation at such a conference as well as consider approaching other credentialing bodies if the recognition offered is desired.

The Role of APA in the Regulation of Practice

Organized psychology, through APA, has no direct role in the regulation of practice. Indirectly, however, through promulgation of policies as well as accreditation of training programs, APA does have a noticeable, albeit delayed, impact upon state regulatory bodies. Regulation issues, in some ways, surpass internal, specialization disputes in significance because the general public, including other mental health care providers, third-parties payers, and consumers, need to know how professional psychology generally defines itself. Because of this need in the general public, as well as the relatively immature status of professional psychology, APA has supported generic, rather than specialty, licensing at the state/provincial level. Thus, while groups such as clinical child pyschology struggle with issues of differentiation within professional psychology, there are vast numbers outside of psychology who still want to know "What is a psychologist?"

In the current *Standards for Providers* (APA 1977), APA defines "professional psychologist" as follows: "Professional psychologists have a doctoral degree from a regionally accredited university or professional school in a program that is primarily psychological and appropriate training and experience in the area of service offered." (APA, 1977, p.4) Further, current policy requires two years of relevant, supervised experience, one of which is postdoctoral for those professionals in independent practice. To a great extent, psychologists are left to self-monitor their adherence to APA's *Ethical Principles* (APA 1981a) requiring that one practice only within one's area(s) of competence. APA has used the term "health care provider" and "clinical" psychologist to include clinical, counseling, and school psychologists in its advocacy efforts to include psychology in various federally funded programs such as those under Medicare. Generic licensing, therefore, assures the public that psychologists offering services to individuals have a minimal level of credentials.

There are many factors impinging on organized psychology which supports a policy of generic licensing at this point in the evolution of the profession. The effects of in fighting upon psychologist's status in the health care marketplace cannot be underestimated. The fact that psychology was not included as an independent provider, for example, in the original Medicare legislation in 1965, may have been avoided if APA had made a uniform and swift response to the legislation when it was proposed. Psychology's exculsion from Medicare has, in turn, resulted in our exclusion from a vast array of programs under Medicare, as well as countless privately-funded programs who copy the provider definitions from the Medicare language. Major factors affecting organized psychology's public stance include:

(1) *Relationships with other professions.* In reference to psychiatry, for example, psychologist views range from those who believe we should do everything they do, including prescribe medications, to those who seem comfortable with a role best described as "assistant physician," often functioning exclusively as a psychometrist.

(2) *An increasingly competitive health care marketplace.* With an increasingly sophisticated consuming public and the integration of business principles with health care administration, the main theme has been cost-effectiveness (i.e., psychologists must demonstrate how our services in general make a difference).

(3) *The relationship between APA and the states.* In the past, APA has mainly offered organizational consultation to state psychological associations, although the current trend points toward more active intervention. APA has worked on a model licensing law which could be disseminated to the states since the late 1960's; such a model has yet to emerge. State legislators have concerns similar to federal lawmakers; again, cost-effectiveness is a major issue, in addition to the continuing issue of definition — who are psychologists and what do they have to offer that is different from physicians or counselors? Most states have adopted parts of APA policy in their practice statutes and the generic rather than specialty descriptions seem to be most appropriate at this time.

(4) *Legal/antitrust environment.* The current legal environment has had, as mentioned above, a profound effect on APA's policy development. Policies which could be construed as promoting the exclusion of practi tioners from the marketplace or increasing vulnerability to malpractice action are viewed with extreme scrutiny. This current climate

has led APA to promote a relatively inclusive definition of psychologist rather than specialty distinctions.

In response to such influences as those listed above, organized psychology has, therefore, focused its energies on arriving at consensus regarding the definition of professional psychologist and generic regulation of practice.

Strategies for Action

In view of the current status of specialization and generic credentialing within psychology, what can clinical child psychology do to have a significant impact on this ongoing process within APA? The following suggestions can be viewed as topics for discussion:

(1) A specialty must be based on a generic foundation. If not, practitioners may find themselves "painted in a corner;" that is, allowed by state law only to practice within a highly circumscribed area.

(2) Academic theories should be weighed against political realities (i.e., any action on the part of the group should be subjected to a cost/benefit analysis). Specifically, possible gains to the group must be balanced with potential alienation of colleagues in the larger group. Further, there may be other subgroups with which the clinical child group could form coalitions based on common concerns.

(3) Motivational issues must be considered. What is the incentive for a practitioner to seek additional training in order to meet criteria deemed appropriate by the group. How can such criteria, once agreed upon, be "enforced?"

(4) Any interest group should start with consciousness-raising efforts within the group itself. The First National Conference, of course, represents such an effort. Once a sufficient level of self-awareness is established, the general public should be considered the most potentially valuable ally. Ultimately, it is the consuming public who will decide whether or not specialties within psychology are important. Thus, a public education campaign can be invaluable in serving the public while simultaneously promoting the interests of the specialty group.

(5) For a group such as the clinical child constituency to influence the governance of APA, it will be helpful to (a) follow through with a specific proposal and track it through the system with the help of APA staff; (b) educate members of relevant governance units such as the Council of Representatives; (c) be prepared to compromise in the face of divergent views but common goals; and (d) attempt to promote members of the clinical child group as members of governance groups such as continuing committees who work on projects of interest.

The National Conference provides an excellent starting point — a way to define what the group seeks to achieve; the next step is to develop a specific action plan and begin to work toward its implementation.

Conclusion

Professional psychology is in a state of rapid change. Groups with a specific interest, such as clinical child psychologists, will need to agree on a balance point between forming coalitions with those who have similar goals and delineating (or fighting for) those characteristics which make the group distinct from other practitioners. Obviously, such a balance is best agreed upon in a forward-thinking, proactive way rather than to allow the group's stance to be passively affected by the many and complex factors affecting national policy from within and without the profession.

Reference

American Psychological Association. (1977). Standards for providers of psychological services, *American Psychologist, 32,* 495-505.

American Psychological Association. (1981a). Ethical principles of psychologists. *American Psychologist, 36,* 633-638.

American Psychological Association. (1981b). Specialty guidelines for the delivery of services. *American Psychologist, 36,* 640-681.

The swift and certain professional advances make those in the science look a bit pallid by comparison. George Miller, in a recent letter to recruit new members for the APA, opened his plea with a memorable statement from his 1969 presidential address:

> In my opinion, scientific psychology is potentially one of the most revolutionary intellectual enterprises ever conceived by the mind of man. If we were ever to achieve substantial progress toward our stated aim — toward the understanding, prediction, and control of mental and behavioral phenomena — the implications for every aspect of society would make brave men tremble (Miller, 1969, p.1065).

Clearly, this was written before the advent of women in psychology; just as clearly, we have yet to achieve the substantial progress Miller envisioned. Indeed, in another presidential address some thirteen years later, Bevan (1982) doubted that the universities (including their psychology departments) could continue to provide intellectual leadership in public life "... because there is no evidence that they can, at present, see reality for what it is — or even if they could, that they would be able, individually or collectively, to get their act together" (p.1310). Bevan felt that this leadership must be assumed by scientific and professional societies, but since the universities guide socialization into science and the professions, the societies will be no better than the members they inherit from the academy. A year later, in a wide ranging summation of a two day centennial celebration of the founding of the G. Stanley Hall laboratory at Johns Hopkins, Bevan (1983) commented that the greatest transformation that has taken place in the past century in psychology is "... that the gentleman scholar has given way, particularly since the end of World War II, to the professional" (p.23). Earlier (1980), he put it even more cogently in saying that "... our graduate schools have become professional schools" (p.133).

The influence of the "professional outlook" (Bevan, 1983) upon scholarship has resulted in greater and greater specialization, corrosive in its effects beyond what evolutionary differentiation would imply. The entire reward system, abetted especially by government research grant funding methods, has led to what Bevan (1983) calls ". . the cult of unbridled individualism that dominates all of our society but that exists in its most extreme form in our colleges and universitites. The problem with the Academy at present," Bevan went on, "is that it is dominated by dedicated operators masquerading as dedicated scholars" (p.25). What might have led a respected scientist-statesman, who. had been a graduate dean, provost at two top rank universities and executive officer of the Amercian Association for the Advancement of Science to such a harsh judgment? What indeed can account for the contrast in what I read as optimism — awesome optimism, but optimism nonetheless — in Millers's 1969 remarks, and the apparent gloom of Bevan in 1983? It so happened that Miller also presented an address at the Hall centennial. The enkindling element in his 1969 paper was not only his vision for scientific psychology but his suggestions for how science could be made useful to people. I asked him if he still believed in his imperishable metaphor that we ought to give psychology away. "Yes," he said, "but nobody wants it." This pithy reply may exaggerate our irrelevance, but is not far off the mark of how we are viewed by the public.

The situation is by no means altogether bleak. Like others, I have a personal list of some exciting developments in psychology. Among them I would include the broadening of cognitive science; the rediscovery of affects and of personality; the promise of work at the interface of cognition, affect, and the neurosciences; burgeoning interest in health and behavior and in prevention (as much for the model they have adopted as for their tangible findings); the prospect of support for research on the process and effects of psychotherapy; interesting strides in research on the family; the emergence of women and minorities, which has changed the notion of who we are and what questions we ask; and the increasing involvement of experimentalists of all stripes in matters of the real world. If I were asked to provide a theoretical anchor in psychology for the next twenty years, it would be lifespan development, the contextual setting for advances in research and in practice and, epistemologically, for the understanding of psychology's own development.

But there are numerous grounds for concern, some of them problems of long standing. We no longer know what constitutes generic education in psychology. Nor, with the accretion of specialized knowledge, do we know what is important and when or how to teach it. Research and practice still coexist uncomfortably in most of our educational programs, with neither adequately informing the other. Boundaries between subfields have become increasingly blurred, but we maintain the illusion of distinctiveness. Entire areas of psychology are grossly undersubscribed by graduate students; other areas, of course, have exploded in popularity, but we lack careful examination and comprehension of what these changes mean. The unselfconscious integration in our teaching of material reflecting ethnic and gender diversity continues to elude us. The recent increase in the number of women applicants for graduate education in psychology will exacerbate this problem. The ratio of women to men admitted is even more lopsided, indicating not only that fewer men are applying but that their quality is not what it had been. The educational process itself, especially in the applied areas, is driven less by the inner sense of curiosity and discovery, by the compassionate desire to help others, or by the needs of society than by credentialing and licensing requirements. A separate, and in my view unequal, professional educational enterprise has proliferated alongside the university graduate establishment. Indeed, the field of psychology, always stretched thin because of its enormous intradisciplinary span, appears to have holes in its middle and losses at both ends. At one extreme, the shift toward complete professionalization results in something so unconcerned with science, and at the other the migration to the neurosciences involves work so molecular and remote from behavior, that their continued inclusion in psychology is debatable. Finally, the public's understanding and support of the behavioral sciences, in general, has been poor because of our ineffectiveness in assuring that what we know and do is meaningful for people's lives.

The issues of specialization and subfield boundaries are almost inseparable. Specialization seems such a natural consequence of the accretion of knowledge that its corrosive effects on the science may go undetected. Henry Gleitman, in a letter to Bevan (1983), put it about as well as I have seen it:

> For the academic system — with competitive research grants, peer review, publish-or-perish, and all the rest of it — has destroyed the audience. Our fellow academicians may be a potential audience, but they have neither the time nor the inclination to act as one. Their only chance of staying in the theatre hall (getting their first job, getting tenure), the price of admission, is to get up on stage as well as be an actor . . . . we are all up there acting, orating, and there is no one in the auditorium seats listening. Even my most scholarly colleagues only read what they must to help them in their own work . . . . As a result, there are fewer and fewer of us — in all fields — who know anything except our own little parts . . .(pp. 26-27).

What has happened in the science has infected the profession as well. Specialization is the subject of exhaustive examination, despite the fact that it hasn't been that easy to distinguish between three of the existing recognized specialities, counseling, clinical, and school psychology. These have fair overlap of function and neither setting nor population characteristics can be used as infallible guides to distinguish them. The fourth specialty is a mite different: industrial/organizational psychologists are fascinating because they seem to have wandered into the wrong party. In reality (i.e., in terms of what people do rather than what they call themselves), boundaries between areas are quite permeable. The professional dilemma is further complicated by the strong growth of an applied research constituency.

In the mid-seventies, when our data began to show a downturn in academic positions, we encourged research training programs to prepare students for career alternatives to academic research and teaching. Most faculty members could not, or did not wish to, make this shift and once again, as in the applied fields, the role models were not completely appropriate to the task. Change was inevitable, given the academic market and the growth of a service economy. The movement of researchers to non-academic research positions has been well documented in a recent article by Pion and Lipsey (1984) and it is a salutory development. Thus, developmental, social, and personality psychologists, and even experimental and physiological graduates began to work in settings that had been dominated by clinical and other applied psychologists. Many of these people perform research on clinical populations, on problems of relevance to service delivery, or do things that research oriented clinicians also do. The health psychologists, an interesting mixture of basic researchers and clinical types, also entered the public system. While this was going on, many "pure" clinicians opted primarily for private practice. But in a short time, it may be very difficult indeed to tell a child clinician from an applied developmentalist. Naturally, the applied researchers also tended to fragment into specializations which, if anything, were even less distinctive than the old professional triumverate. We had psychology that was ecological, environmental, social ecological, transactional ecological, applied social, all shadings of community, applied behavior analysis, plus within-field combinations like social-developmental and across-field programs like psychology and law. The great paradox, of course, is that while one set of forces pushes toward increased specialization, with its rigid codifications and securing of boundaries, another set of forces reflects the great fluidity and rapid change in the total field, As a discipline, it seems we are trying to catch a drop of mercury. Health psychology, which has barely differentiated itself, already shows signs of mitosis into oncological and cardiological psychologists. Not long ago Seymour Sarason, whose incisive writings will be found lurking somewhere behind much of what I say this morning, said to me, "I worry that health psychologists have finally found out how to be the *real* doctors in psychology." The specialities just mentioned give substance to Sarason's concern, and if the health psychologists leap into an identification with medicine, they will have thrown away the best chance they have of really making a difference in medicine. It would be particularly unfortunate, because Arden House, the site of their training conference, was Boulder revisited. Rather than succumb to the detrimental effects of specialization and risk premature rigidity and encrustation, I am inclined to support Leon Levy's (1984) proposal that we think more broadly of human services psychology. Neither our knowledge nor its applications fit neatly into boxes.

I note with pleasure that you have scheduled a session dealing with boundary issues and that a developmental psychologist is presenting on the program. Clinical child psychologists have always had one estimable advantage over the rest of clinical psychology. Because of the importance of families to children — and of children to families — they have never fallen prey to the illusion that they could be concerned solely with the client. That illusion still dominates a good portion of adult clinical psychology, some of which is practiced without context of any kind.Generally, the sensitivity to context does not stop at families, but extends to social institutions, such as schools.

I imagine that an issue in the conference may be whether to establish a specialty. All of the usual professional precedents will dictate that direction, especially if you look to law and medicine. I do not worry about specialization in law. Tax law and admiralty law can usually be practiced without reference to one another. Law has more central dilemmas in the area of the ethics of practice. Medicine runs much greater risks in specialization. When the person becomes the organ, something vital is lost. There is good reason why medical educators are so profoundly concerned with what is happening to medical students today. Medicine somewhere has lost caring for patients as people, and for that matter caring about medical students as people. The risks of specialization are even greater in psychology, where relations with others are central to our concerns. Although we now recognize the importance of biological, psychological, and sociocultural perspectives in graduate education; we study them discretely rather than interconnectedly. The next step would be to recognize the importance of the life span, each period seen in the context of other periods and from the multiple perspectives just mentioned.

I remarked earlier that I would select life span development as the anchor for psychology for the next 20 years. We possess the knowledge base to begin to implement a curriculum whose conceptual, substantive, and experiential crucible is life span development. I include in this concept the biological, psychological, and socio-cultural areas, each presented developmentally and interactively. This means, for example, that something like the history of the elementary school as an institution would be as much a part of learning as biological maturational factors, cognitive and perceptual development, competence, separation, social interaction with peers, and family reactions to a youngster beginning school. It also means a degree of involvement with at least the major age groups in the life span (infancy, early childhood and the preschool years, later childhood, adolescence, young, middle and later adulthood, and the elderly) covering the time from prenatal development to death and bereavement. Normal development, vagaries of development, and developmental psychopathology would be presented so that the full range of biopsychosocial phenomena can be appreciated. Particular attention would be accorded to age and event-related life transitions, to antecedent and consequent possibilities and to factors that lead to resilience and invulnerability as well as those leading to vulnerability. Such a curriculum, covering the entire life span, would be an excellent antidote to narrow specialization, although nothing would prevent students from focusing more intensively on certain age groups, functions, or elements that influence development. Such a process would locate the person in the environment over time, it would emphasize change and the mutual influence of systems on one another, it would embed the individual in society and in a context of personal and social history.

This is not *a* course. It is the backbone of a four to five year program and is the central feature of such a program during the entire time. It cannot be taught by one psychologist and it cannot be taught only by psychologists. At the very least, we shall need considerable help from biological, social, and policy scientists, and I think to do it really well, we should tap historian, novelist, and philosopher. It is a vehicle for making multidisciplinary education real. It must include a strong experiential component, so that the student apprehends the interwoven strands of the developmental process *in vivo*. The experiential component should include work with persons of all ages, both sexes, a diversity of ethnic groups and socio-economic classes. Experience beyond the individual is necessary, with families, small groups, and support networks. This will be the most difficult portion of the program to fashion and implement. If this component were to be carried out with sufficient intensity, caring, and modelling, there would be little need for a separate predoctoral internship which now largely makes up for deficits and detachment in graduate education. Local facilities naturally would be encourged to be active as part of the experiential component. This is not an easy thing to say because internship training has traditionally done an indispensable and excellent job of providing the reality that academic programs so often lack. A coherent program must contain that reality.

Around this central core, one may place methodological, technique-oriented, and in-depth topical courses. Age-related material, such as children's assessment devices, would be introduced at appropriate junctures in the life span. Students will certainly achieve the kind of longitudinal understanding that is now so uncommon, and they can dwell as needed or as desired on a variety of cross-sectional points in their traversal. Ideally, the program should contain research experience with children, adults, and the elderly from a variety of backgrounds in order to sensitize students to research issues with diverse populations. It would be possible, of course, to emphasize one or another life span period, or to include more or less in the way of research and applied interventions so that the program can accommodate differentiation, the development of special expertise and several concentrations, but preparation for multiple career options would characterize the endeavor.

There is no graduate department of psychology (or even of human development or behavioral sciences) that now is able to mount such a program. It would require the full time dedication of three or four faculty members for at least two years to get it started. One of the ways to implement such a radical change would be as an experimental program within an existing graduate program, unless an institution happened to be starting a graduate department *de novo*. Federal training money, if any remains available, might be used appropriately for such a task. Instead of the usual faculty development award, which produces people in the prevailing pattern, a package of four such awards to a single institution for a major program overhaul might serve the nation better in the long run. This is hardly an easy model, either to implement in its own right, or to posit as an alternative to well-entrenched habits. It would go a long way toward counteracting what Sarason (1981) has called the mistake of an asocial psychology.

If you have gleaned from these brief remarks that I think that graduate education in psychology is in need of a large scale overhaul, you are correct. But I try to have very few illusions about the pace at which that may occur, if it gets underway at all. Neverthless, yours is the first of three meetings on this issue that I shall be attending in the short space of three weeks, culcuminating in the Morgantown planning meeting for university based graduate education. Something may actually be happening. Of all the groups meeting, yours has the most natural understanding of development, of a perspective that includes antecedents and consequences. Moreover, you should be sensitive to a dimension unattended by most clinicians, prevention, which will gradually have to displace some of the casualty orientations simply because we shall never have the resources, in people or money, to take care of all the casualties.

The problems that I have mentioned this morning are not trivial problems and they will not yield to trivial solutions or to tinkering. They have to do basically with what kind of profession we want to be, and I use the word profession in the broadest sense to cover research and practice. I must return to George Miller's metaphor because giving psychology away is what its all about. I don't quite agree with Miller that nobody wants it. I do think we don't know how to give it away and that we are not certain we want to do so. Our decision about that will ultimately answer what kind of profession we want to be. But is giving psychology away really a cause for such concern? Isn't that what the best of us do as teachers, scientists, and as psychotherapists? There is a much larger audience out there than Henry Gleitman envisioned. The world is waiting.

References

Bevan, W. (1980). Graduate education for the earthquake generation. *Human Development, 23,* 126-136.

Bevan, W. (1982). A sermon of sorts in three plus parts. *American Psychologist, 37,* 1303-1322.

Bevan, W. (1983, October). *The journey is everything.* Paper presented at the G. Stanley Hall Centennial, The Johns Hopkins University, Baltimore, MD.

Levy, L. (1984). The metamorphosis of clinical psychology: Toward a new charter as human services psychology. *American Psychologist, 39,* 486-494.

Miller, G.A. (1969). Psychology as a means of promoting human welfare. *American Psychologist, 24,* 1663-1675.

Pion, G.M., & Lipsey, M.W. (1984). Psychology and society: The challenge of change. *American Psychologist, 39,* 739-754.

Sarason, S.B. (1981). An asocial psychology and a misdirected clinical psychology. *American Psychologist, 36,* 827-836.

A (Brief) Look Back

Alan O. Ross
State University of New York at Stony Brook

This contribution is entitled "a brief look back" because a brief look into the events leading up to this Conference is all that is warranted. They say that those who fail to learn from history are condemned to repeat it, but, as I hope to show, all we clinical child psychologists can learn from history is that we had better take care of our own interests because nobody else will do it for us.

As most of you know, clinical psychology began as clinical child psychology, for when Lightner Witmer opened his Psychological Clinic in 1896, the majority of his cases were children with academic difficulties. In fact, the first case he described in his new journal, *The Psychological Clinic,* was a boy with inordinate spelling difficulties. The focus soon shifted to juvenile offenders, a more pressing social problem even at that time, when William Healy opened what became the Institute for Juvenile Research, where Grace Fernald was the first psychologist. It also bears mention in this context that behavior therapy began as child behavior therapy with the classical case of Peter whom Mary Cover Jones treated for a phobia in 1924.

In 1959, when I traced these beginnings of our field (Ross, 1959), I expressed surprise that clinical child psychology had not received earlier recognition, in view of the fact that it had its origins that long ago. It was, in fact, not until 1951 that the term clinical child psychology first appeared in the literature. By now, of course, the term is in fairly common use but something else has changed little. It is, and I quote, "that well-trained people are few and that too many psychologists ultimately find themselves working with children without the kind of training and experience which is essential to competence" (p.9). This quote is not from the call for this Conference but dates back to 1955 and comes from a report of a committee appointed by APA's Division 7 and given the charge to look into training standards for working with children. As I said, little has changed. Let me quote some more.

"There now exists a pressing need for well-trained psychologists to do clinical work with children, and it would seem that this need can best be filled by establishing a specialized training program under university auspices, thereby giving recognition to clinical child psychology as a separate professional entity." No, this is also not a sentence taken from the call for this conference. It is a quote from a book of mine called, "The Practice of Clinical Child Psychology," that was published in 1959 (Ross). Why is it that here it is 1985 and we are finally gathering to discuss how clinical child psychologists should be trained? And look at the circumstances. The sponsor of this meeting is not the American Psychological Association or the National Institute of Mental Health, nor the Division of Clinical Psychology. What funding there is comes from the meager resources of Section I, our own grants, our own institutions, or our own pockets. Nor are we talking to the movers and shakers of the psychological establishment as they had at earlier training conferences; we are talking primarily to one another. How different that from the conferences at Boulder, Chicago, and Vail. But more about these later.

I have long felt that the development of clinical child psychology was derailed by the events of World War II, the war to which clinical psychology owes its ascendence. What applied child psychologists there were at the beginning of that conflict were pressed into rendering service to our soldiers, sailors, and airmen. When the war ended and its psychiatric casualties needed help, both the VA and the soon-to-be established NIMH eagerly funded the training of clinical psychologists who could work with adults. Who needed clinical child psychologists? It was felt that what services children might need could be rendered by social workers or by so-called "regular" clinical psychologists whose generic training presumably equipped them to work with people of any age.

Let me say a few words about organizational matters. In 1959 and lacking an appropriately raised consciousness, I referred to the clinical child psychologist as "a man (sic) without a country." APA had no division appropriate for members of our emerging specialty; there was no journal serving as an appropriate outlet for our research; and no one believed in predoctoral training leading to a clinical specialization with children. It was not until March of 1961 when five of us who were attending the Ortho meeting got together in a New York deli on Seventh Avenue to discuss starting an interest group in APA that would be devoted to clinical child psychology. At the subsequent 1961 APA meeting, 48 people gathered around a table in a small room and founded what was to become Section I of Division 12. It will not surprise you to hear that the agenda of that very first meeting included a discussion of where, whether, and how clinical child psychology was to be taught.

I must here mention the remarkable development of our publication. Started in 1961 as a mimographed newsletter of the interest group, edited by Allan Barclay, it grew to the refereed, abstracted, and much-cited *Journal of Clinical Child Psychology*. If Section I had done nothing else, that journal is a real accomplishment and all who had a hand in its development deserve our vote of thanks. It is indeed something we can all be proud of. I shall not bore you with the rest of our history. It is recorded for posterity in a chapter in Wolman's "Manual of Child Psychopathology" (Ross, 1972).

Let me then turn to a review of what earlier training conferences decided to do (or not to do) about clinical child psychology. It is a dismal record.

As you know, the legendary Boulder Conference, which set the direction clinical psychology was to take for some 30 years, was convened in 1949 (Raimy, 1950). You may wonder what they said about clinical child psychology. Here is a quote that should please you: "There are at present no generally recognized specialties within clinical psychology, except for the rather dubious distinction between work with children and work with adults" (p.189). A dubious distinction, indeed! As far as graduate training was concerned, the conferees agreed on broad rather than specialized training, and, while they felt that people should be trained to work at many age levels, they considered "narrow" specialization to be unwise. Some students, they opined, might legitimately plan to specialize in particular kinds of practice, such as clinical work with children, which required specialized knowledge for maximum effectiveness in service and research (ibid.). Just where, when, and how that specialized knowlege was to be acquired, the report of the Conference sayeth not.

In 1965, motivated largely by great discontent with the lack of relevant substance in clinical training programs, loudly voiced by some recent graduates of such programs, APA called a Conference on the Professional Preparation of Clinical Psychologists. This Conference recognized "the increasing emphasis on clinical work with children and the importance of such work," "the need for clinical psychologists competent to work with [children]," and the fact that "our training programs are generally neglecting the preparation of child clinical and school psychologists" (Hoch, Ross, & Winder, 1966, p.53). The participants were then moved to "urge that greater emphasis be placed on the important subspecialty of clinical child psychology" (Hoch, Ross, & Winder, 1966, p.87).

The conference participants kept coming back to the question of specialty training, but, ultimately, it was their consensus that such training should take place in the postdoctoral years. There was, in fact, a vote to require postdoctoral training for anyone planning to teach or practice a specialty such as clinical child psychology. The development of facilities for such training was "to be encourged" (Hoch, Ross, & Winder, 1966). Those of us who had gone to that conference with high hopes went away feeling disappointed. We had gone to the Windy City and got just that — a lot of wind.

It was not much better at Vail in 1973 (Korman, 1976), when the same sponsors called a conference on "Levels and Patterns of Professional Training in Psychology." This time the motivation was a bit different. No longer were young PhD's unhappy about the training they had received but large numbers of underrepresented people and their advocates were unhappy about the training they were unable to get. It was a largely politically-motivated conference and its resolutions reflected that motivation. There were calls for increasing the enrollment of minorities and women, resolutions condemning racism and sexism, and demands for raising the number of people receiving the doctorate.

Yet, despite that crowded agenda, a small band of child advocates managed to work toward the adoption of the following resolution:

> Recognizing the special skills and preparation necessary for working in the area of child and/or developmental psychology, we recommend:
>
> a) The . . . inclusion of preparation in child and/or developmental psychology in all relevant training programs at both the graduate and undergraduate levels.
>
> b) The adoption of the recommendation that all professional training programs heighten the awareness of their graduates that it is unethical to offer professional services for which they are not specifically competent, and that the inclusion of either child, clinical child, school, or developmental psychology be an essential requirement for professional psychologists. (Korman, 1976, p.103)

Such enunciating and endorsing of principles and the raising of consciousness is all most conferences have accomplished, and, as far as clinical child psychology was concerned, that is all Vail accomplished. Vail, however, did one very important thing that changed the face of clinical psychology forever. Vail, as you know, legitimzed the PsyD degree and endorsed graduate training in free-standing professional schools of psychology. I believe that clinical child psychologists and the particpants of this conference can learn a lesson from this.

After attending a number of such training conferences, I have come to the conclusion that whatever effect they may have is to provide a showcase for ideas whose time has come. Boulder did not invent the model that is named after it; that conference served mainly to endorse a report of an earlier committee, chaired by David Shakow, that had recommended the scientist-professional approach to training.

The same was true at Vail. There was a small cadre of single-minded people, mostly from California, who had come to that conference with a plan; a plan which they got the conference to adopt. It was a plan for a professional degree and for training in professional schools. That plan would have come to nothing, however, if those who championed it had stopped with introducing motions and passing resolutions. For as soon as the participants of the Vail Conference had come down from the mountain, these partisans began an explicit, well-orchestrated, targeted campaign to influence the governance structure of APA. Individuals representing that movement brought their message to the Education and Training Board, to the Committee on Accreditation, to the Board of Professional Affairs, and to the Council of Representatives. They did not rest until the accreditation criteria had been modified, the APA by-laws amended, their own people appointed to the E & T Board and BPA, and until their principal spokesman had been elected President of APA. By now, only 12 years later, the PsyD degree and professional schools of psychology are a firmly established part of our world.

For those of us here today, there is a lesson in this. It is that you must use this conference to develop a concrete plan that is ready to be put into action. And you can't hope that others will put it into action for you; you must be prepared to do that yourself. This means you must view this conference as but a step on a long and difficult road. It took a lot of effort to organize this conference, but that effort was nothing compared to the effort that must be expended once this conference is over. It is then that you must enter the political arena and see to it that your recommendations become reality. You must work to have your resolution implemented through changes in the regulations, standards, and procedures of organized psychology, and, if necessary, in the licensing laws of the 50 States. You can't just come to a Conference, engage in lengthy discussions, and pass resolutions recommending steps that *ought* to be taken and actions that *should* take place. Such oughts and shoulds, when published in a conference report, are like a child's wishlist, mailed to the North Pole. It is time we accepted the fact that there is no Santa Claus.

References

Hoch, E.L., Ross, A.O., & Winder, C.L. (Eds.). (1966). *Professional preparation of clinical psychologists.* Washington, DC: American Psychological Association.

Korman, M. (Ed.). (1976). *Levels and patterns of professional training in psychology.* Washington, DC: American Psychological Association.

Raimy, V.C. (Ed.). (1950). *Training in clinical psychology.* New York: Prentice-Hall.

Ross, A.O. (1959). *The practice of clinical child psychology.* New York: Grune & Stratton.

Ross, A.O. (1972). The clinical child psychologist. In B.B. Wolman, (Ed.), *Manual of child psychopathology* (pp. 1287 1296). New York: McGraw-Hill.

Summary of Concurrent Small Groups on Issues Academic Level

Honore Hughes
University of Arkansas

Our group was made up of approximately 25 psychologists working in academic settings, including the traditional university-based departments of psychology and departments set within medical schools, as well as others. Due to both the diversity in backgrounds and interests of the participants and the fact that this meeting was held very early in the conference, the discussion was wide-ranging, with a variety of ideas and viewpoints expressed. The two main issues around which the discussion centered involved (1) the substance or content of clinical child training and (2) the types and quality of the role models who provide this education.

A number of views were expressed regarding the content of training for clinical child psychologists, with little agreement on specifics; however, some consensus was obtained on a few broad issues. Most of the participants seemed to endorse the idea that the aspect of clinical child training that is unique and differentiates it from adult-oriented clinical education is an understanding of developmental psychology from a lifespan and systems perspective. Additional discussion focused upon ways to implement the lifespan orientation as a framework for training. One concrete idea presented as a way in which this developmentally-focused education could be facilitated consisted of establishing a comprehensive psychological services center on the campus that would address the mental health needs of people ranging from infants to the elderly.

In the context of linking lifespan orientation and specialty training, several individuals suggested that a more generic, rather than a specialized, program of training would be appropriate. This viewpoint included the idea that *all* clinical psychologists need to be trained within a lifespan context; thus, clinical child psychology training would serve as the foundation for all clinical psychological training. Several concerns were expressed related to the danger of a specialty area being ignored, swallowed up, or both. Others felt that identifying the content areas that are unique for clinical child psychologists was a vital aspect of advancing an understanding of the field both within and outside of the profession.

Related to the content of training was the issue of role models, discussed in several contexts. General consensus was reached that role models are important and that students benefit most from a variety of role models. One conceptualization of the continuum upon which faculty could be placed in terms of their professional responsibilities consists, at one extreme, of the academic researcher who provides few (if any) clinical services, and at the other end, the practitioner who conducts little (if any) research, with the person who, at least theoretically, embodies the scientist-practitioner model somewhere in between. Some discussion followed centering around faculty as role models and the appropriateness of the scientist-practitioner model of training. Several people expressed the idea that professionals at either end of the continuum were not appropriate role models, while others felt that, since the majority of students fill service positions when their training is complete, the role models should be sought from the more applied area. There was some discussion of the potential pitfalls anticipated if graduate students received too little emphasis on an empirical orientation, including becoming technicians as opposed to problem-solvers.

Another area, which was briefly discussed, concerned the issue of quality, both in terms of role models and the provision of quality training. No operational definitions of quality were advanced. Some group members disagreed with the notion that achievement of ABPP status is an indicator of quality. Quality with regard to clinical services was also briefly discussed, with several views put forth regarding the need to establish our own criteria for standards of quality for both training and service provision.

The discussion of role models evolved into an exchange of ideas concerning the administrative and reward structures within academia and how each functions to restrict the diversity possible in role models for students. There was some agreement that research is the activity which is most highly rewarded within an academic setting (a few exceptions to this are located mostly outside of traditional university-based programs). Some time was spent exchanging ideas about change strategies for use with administrative personnel, with somewhat of a polarity in views reflected in the suggestions made. While some people felt that change must occur from within the system, others were of the opinion that the personnel at the administrative level need to be educated and the structure changed. Several group members expressed the idea that we need to be pragmatic and take ease of implementation into account whenever recommendations regarding training in clinical child psychology are made, whether it is to the E & T Board of APA, or to the university administrators. Others felt that we should not be constrained by logistics and should plan for change as we see it to be necessary. However, there was some agreement that, as a group, we must make an impact upon APA, especially regarding accreditation standards.

Summary of Concurrent Small Group on Issues Internship Level

Anthony P. Mannarino

During the first segment of this discussion group, there was a diversity of opinions expressed regarding the initial position papers. Specifically, there was a focus on how clinical child psychology can be defined and whether it is truly a distinct specialty. In addition, many individuals voiced concerns about what kind of training in clinical child psychology will be provided at the internship level. Most group members felt that training at the internship level would be partly determined by what is offered within graduate training programs.

After these initial deliberations, there were a number of issues addressed specifically related to clinical child psychology training issues at the internship level. One issue raised was whether the training guidelines developed by the Division 37 Task Force have anything to say regarding internship training. There was a general conclusion that this document offered few suggestions regarding specific training requirments at the internship level. Other issues examined included what kind of training should be expected prior to the internship, how much adult training should occur within a specialized clinical child psychology internship program, and what kinds of competencies employers can expect when clinical psychologists have completed their child internship.

Quite a bit of discussion focused on the role of research experiences in a clinical child psychology internship program. Although the group was divided with respect to whether research should be an integral part of the internship program, there was a general consensus of opinion that ample research opportunities should exist for trainees during the internship year.

Finally, regardless of the kinds of training that occur during the internship year, the group expressed concern about funding issues and suggested that alternative sources of funding for trainees need to be developed in the future.

The discussion group saw its deliberations as an initial step in defining training guidelines at the internship level for clinical child psychologists. There was strong opinion expressed at the end of the meeting that a task force should be created that would specifically have as its charge the development of training guidelines for clinical child pyschologists at the internship level.

Summary of Concurrent Small Group on Issues Postdoctoral/Continuing Education Level

Thomas H. Ollendick
Virginia State University and Polytechnic Institute

This small group of twelve was charged with exploring ideas and reactions to the plenary session speakers. Prior to doing so, we first introduced ourselves, shared our professional affiliations and then proceded to disclose the various "routes" we took in becoming clinical child psychologists. Interestingly, only one of the twelve had been trained specifically in a clinical child program.

The remaining eleven were trained in general clinical programs, with one exception; that individual was trained in social and experimental psychology. (It should be noted that this person has served as one of our most distinguished presidents of the Section on Clinical Child Psychology.) Other background information revealed that seven of the twelve completed postdoctoral internships in clinical child or pediatric psychology, while the remaining five completed intense training in clinical child psychology at the internship level. This information was deemed important in that it reveals the various ways in which individuals *can* become clinical child psychologists. Stated simply, there are, and should remain, diverse routes to the attainment of recognition as a competent clinical child psychologist.

The first recommendation of this group captured this position; namely, that we should not lock ourselves into any one training model, but that we should continue to value diversity and heterogeneity.

The second major issue discussed was the need for coursework, or other ways of demonstrating competence, in developmental psychology and systems psychology. These two areas were reviewed as critical, given the diverse roles and responsibilities of practicing clinical psychologists. While there was much discussion on these matters, consensus was unanimous that these developmental and systems views should permeate the training program in clinical child psychology. That is, while coursework in these areas should be considered, it is more important to view these areas as *thematic* approaches to the training enterprise.

Based on these considerations, it was recommended that a *developmental bases of behavior* requirement be implemented for *all* clinical psychology training programs. Just as APA currently requires demonstration of competence in the *biological* and *social* bases of behavior, so too should it require competence in the *developmental* bases of behavior.

The final issue discussed in our group related to the possible requirement of postdoctoral work in clinical child area for acceditation and licensure as a *competent* child clinician. This issue was hotly debated, with ardent supporters on both sides of the aisle. One model suggested was similar to that used in medical settings; namely, if one is to be *board* certified in an area, he or she must complete additional requirements beyond the graduate level. Others raised the issue of whether this would be necessary if the psychologist was trained in a program which specifically addressed such competence at the predoctoral and/or internship level. To reiterate, consensus was not achieved on this very important matter.

Nonetheless, our group wanted to bring this matter to the attention of the Conference as a whole. Accordingly, it resolved that: Subsequent meetings of the conference address this issue in greater detail and deliver a recommendation to us.

In review, Group C of the Concurrent Small Groups had some very lively discussions, with considerable diversity of opinions. We concluded that the training of clinical child psychologists at any level is a complex undertaking and that the resolution of matters set before us will require considerable deliberation.

Roles and Responsibilities
Boundary Issues

Roles and Responsibilities of Clinical Child Psychologists
Boundary Issues

Annette M. La Greca

I'd like to welcome you all to this afternoon's session on "Roles and Responsibilities of Clinical Child Psychologists, and Boundary Issues," which will be cochaired by Dr. Carolyn Schroeder and myself.

We have some very important issues to consider in this afternoon's session. The roles and responsibilities that have been assumed by clinical child psychologists are multiple and complex — and have undergone tremendous growth and evolution in recent years. To adequately address pressing issues in this area, we must closely attend to current professional demands, as well as project ourselves into the future. A forward-looking orientation is essential if we are to successfully anticipate and meet new challenges we will be called upon to face.

With these thoughts in mind, and having had the benefit of previewing the excellent papers that will be presented this afternoon, I'd like to highlight two emergent themes as an orientation to this session.

First of all, I think we need to be mindful that children, adolescents, and families continue to be an underserved population professionally. There is a scarcity of well-trained professionals equipped to meet demands of serving this population. Moreover, the needs of children, adolescents, and families in our contemporary society have become ever more complicated and challenging. This situation has encouraged clinical child psychologists to *take on more roles* and to *be more flexible in their responsibilities* than traditionally has been the case for psychologists with clinical training.

This notion of multiple roles and flexible responsibilities will be addressed more specifically by each of our presenters this afternoon. In attending to their presentations, please consider each of three questions:

(1) Which roles and responsibilities may be viewed as most basic or essential to clinical child psychologists?

(2) Which roles may best be conceptualized as subspecialty areas?

(3) And, in either case, how can training for these roles best be accomplished?

The second theme that I wish to highlight will be clearly emphasized in today's presentations. It concerns the importance of shifting away from a traditional, medical-model orientation to training and service delivery, and, instead, focusing more directly on developmental, community, and systems approaches to working with children and families. The questions we must grapple with here are:

(1) How can we successfully integrate these multiple and diverse influences? and,

(2) How does this translate into successful training goals and experiences?

With these thoughts in mind, let us get on to this afternoon's papers. Before introducing our first speaker, and on behalf of the planning committee, I would like to extend our sincere appreciation to all our afternoon's presenters for their hard work and diligent efforts in the face of demanding time constraints. I think they deserve a special note of thanks for the additional efforts they expended in adapting their papers to the challenge of a difficult topic.

Our first speaker will be: *Dr. Jerome Hanley* who is Director for Health Affairs in the Office of the Govenor of South Carolina. He will be speaking on "Clinical child psychologists serving rural settings."

Our next speaker is: *Dr. David Glenwick* of Fordham University. He will present on "Systems-oriented clinical child psychology." This paper is coauthored with Dr. Steven Neuhaus of Portage Children's Services and Kent State University.

Next we have: *Dr. Frank Fincham* from the University of Illinois speaking on "Clinical child psychologists as research specialists."

Our last presenter before taking a short break is: *Dr. Gary Melton* from the University of Nebraska-Lincoln who is presenting on "Child clinicans as child advocates."

A Broad-Based Approach to the Training of Clinical Child Psychologists Serving Consumers in Rural Environments

Jerome H. Hanley
Division of Health and Human Services, Office of the Governor South Carolina

Between the years 1964 to 1984, the number of distinct divisions in the American Psychological Association has increased from 25 to 44. This expanding number of APA divisions is ample evidence that psychology, as a discipline and as a science, continues to broaden its scope. This expansion has paralleled the specialization in other professions which is necessary to meet the multiple needs of society. At this time, the tide of specialization appears irreversible.

As one who has directly treated children and now is responsible for the development of policy which determines the availability and nature of children's mental health services within a relatively rural state, my perception of the problem of training clinical child psychologists has changed — the importance has not.

It is the intent of this paper to explore the need for, and professional demands placed upon, clinical child psychologists who practice in rural areas.

The following three assumptions form the basis of this paper:

1. Clinical child psychology is a bona fide subspecialty of clinical psychology with its own identity and specific training needs;
2. The purpose of graduate training is to produce functional, competent young professionals prepared to practice upon graduation in varied environments;
3. Mental health needs, clinical skills, techniques and principles, as well as community expectations, differ in rural areas, therefore, require different professional preparation.

The first two assumptions appear confirmed by the existence of this national conference. The third assumption has been confirmed for me both by the literature and experientially.

The limited supply and broad range of functions which define the role of the clinical child psychologists in the southern, predominantly rural, region of the country are the focal points of this presentation. Jeff Koshel (1985), in a National Governor's Association Issues brief, reported that the Joint Commission on Mental Health for Children, the National Consortium on Mental Health Services for Children, and the President's Commission on Mental Health have each identified a chronic and severe shortage of trained professionals to provide mental health services for children and youth. Studying the distribution of mental health professionals in the South, Harding and McPheefers (1979) reported a shortage of mental health specialists serving children and adolescents in both rural and urban areas. They further reported that, in most areas of the South, it is difficult to obtain ongoing treatment services beyond diagnosis for emotionally disturbed children.

To better understand the field against which the supply and role issues are discussed, the following demographics of South Carolina, which are felt to be representative of the Southeastern region of the country, are presented. The total 1980 census was 3.1 million divided among 46 counties with a median county census of 39,999. Using the 1980 census figure, while applying the 1984 federal poverty guidelines, 26% of South Carolina residents fall below poverty level income of $10,200 for a family of four. There are approximately 1.1 million children (0-19) who reside in the state, 48% of whom reside in rural areas. The average daily attendance for public schools, grades K-12, is 603,974, with a total of 40,944 children and adolescents enrolled in programs for emotionally handicapped (5,618; .9%), learning disabled (19,802; 3.3%), educable mentally retarded (13,122; 2.2%), and trainable mentally retarded (2,402; .4%).

To serve these and the less severe, yet undiagnosed cases are a total of 231 licensed psychologists, 148 of whom are clinical psychologists. It was not possible to determine how many were trained to work with children.

The practitioner supply problem in rural areas is intensified by an accompanying scarcity of supportive and therapeutic resources. It is, perhaps, the multiple needs to be met and the varied demands place upon the rare clinical child psychologist in rural areas which must directly affect their decision to locate and remain in these underserved areas.

The work of Clayton (1977) supports the observation that practice within a rural environment requires of the clinician a reappraisal of his/her professional identity. This reappraisal frequently leads to a professional redefinition of self, types of services rendered, and relationships to clients and community, as an adaptation to various cultural and logistical factors. The cultural differences common to rural communities cannot be understated. Pedersen and Marsella (1982) stated the problem as a *moral vacuum* which exists because the values of a dominant culture are often imposed on a culturally different consumer.

Significantly, the President's Commission on Mental Health (1978) reported . . . "that staff preparation is generally inadequate and that pre-service experiences are not sufficiently relevant to the demands eventually faced by personnel working in rural areas." This statement, though not addressing clinical child psychologists directly, should influence the future training of young professionals for the demands of rural practice.

The clinical child psychologist, practicing in a rural area, finds him/herself responsible for the delivery of all clinical, and, oftentimes, non-clinical, activities related to the needs of his/her young clients. The American Psychological Association's Ethical Standards dictate a self-awareness of professional limits, yet a community in need of services will not accept statements of ethics. When a conscientious professional is the only resource, does he/she not attempt to serve a child even if with questionable qualifications/skills in the requisite area? The question is easy to answer when other resources are available, but not so simple when the weight of being the *"doctor"* is singly upon the psychologist's shoulders. Within any given week, the child clinical psychologist can expect to be called upon to impart information on any behavioral or developmental concern raised about a person between the ages of 0 - 18. The practitioner must also have the skills to provide:

1. *Assessments.* Preadoption, foster care, termination of parental rights, pre-family court placement, special education placements, developmental assessment, pre and post commitment reviews and child custody evaluations.
2. *Treatment.* Outpatient and inpatient.
3. *Consultation and Education.* Family court, sheriff, schools, (inservice, case consultation, career day, classroom management, student rap sessions), department of social services, churches, attorneys, day care centers and an array of general public workshops addressing separation/divorce, general child development, school readiness and behavior management, to name a few subjects.
4. *Child Advocacy.* These are more political activities where the psychologist represents the needs and interest of a single family, child, or a group of children. Typical targets of these activities are schools, law enforcement, social services agencies, and government. This role is sometimes viewed as adversative, straining necessary and ongoing relationships within the community or county.
5. *Training and supervision of subordinate staff.* The doctorate level psychologist may be fortunate and have other personel assisting him. Often, due to a limited budget, individuals not trained in children's issues must be hired. In such cases, the clinical child psychologist provides the training in addition to his/her other duties. The logistical constraint of being located miles apart and limited face-to-face contact complicate the supervisory process. The logistical barriers to customary face-to-face supervision and case consultation increase the concerns of liability facing the supervisor. Supervision within these limits takes on a crisis management quality with the supervisor serving as a support and technical resource.
6. *Public Relations.* The psychologist markets his/her product in an effort to gain acceptance and broaden the consumer pool. By broadening the potential consumer pool, the hope is to engage in more preventive activities while garnering community and financial support for the service.
7. *Fund Raising.* Through grants, fees and governmental appropriations, the services by a clinical child psychologist can be maintained or expanded. Public relations and governmental relations are important here.
8. *Administration and Program Development.* The psychologist must run his/her practice or service while continually being sensitive to the changing service needs of the community.

Such varied areas of clinical and non-clinical responsibility require knowledge and skills which can be aquired only through broad-based intensive training with experience in rural communities. It is the responsibility of training institutions, both academic and clinical, to address specific consumer needs as an integral part of professional preparation.

The supply and professional preparation issues

facing child clinical psychologists are not unlike the phsyician supply; distribution and specialty issues being addressed by medical schools as they prepare practitioners for rural communities.

Psychology departments, particularly those within state-supported institutions, must:

1) Recognize the need for clinical child psychologists, in general, and the additional need for, and needs of, those professionals serving rural communities.
2) Recruit students for these programs who are from rural communities and others with an expressed interest in serving rural consumers.
3) Make the need for professionals to serve in these areas known and stimulate interest through seminars and mini-classes on rural mental health issues (culture, values, economics, logistical barriers, clinical resource limitations).

In addition, selected graduate programs should develop practice opportunities in adjacent rural communities through community mental health centers, community health clinics, county human service agencies and the family court.

Selected clinical child psychology internships should develop consortia-like relationships with rural communities allowing for a more intensely supervised preparatory experience.

Without question, implementation of these suggestions entail an increase of both time and money. States have made the physician supply commitment. Psychology has yet to present its case.

States appear on the verge of making a significant commitment to children as reflected in the National Governor's Association policy resolution which states, in part, that "states should support the development of a federal and state health policy which provides equal access to mental and physical health services for children regardless of income or residence."

There are young people who are willing to accept the challenge and who understand the vast rewards, both personal and professional, of work in rural communities; it is our responsibility to prepare them to do the job well.

References

Clayton, T. (1977). Issues in the delivery of rural mental health services. *Hospital and Community Psychiatry, 28,* 673-676.

Hardin, J.R., & McPheeters, H.L. (1979). Distribution of mental health professionals in the south: A research project. *Hospitals and Community Psychiatry, 30,* 772-775.

Koshel, J. (1985).*Providing mental health services for children and youth.* Paper presented at the National Governor's Association Center for Policy Research. Washington, DC.

Pedersen, P.B., & Marsella, A.J. (1982). The ethical crisis for cross-cultural counseling and therapy. *Journal of Professional Psychology, 13,* 492-499.

President's Commission on Mental Health. (1978). *Report to the President* (vol. 1). Washington DC: United States Printing Office.

South Carolina Statistical Abstract. (1984). A publication of the South Carolina Division of Research and Statistical Services.

A System-Oriented, Community-Based Training Model for Clinical Child Psychology: Implications for Role Development and Skill Acquisition

David S. Glenwick
Fordham University

Steven M. Neuhaus
Portage County
Children's Services Center
and
Kent State University

In the past two decades, the range and complexity of problems seen by practicing clinical child psychologists has increased considerably. Unfortunately, the training of graduate students in clinical child psychology has not kept pace with the demands and requests to be made of them when they enter the "real world" as doctoral level practitioners. This situation has often necessitated that much of the learning about how to navigate in the real world has been sink-or-swim, ad hoc learning, *after* receiving one's PhD. Therefore, a curriculum grounded in the contemporary status of children and their problems would seem to contain considerable promise for preparing tomorrow's clinical child psychologists for the tasks they will later face.

The training model to be proposed here has three primary foci: (a) a broadened taxonomy of the *problems* experienced by children in contemporary society, (b) an appreciation of the numerous social *systems* affecting children's functioning, and (c) preparation for the expanded *roles* and *skills* required of clinical child psychologists to effectively intervene in children's problems and the pertinent social systems. Each of these interrelated foci will be discussed, in turn.

Problems

Clinical child programs have conventionally concentrated rather heavily on a fairly circumscribed group of problems (including childhood psychoses, autism, "neurotic" behaviors, and psychosomatic disorders) that are often conceptualized in terms of "mental illness" and treated in medically oriented settings, both in- and out-patient. However, these problems comprise a minority of the total spectrum of youngsters and families seen by practicing clinical child psychologists. We propose that the training curriculum reflect more closely this total spectrum. Among the problems that would merit major attention, in addition to the traditional categories, are: developmental disabilities and learning problems (e.g., mental retardation, learning disabilities, hyperactivity); physical disabilities and handicaps; physical and emotional abuse and neglect, and sexual abuse; aggressive behavior, delinquency, and status offenses; parental separation and divorce; parental death; and social/interpersonal deficits (e.g., shyness and withdrawal). While study of these topics would include consideration of their psychological (e.g., cognitive, affective, behavioral) and physical aspects, interpersonal and social/societal ramifications of each category would also be worthy of exploration, as each of these problem categories has potential implications for the total functioning of the individual (and of significant others, as well). In considering each category, such facets as the extent and nature of the problem, theories of causality (from a variety of perspectives-e.g., biological, psychodynamic, ecological), and appropriate interventions (again, from a variety of viewpoints) would be included.

Systems

The displaying of most of the above behaviors affects (a) the child's functioning within several of our social systems and (b) the systems' response to the child (Hobbs, 1979). (Some might argue that these systems also contribute to the development of the above-mentioned problems.) Thus, to respond effectively to a given child's needs, the clinical child psychologist often must venture forth from his/her office and come into intimate contact with these real world systems (Wohlford, 1979). Among the major systems impacting upon children are the family, educational (pre-school and school), juvenile justice, welfare, and medical systems. Each system is more intimately involved with some problem categories than with others. Obviously, for example, delinquency and status offenses are central concerns of juvenile justice authorities (who are the agents labeling certain behaviors as such). Some problem categories (e.g., developmental disabilities) may result in the simultaneous participation of more than one system, and a sizable percentage of children seen by child clinicians will be members of multiproblem families who have attracted the attention

Table 1. *Network of Possible Interactions among Children's Problem Categories and Social Systems Involved with Youth*

	Problem Category																
Social System	Mental Retardation	Learning Disabilities	Hyper-activity	Other Develop-mental Disabilites	Physical Disability	Physical & Emotional Abuse & Neglect	Sexual Abuse	Parental Separation & Divorce	Parental Death	Delinquency & Status Offenses	Drug & Alcohol Abuse	Depression & Suicide	Behavior Disorders	Social "Maladjust-ment" Dis-orders & Deficits	Neurotic Disorders	Psychotic Disorders	Autism
Family																	
Peers																	
School (Educational)																	
Criminal Justice																	
Welfare																	
Medical and Health																	

Note: The problem categories and social systems listed are offered as examples and are not intended to be comprehensive.

of authorities from several systems. Table 1 depicts a network of potential interactions between problem categories and social systems.

Consideration of the numerous "nonmental health" agents who may be involved in a given case introduces an element of complexity not faced by the clinician who defines all cases in terms of circumscribed mental illness or behavioral deficits. To aid students in becoming familiar and comfortable with these child-related systems, the following sets of questions should be addressed during training: (a) What are the structure and mode of operation of each of these systems? What are the goals, powers, and procedures of the systems? What are the constraints within which these systems function? Who are their personnel? (b) What is the impact (intended and unintended) of each system upon children? How successful are these systems as "helpers?" (c) How do these systems interrelate with one another? (d) How does each system conceptualize behavior, its causation, and its treatment? How do these conceptualizations overlay or conflict with the approach of the behavioral sciences (e.g., legal vs. psychological views of anti-social/dysfunctional behavior?) (e) How do these systems regard, and for what roles and purposes will they seek out, clinical child psychologists? (f) What does the clinical child psychologist need to know to work effectively with these systems?

Exploration of such questions should assist prospective clinical child psychologists in developing an awareness of children's behavior, both functional and dysfunctional, as developing within a context containing biological, interpersonal, and cultural components. There are several levels of social systems that influence individual behavior, ranging from the small group (e.g., family) to the organizational (e.g., school) to the community (e.g., neighborhood, small town, or urban area) to the societal (e.g., laws regarding corporal punishment); knowledge of these systems will enlarge a clinical child psychologist's view of the determinants of behavior and of possible targets of intervention and change.

Roles and Skills

The clinical child psychologist's core functions have traditionally been those of assessor and therapist. While preparation for these functions should remain *necessary* aspects of training, the roles of therapist and assessor are not *sufficient* for the clinical child psychologist trained in a systems-oriented approach. To be effective in facing the array of problems experienced by troubled youth (and youth in trouble) and in working with the several child-related systems, the clinical child psychologist must possess skills that go beyond therapy and assessment. Some of these skills are helpful in working with an *individual* case (i.e., child or family); others are vital if the clinical child psychologist is to have an impact as a *systems* changer upon groups, organizations, communities, and society. Among the individual case-related skills are the following: (a) consultant to a system regarding a specific child (e.g., as expert witness in juvenile court or as advisor to a school regarding the program for a pupil with special needs); (b) case manager and coordinator (e.g., in working with multi-problem children or families to ensure that such clients don't "fall through the cracks" and that all participating systems are on the same wavelength in their approach to a given case); (c) mediator among systems (e.g., serving as a go-between in smoothening relations between a child's parents and school officials who may be in conflict over the child's educational placement); and (d) interdisciplinary team member (e.g., in a pediatrics department or a rehabilitation setting).

Among the roles that the clinical child psychologist interested in improving *systems* may have to assume are the following: (a) *consultant* to organizations, agencies, government bodies, etc. concerning programs rather than single cases; (b) *advocate* and *lobbyist* for children's rights and services; (c) *program evaluator,* to aid in determining a program's efficacy and suggesting possible modifications; (d) *administrator/program developer/policy planner* (an overlapping set of roles in which an increasing number of psychologists are finding themselves); (e) *community educator,* both in person (e.g., as speaker to parent and church groups, schools, police departments) and through the media (e.g., newspapers, magazines, radio, television); (f) *supervisor/trainer,* to pass along one's skills to those working with children (e.g., interns, professionals in other fields, paraprofessionals) (Glenwick & Stevens, 1980); and (g) *spokesperson* for, and mounter of programs in, *prevention,* such that by fostering prevention and the building in of competencies in children the number of youngsters developing dysfunctions severe enough to require intensive intervention will be reduced (Felner, Jason, Moritsugu, & Farber, 1983; Jason & Glenwick, 1980a).

Achieving success in these roles requires competencies that are, in large part, learnable. For example, in addressing a community group, how does one handle difficult questions or audience hostility? As an administrator of a children's mental health program, how does one conduct a needs assessment in the community? What are various procedures for evaluating the costs and benefits of a children's program? Although such questions are too seldom addressed in the training of psychologists, it is precisely such issues and roles that need to be considered if clinical child psychologists are to be comfortable and successful in dealing with multiple target levels (individual, group, organization, community, and society) (Reiff, 1975) and time points of intervention (primary, secondary, and tertiary prevention) (Caplan, 1964; Jason & Glenwich, 1980b).

Having outlined *what* a community-and systems-oriented prospective clinical child psychologist should be conversant with, let us discuss *how* such material can best be presented in the curriculum and training program. While a solid psychology background, as well as course work in child psychopathology, psychotherapy, and assessment, are important components of any clinical child program, the orientation sketched here requires additional training experiences besides lectures and practica in "traditional" subjects. Specifically, to foster familiarity with diverse systems and roles, the following have promise as aspects of the curriculum and training: (a) courses in areas not usually considered integral to clinical child psychology, both within psychology (e.g., community psychology, organizational psychology, program evaluation, mental health administration) and in other disciplines (e.g., law, urban planning, public administration, criminal justice, communications, education, public health); (b) courses that include such features as (1) guest speakers from the outside world who are involved in the systems and roles discussed above and (2) field experiences in various settings pertaining to children (both normal and "deviant"); and (c) practicum and internship experiences in which clinical child students have the opportunity to develop competence in the roles delineated above.

With respect to field, practicum, and internship experiences, we suggest that clinical child placements need not be restricted to residential facilities, hospital psychiatric in-patient units or community mental health center out-patient locales, in which the overwhelming majority of trainees' time is spent in conventional therapy and assessment. Thus, settings such as preschool (e.g., nursery school, day care, and Head Start), "regular" education, and special education programs; juvenile courts, detention centers, and probation departments; and pediatric, physical rehabilitation, family medicine, and other hospital departments are all suitable environments for such experiences. Somewhat more radical, but quite appropriate, placement sites would be state and local departments of mental health, health, welfare, and human services (with students discovering firsthand the intricacies of policy formulation and implementation concerning children); legislative bodies at the federal, state, and local levels (with students learning how legislation related to children's mental health and impacting upon children evolves); children's rights organizations (with students involving themselves in advocacy activities); and media outlets — radio and television stations, newspapers, and magazines (with students becoming aware of how the media present children's mental health issues to the public and gaining experience in print and broadcast journalism). In these, as well as in the more conventional settings, trainees should have the opportunity to engage in (or at least observe) several of the roles discussed above. This can be arranged even in nonradical placements, such as community mental health centers, where, in addition to traditional functions, interns can perform such activities as (a) consulting to other child-related agencies and groups, both professional and lay (examples of the latter being such self-help organizations as Parents Anonymous and Parents Without Partners), in the community; (b) presenting talks to community groups; (c) supervising others (e.g., more junior graduate students, undergraduates, paraprofessionals, community volunteers); (d) helping to design the center's evaluation program; and (e) participating in mental health levy campaigns.

Conclusion

Most clinical child programs would likely feel that, in trying to provide or make accessible course work and training in all of the systems and roles presented here, they would be spreading themselves too thin. It is the rare (and probably nonexistent) program that would be capable of touching all of the above bases. Programs could therefore, decide to concentrate on certain subareas within clinical child psychology (e.g., clinical child in relation to the criminal justice system; children in rural populations) in addition to offering the basic foundation in clinical child psychology. Factors determining a program's subareas of concentration might include the competencies and interests of the clinical child program's and the psychology department's faculty, the resources of the university, the backgrounds and desires of the program's graduate students, the nature and needs of the community in which the program is located, and the opportunities (actual and potential) that exist in the community. It is our belief and hope that discussion of innovative roles and skills for clinical child psychologists can serve as a jumping off point for the development of creative and imaginative training programs involving the collaborative partnership of psychology departments, their universities, and the geographical and psychological communities of which they are a part.

References

Caplan, G. (1964). *Principles of preventive psychiatry.* New York: Basic Books.

Felner, R.D., Jason, L.A., Moritsugu, J.W., & Farber, S.S. (Eds.). (1983). *Preventive psychology: Theory, research and practice.* New York: Pergamon.

Glenwick, D.S., & Stevens, E. (1980). Vertical supervision. In A.K. Hess (Ed.), *Psychotherapy supervision: Theory, research and practice* (pp. 226-241). New York: Wiley.

Hobbs, N. (1979). *Helping disturbed children: Psychological and ecological strategies, II; Project Re-Ed, twenty years later.* Nashville: Vanderbilt Institute for Public Policy Studies.

Jason, L.A., & Glenwick, D.S. (1980a). Future directions: A critical look at the behavioral community approach. In D.S. Glenwick & L.A. Jason (Eds.), *Behavioral community psychology: Progress and prospects* (pp. 409-464). New York: Praeger.

Jason, L.A., & Glenwick, D.S. (1980b). An overview of behavioral community psychology. In D.S. Glenwick & L.A. Jason (Eds.), *Behavioral community psychology: Progress and prospects* (pp. 4-37). New York: Praeger.

Reiff, R. (1975). Of cabbages and kings. *American Journal of Community Psychology, 3,* 187-196.

Wohlford, P. (1979). Clinical child psychology: The emerging specialty. *The Clinical Psychologist, 33,* 25-29.

Training research specialists in clinical child psychology

Frank D. Fincham
University of Illinois

"Would you tell me, please, which way I ought to go from here?"
"That depends a good deal on where you want to get to," said the Cat.

Lewis Carrol, *Alice in Wonderland*

It is a truism that the form of training programs in clinical child psychology will depend on the nature of the specialist they are intended to produce. In this regard, much ink has flowed concerning the quality of training received by psychologists engaged in clinical work with children (e.g., Roberts, 1982; Wohlford, 1978) and how to improve the service delivery skills of such professionals (Goldman, 1982; Tuma, 1982; Wohlford, 1979). However, a viable clinical child psychology requires training programs which not only foster competent clinical practice but also advance knowledge directly relevant to clinical practice in this new specialty area. Little attention has been paid to this latter goal, yet few would dispute that the field would soon become sterile were it completely neglected. It seems to have been implicitly assumed that the existence of Boulder model programs in clinical psychology will automatically result in the achievement of this goal. The present paper questions this assumption and addresses several issues specific to the training of research specialists in clinical child psychology.

Defining the problem

There are two major reasons to believe that traditional scientist-practitioner training programs in clinical psychology are not optimal for providing an empirically grounded service delivery in clinical child psychology. First, some 35 years have passed since the Boulder Conference and there remains concern regarding the scientist-practitioner schism in clinical psychology (e.g., the 1980 annual conference of the Association for the Advancement of Behavior Therapy focused on this rift in an attempt to lessen the gap between the two areas). Whatever forces have prevented the full realization of the Boulder model in adult clinical psychology are likely to prevent its realization in the clinical child area. The adage that those who ignore history are destined to repeat it, bears mention. Second, specialists in the clinical child domain need to acquire many of the skills of their counterparts in adult clinical psychology in addition to those targeted at their child specialty.

As a *practitioner,* the child specialist must learn to work with adults not only as parents, teachers, and other helpers, but as individuals at the adult level of development. Given the recent recognition that adulthood comprises different phases of development each with its own life tasks, mastery of this goal is no mean feat. Consequently, what is at issue in this regard is not whether such training is necessary for the child specialist, but how much training is optimal (Goldman, 1982). In addition, the considerable skills needed to work with children have to be acquired. In many ways, this task is even more difficult than learning to work clinically with adults, as it involves decentralization from the adult world and exploration of several different universes which vary as a function of the developmental level of the child. Hence, for example, the clinician skilled at working with the preschooler is not thereby necessarily competent to work with the teenager and vice versa.

As a *scientist,* the child specialist is confronted with similar additional problems. Not only must he/she master general scientific methodology, but also increasingly specialized techniques used to study development (Achenbach, 1978). Many of the relevant methodologies (e.g., panel designs, quasi-experimental designs etc.) and data analytic techniques (e.g., time series analysis, lag sequential analysis) are not taught in the general research design and statistics courses required of students in Boulder model clinical training programs. Moreover, whether one traces the origins of clinical child psychology to the marriage of clinical psychology and academic psychology (Ross, 1959) or to child psychiatry and the emergence of the Child Guidance Movement (Santostefano, 1978), it is clear that this specialty is interdisciplinary in origin. It rightly maintains this tradition and, consequently, the child specialist as scientist is confronted with all the conceptual and pragmatic problems associated with interdisciplinary research (Campbell, 1969).

Given the above observations, is it realistic to expect graduates of programs in clinical child psychology to be professionally competent (that is, to possess requisite knowledge, skills and abilities *and* the ability to apply these to actual problems they encounter) (Ollendick, 1984) as both scientist *and* practitioner? It is a rare individual who meets such requirements. Moreover, the advancement of the field does not require such Renaissance persons. The focus on service delivery in the recent literature on training seems implicitly to recognize this fact. In the remainder of this section, the arguments in favor of the above viewpoint will be developed before discussing issues relevant to the training of research specialists in clinical child psychology.

The emergence of clinical child psychology as a specialty has been paralleled by the appearance of several areas (e.g., social-clinical psychology, developmental-social psychology) standing at the interface of subdisciplines within psychology (Fincham, 1985). These developments have focused considerable attention on the problems of interdisciplinary research (cf. Fincham & Cain, 1983; Maddux & Stoltenberg, 1983; Masters, Yarkin-Levin & Graziano, 1984). Of particular relevance is the observation that any attempted mastery of more than one subdiscipline tends to be self defeating as such mastery normally occurs at the expense of the intense specialization necessary for scientific productivity. Moreover, as Campbell's (1969) analysis of interdisciplinary research points out, the locus of knowledge is social: integration occurs in the collective wisdom and language of the scientific community and not in the minds of individuals. Thus, even the clinical child psychologist as researcher need not necessarily master *all* the skills relevant to this role.

A parallel argument can be applied to the scientist-practitioner ideal. To the extent that a single person attempts to master truly the skills of each role, there is the danger that their efficacy as either scientist or practitioner will be diminished. This is not to suggest that a critical approach to knowledge or an appreciation of the scientific endeavor should not be part of the training of the clinical child psychologist as practitioner. Nor is it implied that the clinical child psychologist as researcher need not be familiar with the problems encountered in practice. On the contrary, this is critical to the successful training of clinical child researchers, as outlined below. However, it behooves us to recognize the impact of Boulder model training on the generation of research in clinical child psychology.

The research productivity of scientist-practitioners in clinical child psychology is, in part, responsible for the phenomenal progress made in this domain during the last two decades. Notwithstanding this laudable contribution and many examples of fine research, there is a relative paucity of theoretical integration in the field, while the ratio of methodologically sophisticated to methodologically flawed research remains alarmingly low. Our increased knowledge of child disorders brings with it the demand for more concentrated attention and greater sophistication from the investigator whose research is to advance the field. In short, there is a need for the research specialist in clinical child psychology. Lest it appear otherwise, it must be explicitly stated that this should not be seen as a call to end the training of scientist-practitioners and to establish "professional" schools in the clinical child domain. Rather, the call is for an addition, not a replacement, to our field: the training of the research specialist.

Towards a solution

In seeking a model for research training in the clinical child area, it is again necessary to consider explicitly the nature of the specialist trained. Ideally, the graduates of such a program will produce knowledge which directly addresses problems encountered in the practice of clinical child psychology. Unfortunately, as Patterson (1982) points out, most current research in "clinical child psychology is a piecemeal affair ...investigators ...select problems which fit within some favored paradigm...the strategy becomes that of searching for phenomena *fitting the explanation.* The phenomena that do not fit the explanation are set aside in favor of those that will". (p. 7) Thus, it is not sufficient to simply have students in an ideal program learn sophisticated research skills; proactive measures are needed to direct these skills toward programmatic, problem-oriented research, which will ultimately address the needs of the practitioner in clinical child psychology.

The problems encountered by the clinical child psychologist are numerous. Currently, clinicians serve children of all ages with severe psychopathology through mild problems in adjustment, in settings as diverse as inpatient psychiatric wards, group homes, schools, community mental health centers and private practice and utilize multiple skills appropriate to different levels of intervention (e.g., individual, family, community). A variety of different perspectives, rather than a single monolithic approach, are needed to address the range of problems encountered by clinical child psychologists. Consequently, it is questionable whether the needs of our field will be adequately addressed by persons trained only in clinical psychology. At the very least, it seems necessary to actively recruit trainees from other relevant subdisciplines of psychology, such as social, community, developmental psychology, and so forth. Indeed, the interdisciplinary approach to child disorders could justify the recruitment of trainees from various disciplines. This raises a question as to the level at which the training is best instituted. In this regard, it would probably be best to conduct specialized research training at the postdoctoral level.

A second issue concerns the clinical component of the research training. It would seem important to structure the training so that students are exposed to the content of clinical child psychology at both a theoretical *and* a practical level from the very beginning. How would this be achieved other than via the practica and internship already found in Boulder model clinical training programs? One possibility is for the trainee to have an ongoing "research" internship in the clinic which would be integrated with the coursework and research project components of their training.

The "internship" would differ from one for a trainee practitioner in that its goal would be to expose the student to clinical phenomena and the problems encountered in clinical practice, rather than to train him/her in the delivery of services to children. The difference need not be an absolute one, but rather one of relative emphasis. Where appropriate, research interns might be involved in service delivery. However, the goal here is simply to familiarize them with particular problems and, hence, service delivery experiences would be extremely limited. Active measures might be needed to avoid the danger of trainees becoming too involved in service delivery. For example, primary responsibility for service delivery might rest with someone other than the trainee whose role would always be limited to that of a secondary or adjunct service provider. In addition, involvement in service delivery would only occur when it can be shown to be directly related to the trainee's development as a researcher.

A second purpose of the internship would be to socialize the student into the community of practitioners, an important factor which should not be overlooked. The ability to communicate and collaborate with practicing clinicians is essential to conducting the kind of research envisioned in an ideal training program. Like the interventions of a clinician who works with the parents or teacher of a child, research ideas are valuable only to the extent that they are implemented. To facilitate this goal, a structured meeting with one or more practitioners analogous to the supervisory sessions of trainee practitioners might be instituted. Here, the student would learn first hand, either directly or by inference, the kind of information yielded by research that may address the problems encountered by practicing clinical child psychologists. Perhaps more importantly, the student would be exposed to a rich repertoire of potential research ideas, the insights of clinicians culled from years of clinical practice. This exposure to clinical practice would, thus, serve as a springboard for the student's research. Moreover, the integration of practitioners in the training program might help ensure the "social validation" (Kazdin, 1977) of any proposed project by, for example, requiring that the project be evaluated by them before its eventual implementation. Thus, the research conducted would meet both scientific and practical, applied critieria.

Besides the clinical component of the research training, what coursework requirements might there be? The core clinical child courses (e.g., developmental psychopathology) in a regular clinical training program (without associated practica and emphases on service delivery), supplemented by a seminar on professional conduct/ethics, might represent the minimal 'clinical' component of the coursework. A parallel course sequence which taught methodologies not covered in traditional experimental design courses (e.g., time series, single subject experimental designs, etc.) would also be needed. Both clinical courses and the internship experience would provide material for exercises in the application of these designs. During this time, the student would, in consultation with their internship and research advisors, design and later implement their own research project which would be a requirement of the research training.

Given the content of the research training outlined above, a question arises as to the amount of time needed to complete such training. It is difficult to envision a program that requires less than two years: the first year would cover the basic clinical and research design coursework, while the second would focus on a research project and possibly, further, individually tailored seminars to address the trainee's specialized needs in a particular clinical area or research methodology. Throughout the training, the student would continue his/her internship.

The implementation of the research training outlined above may appear to be straightforward. Indeed, it might be, were it not for the fact that the much vaunted close relationship between psychological research and clinical practice exists more in theory than in fact. It is this de facto schism between researcher and practitioner and the values espoused by each which represents an obstacle to the smooth implementation of the training. It is, therefore, imperative that any research training program entail a genuine respect for the practice of clinical child psychology. One concrete means of communicating this respect is to locate the training program in the clinic rather than in an academic department of psychology. At the present time, the kind of research training outlined is unfortunately only likely to be realized in clinical settings with an academic emphasis. However, by according the practitioner an important role in the training of the researcher, it is hoped that the ideal relationship between research and practice may be more closely approximated. As we move towards this ideal, it should be possible to locate research training programs in more diverse clinical settings. Clearly, the proposals made above run counter to the prevailing trend in clinical psychology. Their realization is, therefore, likely to be difficult but with the commitment on our part and a good deal of dogged determination they may be achieved.

Conclusion

Like Alice in Wonderland, we are confronted with a choice of paths we might potentially travel. Presumably we, unlike her, are concerned about our untimate destination. It, therefore, behooves us to consider the role of research in clinical child psychology and how this role is best achieved. The above picture of specialized research training is admittedly painted in broad strokes. The intention has been to make the case for such training in clinical child psychology and to indicate briefly what the training might entail in concrete terms. The suggestions made are designed to facilitate close links between clinical research and clinical practice in the belief that the kind of problem-oriented, applied research vital to the sustained growth of clinical child psychology will not be fully realized within existing organizational structures. Its proposal does not in any way deny the need for basic research nor its potential relevance for clinical child psychologists. Indeed, the existence of a research specialist in clinical child psychology, unencumbered by a case load of patients, increases the probability of realizing the clinical relevance of basic research. In essence, what is proposed is an attempt to ensure that the kind of research most useful to the clinical child psychologist as practitioner is, in fact, carried out.

The present paper began with a critique of the Boulder Model in the domain of clinical child psychology. To the extent that the scientist-practitioner role embodied in this model can be split between closely collaborating professionals, the paper is not much different in intent from the Boulder Model in its affirmation of the need for an empirically-based clinical child psychology. Its point of departure is the recognition of the limits of what most individuals can master and recognition of the fact that knowledge is social. After all, were this not the case, this national conference designed to utilize our collective wisdom in defining the domain of clinical child psychology and determining appropriate training in this domain, would not have been necessary.

References

Achenbach, T.M. (1978). *Research in developmental psychology: Concepts, strategies, methods.* New York: Free Press.

Bush, M., & Gordon, A.C. (1978). Client choice and bureaucratic accountability: Possibilities for responsiveness in a social welfare bureaucracy. *Journal of Social Issues, 34,* 22-43.

Campbell, D.T. (1969). Ethnocentrism of disciplines and the fish-scale model of omniscience. In M. Sherif & C. Sherif (Eds.), *Interdisciplinary relationships in the social sciences* (328-348). Chicago: Aldine.

Fincham, F.D. (1985). The emergence of research at the interface of social, clinical and developmental psychology. *Journal of Social and Clinical Psychology, 4,* 385-390.

Fincham, F.D., & Cain, K.M. (1983). An interface of social, clinical *and* developmental psychology: Possibility or pipedream? *Society for the Advancement of Social Psychology Newsletter, 9,* 27-31.

Goldman, J. (1982). Clinical child psychology training and credentialing. *Journal of Clinical Child Psychology, 11,* 8-12.

Kazdin, A.E. (1977). Assessing the clinical or applied importance of behavior change through social validation. *Behavior Modification, 1,* 427-451.

Maddux, J.E., & Stoltenberg, C.D. (1983). Clinical social psychology and social clinical psychology: A proposal for peaceful coexistence. *Journal of Social and Clinical Psychology, 1,* 289-299.

Masters, J., Yarkin-Levin, K., & Graziano, (1984). Boundary area research. In J. Masters & K. Yarkin-Levin (Eds.), *Boundary areas between developmental and social psychology* (pp. 1-14). New York: Academic Press.

Ollendick, T.H. (1984). Training in clinical child psychology: The role of continuing education. *Journal of Clinical Child Psychology, 13,* 90-91.

Patterson, G.R. (1982). *Coercive Family Process.* Eugene, OR: Castalia Publishing Company.

Roberts, M.C. (1982). Clinical child psychology programs: Where and what are they? *Journal of Clinical Child Psychology, 11,* 13-21.

Ross, A.O. (1959). *The practice of clinical child psychology.* New York: Grune & Stratton.

Santostefano, S. (1978). *A biodevelopmental approach to clinical child psychology.* New York: Wiley.

Tuma, J.M. (1982). Proposal for a national conference on professional preparation of clinical child psychologists. *Journal of Clinical Child Psychology, 11,* 3-7.

Wolhford, P. (1978). A challenge to clinical psychology: Better training to serve children. *Journal of Clinical Child Psychology, 7,* 89-90.

Wolhford, P. (1979). Clinical child psychology: The emerging specialty. *The Clinical Psychologist, 12,* 25-26.

Training Child Clinicians to be Child Advocates[1]

Gary B. Melton
University of Nebraska-Lincoln

In 1970, the Joint Commission on the Mental Health of Children issued a call for child advocacy. The report was predicated on an assumption that, given children's dependent status, they required adult advocates to ensure that their interests were advanced and protected. This need was to be met through establishment of a national system of child advocacy councils and centers.

The primary problem with the Joint Commission's report (and many of the "advocacy" programs which developed in response) was political naiveté (Knitzer, 1971, 1976). There was an implicit belief that bringing together a critical mass of sensitive individuals committed to children's welfare would result in significant social change. The Commission ignored the persistent, frustrating reality that there will always be strong sociopolitical resistance to redistribution of "loot and clout" (cf. Ryan, 1971). No attention was given to the technology of child advocacy, and little attention was given to sorting the diverse and often competing values and interests underlying the children's rights movement (see Melton, 1983a; Mnookin, 1978; Rogers & Wrightsman, 1978; Steiner, 1976). The result has been that self-described child advocacy agencies are often nothing more than warmed-over child guidance agencies (Kahn, Kamerman, & McGowan, 1972). As I have put it elsewhere (Melton, 1983a), child advocacy has often stagnated because it has been confused with simply "being nice to kids."

The delivery of services to children is not coextensive with child advocacy. Although performed (one would hope) in a child's best interests, child psychotherapy as usually practiced is not child advocacy. "Just doing something for or to a child ostensibly in his or her best interests does not constitute child advocacy. Rather, child advocacy is distinguished from other interventions said to be in children's best interests by the emphasis on increasing the accountability and responsiveness of social institutions affecting children" (Melton, 1983a, p. 65) (also see Kahn et al., 1972, p. 63). Indeed, service providers, including child clinicians, are necessarily often the target of advocates' efforts. The purpose of child advocacy is to *enable* children to make use of societal resources. Advocacy thus entails social and political action at various systemic levels to ensure that the purported societal interest in child welfare is met, or to provide children with forums to express their own interests and to participate in determining their own fate (see Melton, 1982, 1983a, 1983c).

There have been some encouraging developments in child advocacy within organized psychology; notably, the rapid evolution of APA Division 37 as a community of psychologists committed to analysis of child and family policy and the establishment of a position, albeit still a single position, in APA's Central Office for governmental relations on child and family issues. Nonetheless, psychology still has far to go in recognizing a collective responsibility to advocate for children's interests. The proposed establishment of a standing committee on children, youth, and families, continues to be resisted, ostensibly because of the rather quaint notion that every APA board or committee should represent a constitucncy of psychologists.[1] (Maybe the issue we should be discussing is the training of *child* psychologists.) More to the point of this conference, clinical child psychologists rarely deviate from the in-office 50-minute hour. Koocher and Pedulla (1977) found, for example, that the model number of contacts by child therapists with their clients' teachers was two per year. With the appearance of block grants and the concomitant disappearance of any financial incentives even for community mental health professionals to engage in consultation, I suspect that the frequency of clinicians' involvement in the child's world outside the clinic is even less than at the time of Koocher and Pedulla's study.

I do not mean to minimize the structural (read financial) impediments to psychologists' assuming an advocate's stance on behalf of their child clients. However, the training and socialization issues may be even more profound. "Psychologizing" too often results in blaming the victim and missing the root issues (Ryan, 1971). Even midst the Great

[1]For comprehensive discussion of the issues presented in this paper, see Melton (1983a).

Society's efforts to create Model Cities, mental health professionals were viewed, even by mental health professionals themselves, as having little to offer to the resolution of social problems (Warren, 1971). Put in its best light (and the framework most relevant to this conference), professional psychologists are ill-prepared to engage in politics in order to change schools, housing projects, health centers, and so forth, on children's behalf.

Some may argue that the current state of affairs is the proper one: that child clinicians have enough to do without becoming involved in life beyond the clinic. A somewhat more enlightened view might be that it is appropriate to venture beyond the walls of the clinic but that clinicians who do so should stick to the technology they know well (in this instance, mental health consultation, most likely of the case-centered variety). With all due respect, I believe that both views are wrong. Without child advocacy, clinical child practice is destined to fail on both ethical and pragmatic grounds.

Ethically, as psychologists, we subscribe to a primary obligation to guard the dignity and welfare of our clients (Ethical Principles 1 and 6) (APA, 1981). This obligation becomes particularly acute when clients are unable to act to guard their own interests, whether because of de facto incompetency or legally and socially enforced dependency (Ethical Principle 5d) (APA, 1981). Respect for persons demands attention to the provision of primary goods for children (Brown, 1982; Worsfold, 1974). Psychologists' ethical principles require protection of clients' civil rights (Ethical Principle 3c) (APA, 1981), but the broader ethical principle clearly is to protect clients' *human* rights, to ensure that basic needs are met.

Although there are few social groups whose rights are more fragile than children's, there are also few classes of clients who are less likely to be protected by the professionals who purport to serve them. Services to children are extraordinarily fragmented. Essentially the same services are often rendered to essentially the same groups of children by educational, social service, juvenile justice, and mental health agencies (Knitzer, 1982; Melton & Spaulding, in press). There has been no significant movement toward the Hobbs (1975) Commission's major recommendation to consolidate children's services structurally and philosophically (within an ecological framework). The result, as Koocher (1979) has pointed out, is a persistent assumption that it is someone else's job to safeguard the child's interest. Responsibility is diffused, and no one assumes the advocate and coordinator roles. The pernicious paradox is that such roles are especially key precisely because the system of services is so fragmented. At best, the result is relatively benign; a child does not receive services which would enhance his or her development. At worst, such lack of affirmative action on a child's behalf results in actual harm to the child (what Polier [1975] has termed the "professional abuse of children"). The phenonomen, for example, of children being *lost* in foster care (the context in which the state's responsibility for children is clearest) is so widely acknowledged now (e.g., Mnookin, 1973) to seem almost trite.

Pragmatically, then, unless a clinician assumes an advocate's role, the social realities of the child client's life are often such that they will more than negate whatever good is done in the therapist's office. Even if their behavior is not consistent with their beliefs, most clinicians, I think, intuitively accept this proposition. It is remarkable that there has never been a hue and cry in response to Levitt's (1957, 1971) Eysenck-like claim that there is no evidence for efficacy of child therapy when spontaneous remission rates are taken into account. Although there are several possible explanations for the lack of response (see Melton, 1983a, pp. 66-68), the most persuasive to me is that child clinicians were unsurprised by the results of Levitt's meta-analysis of child therapy outcome studies.

A review of the treatment outcome literature is well beyond the scope of this paper (see Melton, 1983a, chaps. 3 and 4), but it is clear to me that, with the possible exception of behavior therapy for circumscribed problems (e.g., enuresis, phobias), the most successful child and family interventions have combined a careful ecological assessment, educational interventions aimed at building relevant skills, and social interventions to enhance the fit between child and setting. Some of the programs have been sufficiently oriented toward changing the social reality that they border on what I have termed *clinical child advocacy* (Melton, 1977, 1983a). Massimo and Shore's (1963) classic *vocationally oriented psychotherapy* is illustrative:

> Motility and action were emphasized. The therapist had no central office, and made frequent field trips when necessary. In essence, the therapist entered all areas of the adolescent's life. Job finding, court appearances, pleasure trips, driving lessons when appropriate, locating and obtaining a car, arranging for a dentist appointment, going for glasses, shopping for clothes with a first pay check, opening a bank account and other activities require this maximum commitment. (Massimo & Shore, 1963, p. 636)

Actually however, even Massimo and Shore's program, as described, did not quite reach the point of being an advocacy program. It was oriented toward building skills for the youth within the context of a consistent relationship, but it apparently did not focus on changing the system so as to maximize the opportunities for clients. To go that far, though, does constitute clinical child advocacy. Clinical child advocacy, in turn, offers a bridge between clinical and community psychology. When a clinician "goes the extra mile" to ensure bureaucratic accountability, the likely result is not simply heightened probability of efficacious treatment in the particular case. Particularly when a policy issue is at stake, there is a likelihood that the effort will generalize to other children in similar cases.

Moreover, child advocacy itself may be therapeutic. Advocacy aims toward *empowerment* (cf. Rappaport, 1977). Such heightened control has substantial positive effects on general mental well-being for both children and adults (Melton, 1983a, pp. 98-100; Melton, 1983b). Besides providing a sense of personal control, successful advocacy may also provide models of how to increase one's control over the environment. Thus, there may be significant long-term psychological and social effects.

Being an effective advocate requires substantial knowledge of the legislative, administrative, and judicial processes (or at least knowledge of where to go for help with respect to these issues). It also requires knowledge of how to manipulate these processes. The successful child advocate needs a solid background in the sociology and politics of children's services and children's status itself (see generally Melton, 1983a). The advocate also should have practical experience in the application of social science to policy matters. Where advocacy originates from clinical cases, there should also be supervised experience in blending more conventional psychological interventions with advocacy (in my terminology, clinical child advocacy).

I have previously described one model for such training (Melton, 1977). The central feature of this model is involvement with change agents in settings with an explicit advocacy function. The assumption is that supervision by professionals (and sometimes paraprofessionals) from disciplines oriented toward systems change will enrich the repertoire of interventions available to a clinician:

> There is much to be gained from experience in settings which are problem- rather than discipline-oriented. Most of us train in facilities which claim to be multidisciplinary. Usually, though, the disciplines represented are all in the mental health field (psychiatry, psychology, social work, and nursing). However, skills as change agents are not limited to clinicians. Experience in settings including attorneys, advocates, and community organizers provides a broader perspective and particular skills in changing bureaucracies. One also becomes keenly aware of how mental health, welfare, and legal problems are so intertwined and of the necessity for a coordinated treatment plan for a client. An important side effect is that non-clinicians become more aware of what it is that mental health professionals have to offer. They can informally learn from the clinicians as well as the converse. The learning process can be further enhanced when there is an opportunity for supervision around clinical contributions to advocacy by a clinician who is sensitive to the systemic elements in psychopathology. In short, a practicum [or internship] experience which includes both conventional mental health training and training in other change methods can be an effective way of learning to advance and protect a child's total welfare. (Melton, 1977, p. 29.)

As implicit in the quote above, the clinical trainee can broaden the perspective of the professional advocate. Through knowledge of group dynamics and of the needs of children (cf. Westman, 1979), the clinician can help to build the clinical skills of full-time advocates and to assist them in development and implementation of service plans for individual children or classes of children. Psychologists can also assist in systematically evaluating various strategies of child advocacy, a topic which is still largely unresearched (Davidson & Rapp, 1976), although existing literature in sociology and political science is often at least tangentially relevant (see generally Melton, 1983a, especially chaps. 6-8).

My own internship was exemplary of the sort of training opportunity I have described. I blended work in an inner-city community mental health center with training in the Massachusetts Office for Children, a state child advocacy agency. Many states now have such gadfly agencies with either state or foundation support. (How stinging the gadfly is varies markedly, of course.) The kind of training which I am endorsing could come in other agencies with an advocacy focus as well (e.g., public-interest lobbying groups, legal aid societies, community action agencies, self-help groups, neighborhood associations, etc.)

The key element which needs to be provided to clinical students in such settings is assistance in bridging the advocacy training with their clinical child work. This bridge can be accomplished in at least two ways. First, supervision of the advocacy work should be available from an advocacy-minded clinician or a psychologically-minded advocate. Second, joint seminars among advocates and clinicians can help to illuminate areas in which psychology can inform child advocacy and, conversely, areas in which techniques of advocacy can facilitate clinical practice. In that regard, although I have emphasized practical training, many of the advantages of the model I have proposed could be obtained through careful selection of courses in the other social sciences, community planning, and law.

Such didactic experiences in combination with practical experience in child advocacy should provide trainees with skills in assessing a child's needs in a particular settings and in developing and implementing a strategy for enabling the child to obtain access to needed services. (The same sorts of skills are relevant, of course, to enabling children to enjoy some measure of privacy and autonomy; see Melton, 1983c). It is likely that training in child advocacy would also have the effect of desensitizing the clinician's anxiety in response to the need for politics in advocacy for children.

Presumably, then, when clinicians who have been trained in advocacy encounter that occasional case in which a child is somehow lost midst a dozen agencies who have some responsibility for the child (or at least a part of the child), they will be more likely to know what to do to break the logjam to feel motivated to do so. And while I have implicitly focused on case advocacy, most of the same issues apply to class advocacy. Child clinicians should be able to move from observations of mistreatment of a particular child to an understanding of the need for changes in legislation, formal regulation, or administrative custom. They should have a sense of how to use the system to effect changes at various levels, depending on the need and the relative costs and benefits.

There should also be positive side effects of the sort of training which I am recommending. First, by learning to analyze child and family policy, clinicians should become more sensitive to issues about children's status, issues which affect the formulation of children's problems and the ethics of intervention with children. Second, mastery of techniques of child advocacy may give clinicians a better feel for administering complex agencies and implementing programs (cf. Reppucci & Saunders, 1983), tasks which psychologists are often asked to perform but which they are also often untrained to fulfill. Given the complexity of children's services, education about the factors affecting the delivery of services to children and training in maneuvering through the bureaucratic maze may be especially important for psychologists who assume administrative positions in children's agencies. Third, training in child advocacy should provide an interdisciplinary flavor to training in child advocacy. Besides providing intellectual enrichment, such interdisciplinary education is likely to give clinicians a broader, perhaps more accurate view of the world of childhood than is obtained in conventional clinical child training and to suggest new approaches to clinical evaluation and intervention.

In conclusion, lest I be misunderstood, let me make clear that I am not suggesting that clinical child psychologists should forsake their identity as psychologists and assume the role of full-time professional child advocates. Just as being a psycholegal scholar does not necessarily require full legal training (Melton, in press), a psychologist need not pursue the full training of a community organizer, a social planner, a lobbyist, or a lawyer, to be an effective advocate for children. However, I do wish to make clear that the role of advocate is necessarily one aspect of clinical child psychologists' identity, if their practices are to be ethically and pragmatically sound. Moreover, to understand and fulfill such a role requires special training. An appreciation of the social influences on children's lives and expertise in manipulation of such systems to enhance the fit between children and their environment typically do not come naturally. Clinical child training should be broadly interdisciplinary and provide specific didactic and practical training in child advocacy.

References

American Psychological Association. (1981). Ethical principles of psychologists. *American Psychologist, 36,* 633-638.

Brown, P.G. (1982). Human independence and parental proxy consent. In W. Gaylin & R. Macklin (Eds.), *Who speaks for the child? The problem of proxy consent* (pp. 209-222). New York: Plenum.

Bush, M., & Gordon, A.C. (1978). Client choice and bureaucratic accountability: Possibilities for responsiveness in a social welfare bureaucracy. *Journal of Social Issues, 34,* 22-43.

Davidson, W.S., II, & Rapp, C.A. (1976). Child advocacy in the justice system. *Social Work, 21,* 225-232.

Hobbs, N. (1975). *The futures of children: Categories, labels, and their consequences.* San Francisco, CA: Jossey-Bass

Kahn, A.J., Kamerman, S.B., & McGowan, B.G. (1972). *Child advocacy: Report of a national baseline study.* New York: Columbia University Press.

Knitzer, J.E. (1971). Advocacy and the children's crisis. *American Journal of Orthopsychiatry, 41,* 799-806

Knitzer, J.E. (1976). Child advocacy: A perspective. *American Journal of Orthopsychiatry, 46,* 200-216.

Knitzer, J.E. (1982). *Unclaimed children: The failure of public responsibility to children and adolescent in need of mental health services.* Washington, DC: Children's Defense Fund.

Koocher, G.P. (1979). Child advocacy and mental health professionals. In P.A. Vardin & I.N. Brody (Eds.), *Children's rights: Contemporary perspectives* (pp. 84-98). New York: Teachers College Press.

Koocher, G.P., & Pedulla, B.M. (1977). Current practices in child psychotherapy. *Professional Psychology, 8,* 275-286.

Levitt, E.E. (1957). The result of psychotherapy with children: An evaluation. *Journal of Consulting Psychology, 21,* 186-189.

Levitt, E.E. (1971). Research on psychotherapy with children. In A.E. Bergin & S.L. Garfield (Eds.), *Handbook of psychotherapy and behavior change: An empirical analysis* (pp. 474-494). New York: Wiley.

Massimo, J.L., & Shore, M.F. (1963). The effectiveness of a vocationally oriented psychotherapy. *American Journal of Orthopsychiatry, 33,* 634-643.

Melton, G.B. (1977). The psychologist as clinician-advocate: Issues in practice and training. *Journal of Clinical Child Psychology, 6,* 27-29.

Melton, G.B. (1982). Children's rights: Where are the children? *American Journal of Orthopsychiatry, 52,* 530-538.

Melton, G.B. (1983a). *Child advocacy: Psychological issues and interventions.* New York: Plenum.

Melton, G.B. (1983b). Decision making by children: Psychological risks and benefits. In G.B. Melton, G.P. Koocher, & M.J. Saks (Eds.), *Children's competence to consent* (pp. 21-40). New York: Plenum.

Melton, G.B. (1983c). Towards "personhood" for adolescents: Autonomy and privacy as value in public policy. *American Psychologist, 38,* 99-103.

Melton, G.B. (in press). Training in psychology and law. In I.B. Weiner & A.K. Hess (Eds.), *Handbook of forensic psychology.* New York: Wiley.

Melton, G.B., & Spaulding, W.J. (in press). No place to go: *Civil commitment of minors.* Lincoln: University of Nebraska Press.

Mnookin, R.H. (1973). Foster care: In whose best interest? *Harvard Educational Review, 43,* 599-638.

Mnookin, R.H. (1978). Children's rights: Beyond kiddie libbers and child savers. *Journal of Clinical Child Psychology, 7,* 163-167.

Polier, J.W. (1975). Professional abuse of children: Responsibility for the delivery of services. *American Journal of Orthopsychiatry, 45,* 357-362.

Rappaport, J. (1977). *Community psychology: Values, research, and action.* New York: Holt, Rinehart & Winston.

Reppucci, N.D., & Saunders, J.T. (1983). Focal issues for institutional change. *Professional Psychology: Research and Practice, 14,* 514-528.

Rogers, C.M., & Wrightsman, L.S. (1978). Attitudes toward children's rights: Nurturance or self-determination. *Journal of Social Issues, 34,* 59-68.

Ryan, W. (1971). *Blaming the victim,* New York: Vintage.

Steiner, G.Y. (1976). *The children's cause.* Washington, DC: Brookings Institution.

Warren, R.L. (1971). Mental health planning and model cities: "Hamlet" or "Hellzapoppin." *Community Mental Health Journal, 7,* 39-49.

Westman, J.C. (1979). *Child advocacy: New professional roles for helping families.* New York: Free Press.

Worsfold, V.L. (1974). A philosophical justification for children's rights. *Harvard Educational Review, 44,* 142-157.

Training of Clinical Child/Community Psychologists

Douglas G. Ullman
Bowling Green State University

Howard J. Markman
University of Denver

William O. Donnelly
Children's Resource Center

As clinical child psychology continues the development of its professional identity, increasing attention has been paid to the establishment of boundary lines as to what is inside and what is outside the domain of the profession (e.g., Wohlford, 1979; Maurer, 1975). One way to delineate clinical child psychology has been to focus on the factors which differentiate it from adult clinical, developmental and community psychology. While the emphasis on differences is understandable in this light, we feel that much can be gained from analysis of the areas of overlap, particularly with respect to identifying the background knowledge, skills and perspectives appropriate for a training program in clinical child psychology. More specifically, we feel the overlap of conceptual, research and practical issues between clinical, developmental and community psychology should provide the core of a clinical child psychology training program. We refer to this as a clinical child/community model.

Wohlford (1979) proposed a *community mental health model,* which essentially involved extending clinical services to children in community settings and serving as consultants to community agencies. We have expanded this to a broader, clinical/community model, and have included interventions and concepts from community psychology, such as prevention, systems perspective and community organization (Heller & Monahan, 1977).

The term *model* has been used by different authors to convey different meanings. Roberts (1982) for example, used the term *models* of clinical child psychology training as essentially synonomous with the type of program in which the training took place. Thus, the four models he described corresponded to four types of university-based training programs. While our use of the term model also refers to a philosophy and approach to training doctoral students to meet what we believe are important roles and responsibilities expected of clinical child psychologists, it is not restricted to any one specific type of training program. Indeed, the clinical child/community model to be described characterizes both Bowling Green State University and the University of Denver, the home universities of the first two authors. Bowling Green would probably be described as a general clinical training program with a clinical child track, while the University of Denver is one of the oldest examples of a specialized child clinical program. In this paper we will provide the basic rationale for this model and a brief overview of the goals we see as appropriate in a training program.

Rationale

As Ross (1972) notes, most of clinical child psychology's key concepts and theories, research questions and methodologies, and developmental perspective on normal and abnormal behavior have their roots in clinical or developmental psychology. The continued importance of the clinical roots can be seen in that most clinical child psychologists report that their doctoral degree is in clinical psychology and that it remains their major interest, broadly defined (Routh, 1977). Indeed, *traditional* clinical child psychology has been defined in terms of its clinical *core* (a primary emphasis on diagnostic testing and individual psychotherapy with children) (Cummings, 1974).

As the profession developed, the interest in assessment and treatment appears to have remained, but what is meant by those terms has been broadened considerably. Assessment may now range from traditional tests of psychological factors operating within the child, to evaluations of the child's interaction with his/her environment, to assessment of the key people and systems in the child's world. That is, the kinds of assessment questions now being asked of child clinicians include a good deal more than just what are the key psychopathology/personality factors involved. Questions such as "Which parent can best meet the needs of this child?" in a custody case, or "Should this child be placed in a foster home?" in an abuse case, or "What could be done to reduce hyperactive behaviors in this setting?" in a school related case, are all reflections of this expansion. Similarly, treatment has come to refer to a broad spectrum of interventions. These range from an increasing variety of one-to-one therapies with the child as the identified patient, to family systems-oriented therapies, to therapeutic interventions with those who are already involved with the child (e.g., parents, teachers, welfare workers, pediatricians). For example, in a case in which a child has been abused by his/her parents, the psychologist may be asked to treat (or make treatment recommendations for) the child, the parents, the family, the foster parents during placement, the case worker, the school, the courts, and so forth. There are no indications that the tremendous growth in range and types of clinical interventions will slow down in the near future. Indeed, perhaps as a function of the increasing complexity of children's problems and the large number of factors to be dealt with, modern clinical child psychologists have expanded their activities to include such wide ranging topics as prevention, child advocacy, consultation, program development and evaluation, and so forth (Wohlford, 1979, Roberts & Peterson, 1984). Thus, there remains a common core clinical interest in children and their problems, but the ways clinical child psychologists become involved in trying to do something about them have become quite vast.

The roots in developmental psychology include more that just a common interest in children. A solid background in developmental psychology is not only necessary to address many clinical questions, but also to put normal and abnormal development in perspective (e.g., Cass, 1974). The primary importance of a developmental perspective is one of the major distinguishing features between child and adult approaches. This means more, however, than simply preparing the child clinician to answer questions from parents, teachers, and physicians, such as "Will this child outgrow it?" or "Is this normal for a child of this age?" It involves a basic understanding of the psychological processes and environmental factors involved in normal psychosocial development. For example, the child clinician might be asked to evaluate the effects of periods of prolonged abuse or neglect on a child and would need to know which psychological processes might be affected and how. Similarly, appropriate intervention and prevention strategies in such cases depend heavily on this kind of knowledge. In addition, one of the relatively unique contributions clinical child psychologists can make relative to other child professionals is a knowledge of the research data base, models, methodologies and limitations of relevant areas in developmental psychology. It is this background which enables one to put such questions as "Will a divorce affect this child?" or "What psychological factors might be affected by being a 'latch-key' child?" in proper perspective, as well as to appreciate how complex such questions really are. Further, the emergence of areas like applied developmental psychology have served to highlight some of the overlap in terms of scientific and applied concerns.

While the commonalities with clinical and developmental psychology are relatively straightforward, the overlap with community psychology is perhaps less obvious, but also important. Analyses of recent major clinical child and community psychology journals suggest increasing areas of overlap between the two in terms of conceptual, research and practical issues (Markman & Ullman, 1980). The core concepts of community psychology, far from being antithetical to a clinical child model, are often complementary to it. These concepts include: (1) a focus on work with "systems," with particular emphasis on powerful people within the systems; (2) a focus on "prevention," ranging from primary prevention to crisis intervention; and (3) a focus on coping skills (or "adjustment") related to critical life stresses (Donnelly, 1980). These concepts play important roles in the thinking and application of both areas, although discussed in different jargon.

To illustrate some of the areas of overlap between clinical child and community concepts and models of psychological service delivery, Donnelly (1980) assessed services provided by clinical child psychologists in a multi-disciplinary center providing direct clinical and "indirect" community services for children and families in a rural county. The convergence between the goals, activities, and focus of the clinical and community programs was apparent. For example, analyses of the treatment plans of the clinical programs indicated that 87% called for some specific treatment involving the parents; 43% called for intervention or mutual planning with a school system; 32% involved some collaboration with a local welfare department; and 12% involved contact, consultation and/or planning with the court system. Further, in more than half the cases, clinical services were provided at least as much, if not more, to the child's family system than to the child alone. In turn, many of the community programs, such as early identification and screening programs, consultation to Head Start, and so forth, frequently led to the delivery of direct clinical services. At times, the distinction between clinical and community became blurred, as in a program providing guidance, support and child development information to adolescent mothers and their infants. The infants were without symptomology, but clearly an "at risk" community concern, while the teenage mothers could be considered a clinical population.

Although obviously not characteristic of all clinical child psychologists, the preceding description of services is an attempt to illustrate some of the things they are currently doing which are outside the range of the traditional clinical activities and which require a community psychology perspective. There are a number of indications that the range and scope of these activities are expanding rapidly. Prevention programs, for example, have targeted specific child problems, or settings, or developmental stages or milestones as points for intervention (Roberts & Peterson, 1984). As such, we feel the traditional models of training need to be re-examined and modified to accommodate the clinical, developmental, and community psychology background required to confront the expanding research and practical issues faced by clinical child psychologists.

A Clinical Child/Community Training Model

Overview

Obviously, there are a number of general issues which must be considered in describing a training model and it is simply not possible to discuss all of them here. Instead, the focus will be on the core clinical, developmental, and community components, which, as noted earlier, might be provided in a number of different types of training programs or settings. It should be noted, however, that the underlying assumption of the model is that the training takes place within a Boulder Model scientist-practitioner program. One of the distinguishing features of psychologists relative to other mental health professionals is a background in research. Among the advantages which a research background offers include: (a) the ability to critically evaluate developments within the field and to potentially contribute to its knowledge base; and (b) the ability to raise the kinds of questions that need to be addressed as the field evolves, and, in turn to identify areas of needed skill development. Further, many (e.g, Price & Cherniss, 1977) feel that evaluating the impact of social programs on the consuming public is an ethical imperative for social scientists. The practitioner-side must also be kept current and receive equal emphasis if one is to apply the limited knowledge base to meet the needs of children and their families. We strongly believe that research and intervention programs are not mutually exclusive and that one may lead to the other. For example, research findings lead to ideas for clinical interventions and, likewise, clinical experience leads to hypotheses to be tested in empirical studies. The overlap between research and intervention can be facilitated by academic training centers joining with child-oriented community agencies in endeavors relevant to both.

Clinical Core: The traditional clinical model focuses on psychopathology, diagnostic testing, and individual psychotherapy. A clinical/community model would call for an extensive broadening of these categories and would include assessment, formulating treatment plans, therapeutic interventions (broadly defined), and behavior disorders in children, as well as the community perspective described later. More specifically, an assessment sequence of courses and practica would range from individual assessment (e.g., interviewing, intelligence, personality, neuropsychological testing) to assessment of the child's environment and relevant systems (e.g., family, schools). Practicum experiences would facilitate the combination of such assessment data with other information into the formation of treatment plans. The academic focus would provide the background on the research issues relevant to assessment in general, as well as at least the fundamentals of what is involved in the development of tests and other needed assessment tools. Similarly, the therapeutic interventions sequence of courses and practica would range from a focus on individual treatment (e.g., play therapy, behavioral approaches, etc.) to a focus on the people in the child's relevant systems (e.g., school consultation, parent training) to a focus on both (e.g., family therapy). The goals would include both conceptual development and practicum experiences with a variety of such interventions. The research component would range from the more traditional therapeutic process and outcome issues to program evaluation research.

Developmental Psychology Background: Many of the reasons to provide a solid background in child development were described briefly earlier. Clearly there are many child behaviors which could be considered normal at one age, but quite pathological at another. The understanding of the sequence and range of normal development is critical in determining what is abnormal or atypical. Similarly, one can be easily misled by focusing solely on clinical populations. For example, a frequently reported observation of young elementary school age children referred for a clinical evaluation was that they showed mixed or inconsistent lateral preference. Consequently, a number of clinical and etiological speculations were generated. However, when normal elementary school age children were studied (Ullman, 1977) mixed and inconsistent lateral preference patterns were found quite frequently and there was no relationship between these and problems. As a final example, from a community perspective, there is a tremendous emphasis on the enhancement of competencies and developmental skills. Obviously, one needs to know what the relevant age appropriate competencies and skills are.

All of the above illustrate the importance of providing the student with a solid background in cognitive, emotional, motor and social development in children and adolescents. An appropriate set of developmental psychology courses would also provide a foundation in observational and interactional research strategies and developmental research designs.

Community Perspective: A community perspective involves an attitude rather than a concrete set of skills or techniques. Components of the attitude include an understanding of and commitment to systems, competencies, naturally occurring community resources, and prevention. A child is actively involved in a number of important social systems (e.g., family, schools) and it is important to learn that the child's behavior affects these systems and vice-versa (Lewis & Rosenblum, 1974). Thus, the community systems perspective implies that diagnostic efforts will be devoted to understand the target child in the context of a number of social systems. Family and school observations techniques, therefore, are important additions to the child clinician's repertoire.

A competency perspective directs the child diagnostician to assess competencies as well as deficits, and the child therapist to enhance competencies in addition to, or rather than, eliminating deficits. For example, as noted by Hartup (1979), the traditional clinician may ask, "What effect did trauma X have on the child?" In contrast, the competency-oriented clinician may ask, "How did the child *cope* with trauma X and what generalized coping skills did the child develop in the process?"

The community perspective also highlights the importance of utilizing naturally occurring community resources, such as friends, church, relatives, and so forth. Assessment of the strengths and weaknesses of such resources may be critical in determining the feasibility of treatment plans. Furthermore, utilization of these resources may enhance treatment by professionals or may obviate the need for treatment (Donnelly, 1980).

A prevention perspective implies that we need not wait for clients to come to our doors. Rather, intervention can be developed to enhance competencies of children and their families, alter social systems so as to more positively affect mental health and to help children and families through stressful milestone periods in their lives.

Finally, the community perspective allows for an expanded vista regarding practicum opportunities. There are a variety of settings that serve children and have a tremendous impact on them, but have not been traditional training settings for clinical child psychologists. These include pediatric settings, schools, day care centers, health agencies, social service agencies. However, they are potentially valuable training resources and student placements could be mutually beneficial. That is, the students not only *get* supervised experience with the psychological needs and questions relevant to the children in these settings from a multi-disciplinary perspective, but also *give* the clinical and research skills being developed in their program.

Summary

As clinical child psychology moves into the mid-1980s, we feel it is time to re-examine the models which have provided the basis for traditional graduate programs. As one alternative, we have described our model of training clinical child/community psychologists. It consists of an integration of clinical, developmental, and community psychology perspectives in terms of theoretical, research and applied issues.

References

Cass, L.K. (1974). The training of clinical child psychologists. In G.J. Williams & S. Gordon (Eds.), *Clinical child psychology: Current practices and future perspectives* (pp. 463-482). New York: Behavioral Publications.

Cummings, S.T. (1974). Is traditionl clinical child psychology obsolete? In G.J. Williams & S. Gordon (Eds.), *Clinical child psychology: Current practices and future perspectives* (pp. 485-506). New York: Behavioral Publications.

Donnelly, W. (1980, May). *Convergence of clinical and community practice in a children's community mental health program.* A paper presented at the annual meeting of the Midwestern Psychological Association, St. Louis, MO.

Hartup, W. (1979). The social world of childhood. *American Psychologist, 34,* 944-950.

Heller, K., & Monahan, J. (1977). *Psychology and community change.* New York: Dorsey.

Iscoe, I. (1974). Is clinical child psychology obolete? Some observations on the current scene. In G.J. Williams & S. Gordon (Eds.), *Clinical child psychology: Current practices and future perspectives* (pp. 507-514). New York: Behavioral Publications.

Lewis, M., & Rosenblum, L.A. (Eds.) (1974). *The effect of the infant on its caregiver.* New York: Wiley.

Markman, H.J., & Ullman, D.G. (1980, May). *A comparison of clinical child and community psychology.* A paper presented at the Annual meeting of the Midwestern Psychological Association, St. Louis.

Maurer, A. (1975). Letter to the Editor. *Journal of Clinical Child Psychology, 4,* 53.

Price, R., & Cherniss, C. (1977). Training for a new profession: Research as social action. *Professional Psychology, 8,* 222-231.

Roberts, M.C. (1982). Clinical child psychology programs: Where and what are they? *Journal of Clinical Child Psychology, 11,* 13-21.

Roberts, M.C., & Peterson, L. (Eds.) (1984). *Prevention of problems in childhood.* New York: Wiley.

Ross, A.O. (1972). The clinical child psychologist. In B.B. Wolman (Ed.), *Manual of child psychopathology* (pp. 1287-1296). New York: McGraw-Hill.

Routh, D.K. (1977). What is a clinical child psychologist? *The Clinical Psychologist, 30,* 23-25.

Ullman, D.G. (1977). Children's lateral preference patterns: Frequency and relationships with achievement and intelligence. *Journal of School Psychology, 15,* 36-43.

Wohlford, P. (1979). Clinical child psychology: The emerging speciality. *The Clinical Psychologist, 33,* 25-29.

Roles and Responsibilities of Trainees Working with Children with Multiple Problems

Sandra W. Russ **Donald K. Freedheim** **Jane W. Kessler**
Case Western Reserve University

There is increasing diversity in the child populations served by mental health professionals (Wohlford, 1977). Each unique subgroup has special assessment and intervention requirements. Children with multiple problems include those with emotional problems coupled with other conditions. Our graduate program at Case Western Reserve University has chosen to focus on children with emotional problems coupled with physical handicaps, chronic illness, mental retardation, or abused and neglected backgrounds.

Need for Graduate Training Programs

All of these specialized child populations require different methods of assessment and intervention, a separate knowledge base, and different conceptual frameworks (Drotar, 1975; Russ, 1981). For example, few tests have been normed for handicapped children and there is a need to adapt current available tests for use with these children (Ho, Glanville, & Brave, 1980). Family assessment techniques are important in identifying etiological factors in psychosomatic disorders in children (Drotar, 1975). It is difficult to set priorities for intervention with these multi-problem families and a framework of prevention is often utilized since there is early access to at-risk populations at critical times (Drotar, 1981). Consultation with hospital staff is crucial in creating a supportive environment for hospitalized children (Drotar, 1975, 1978). Few training programs have prepared students to work with these populations (Tuma & Pratt, 1982; Stearns, 1982). As a result the needs of children and of the field have not been fully met.

Emotionally disturbed, mentally retarded children are also underserved (Reiss, Levitan, & McNally, 1982). Mental retardation is broadly defined to include children with over-all measured intelligence below 70 IQ as well as children with major cognitive deficits, particularly in the language area. The fact that these children have adaptive behavior deficits is inherent in the classification, but, traditionally, these psychosocial problems have been viewed as the direct by-product of the intellectual limitation. Discrimination of the preventable and treatable facets of the behavioral problems is a diagnostic challenge which requires specialized knowledge. Mentally retarded persons, although known to be particularly vulnerable to the full spectrum of psychological disorders, including psychosis, have not been well served by mental health professionals.

Child abuse and neglect have become problems of major psychological consequence in our society. Since the publication of the work of Henry Kempe and his associates at the University of Colorado Medical School, which introduced the term "battered child syndrome," a broad spectrum of negative parental behavior has been the focus of national attention (Kempe et al., 1962).

Studies of etiology (Gil, 1975; Steele & Pollack, 1974) have pointed out the cycle of abuse which is passed down from generation to generation (Sweet & Resnick, 1979). Recent investigations have emphasized the serious psychological consequences of continous emotional stress and/or physical trauma in childhood (Kinard, 1980; Martin & Beezley, 1977; Steele, 1977). Ultimately, the problems of child abuse/neglect must be viewed in the larger context of family violence and its impact on the individual (Gelles & Strauss, 1979).

The clinical psychologist has a prominent role in the prevention and treatment of child abuse/neglect. First, there is urgent need for adequate research in the area (Sweet & Resnick, 1979; Baker et al., 1976). Next, all clinical child psychologists must have the diagnostic skills and sensitivity to recognize the signs of abuse in children (Green, 1978; Reidy, 1977). Treatment of parents and children requires an understanding of the developmental sequence of maturation as well as experience in working with "at risk" populations. It is also incumbent upon all practicing psychologists, whether they work in agencies, mental health centers, or independent settings, to be knowledgeable as to the programs available in the community concerned with child abuse/neglect (National Institute of Mental Health, 1977).

Program Development

A sub-specialty program in children with multiple problems was developed within an existing clinical child graduate program track. The clincial child program itself is within a clinical psychology graduate training program. The sub-specialty program has been formally in existance for two years and has been supported by an NIMH Child Mental Health Clinical Training Grant. General clinical child program goals are to develop in the student a broad base of knowledge of fundamental principles of child development and behavior, sound clinical skills in assessment and intervention with children, strong research base in approaching problems of children, and knowledge of current issues in the field of clinical child psychology. Key features of the clinical child program include early client contact in a variety of settings, early introduction to research methods and a research apprenticeship in the first year, and extensive clinical experience in community settings prior to the internship year. The goal has been to develop a flexible base in students which enabled them to specialize late in their training, but, increasingly, training in specialty areas is beginning early in the program.

Specialty training in children with multiple problems begins in the first year of the program in limited ways. Students may emphasize one of three areas within the sub-specialty track: (1) physically handicapped and chronically ill children with emotional disturbance, (2) mental retardation and emotional disturbances, (3) abused/neglected child. These three areas were chosen based upon the expertise of the faculty, current programs within the Psychology Department, and nature of the child populations available in clinical placement settings. In essence, in developing a specialty emphasis, we built on the existing strengths of the program and formalized experiences that students were already obtaining. Students in this track now take basic clinical child courses in assessment, which teaches a general problem-solving approach to assessment (Russ, 1978), in intervention, and research. New courses and more highly focused clinical practicum experiences were developed for the sub-specialty program. Research projects are also carried out focusing on the multi-problem child.

In addition to basic child courses, important specialty courses include:

- Specialized Assessment Methods with Children with Multiple Problems
- Specialized Assessment Practicum
- Case Conference on Intervention with Children with Multiple Problems
- Theories, Research, Legal and Community Issues Related to Children with Multiple Problems

Two, year-long 16 hour/week placements in specialized settings in the second and third year are essential features of the program. Also, 6 week mini-seminars cover topics such as child abuse and program evaluation.

Roles and Responsibilities of Trainees in Clinical Placements

One of the most important features of our sub-specialty program is the two day per week clinical placement. Students are placed in two of three clinical settings, one in their second year and another in their third year. Students participate in in-service training, receive intensive supervision, and carry out a variety of clinical activities.

At Rainbow Babies & Children's Hospital, under the direction of Dennis Drotar, students are introduced to working within a pediatric setting (Drotar, 1982). They gain experience with specialized assessment techniques with children who present with a wide variety of problems, such as delayed intellectual development, poor school performance, problematic adaptation to chronic illness and/or child abuse and neglect. Students also engage in short-term psychotherapy with children and families and case-centered consultation to hospital staff. There is extensive training in infant assessment for failure to thrive infants, infants with developmental delay, and infants with physical illness and handicapping conditions. Students also assess the psychosocial environment and parents' coping skills, carry out home visits, and follow-up families.

The Mental Development Center is a university-based outpatient facility funded by the local community mental health board and directed by Laurel Schauer. The child population served is heterogeneous but giving priority to developmentally disabled and mentally retarded children (Freedheim, 1973). These children come to the Center because of combined emotional, family, and cognitive problems, which confound the standard assessment and treatment practices. Students receive close supervision in intake, comprehensive assessment activities, treatment with children, and parent counseling. Students also consult with schools and carry out extensive work with parents in multi-problem families whose children are enrolled in the preschool program.

At Cleveland Metropolitan General Hospital, Child Mental Health Unit, students are trained in specialized assessment techniques, early detection, short-term treatment approaches, consultation to pediatric units, and follow-up activities. They also are involved in detection and intervention with sexually abused children.

In addition, as a supplemental practicum experience, students participate in programs at Bellflower House. Bellflower House is a walk-in center for parents which provides a number of educational and counseling programs directed toward high risk mothers to help prevent child abuse and neglect. Students serve as co-sponsers for the Parents Anonymous groups, as well as give consultation to a number of other programs. For example, the teenage parent program offers group and individual counseling to young mothers on personal and child development issues. Students have assisted the professional and volunteer staff in organizing and developing the program.

Goals of Training

The basic goal of our specialty training program is to teach graduate students in clinical child psychology to work effectively with children with multiple problems. As students become more advanced, they should have increasing expertise in their area of specialization.

By the end of the first year, students should have acquired the following skills:

- Decide when testing is necessary; competently put together an assessment battery which is relevant to the purpose of the testing
- Competently administer, score, and interpret standard tests used in clinical child settings
- Make appropriate basic recommendations for intervention
- Write clear and accurate psychological reports for various purposes
- Give feedback to child, family, and school in an effective manner
- Be aware of specialized assessment techniques with the multi-problem child and family and be competent in administration and interpretation of several
- Know basics of preschool and infant assessment
- Be aware of ethical issues in assessment
- Have grounding in research issues and problems of multi-problem children

By the end of the second year:

- A basic foundation in child psychopathology and intervention
- Basic intervention skills with children and families
- Basic intervention skills with multi-problem child and families
- Knowledge base in specialty area
- Evolving research skills in specialty area

By the end of the third year:

- Thorough knowledge base in children with multiple problems
- Refined assessment and intervention skills with children with multiple problems
- Basic consulation skills for children with multiple problems
- Basic research skills and grounding in research issues with multi-problem child

Sub-specialty Training Issues

In developing a sub-specialty program, our faculty had to deal with a number of difficult issues. Major questions were:

1. What is the appropriate balance between general child training and specialized child training?
2. What are the fundamental courses and experiences in child training at the graduate level?
3. What are realistic goals of graduate training in clinical child psychology?
4. How should research be integrated into the program?

The key to achieving a balance between a general clinical child and specialized clinical child background is accurate identification of the fundamental courses and experiences in clinical child psychology training. In deciding what to teach and how to teach it, we must identify fundamentals of current knowledge and problem solving skills (Russ, 1980). The guidelines for training by the National Training Committee of the Section on Clinical Child Psychology (Johnson & Tuma, 1983) helped with this process as did years of experimenting in our own child program. Also, general principles of clinical child psychology can be taught within specialized child courses. In addition, pacing of the specialized child experiences is essential. For example, during the first year of the program, the only major specialized experience is in assessment, which follows the basic child assessment course. In the second year of the program, when clinical placements begin, it is important that general child experience also be obtained. Students also take at least one adult psychotherapy practicum within the Psychology Department to ensure some intervention experience with adults.

All students participate in a research clerkship during their first year. This is a one day per week research apprenticeship in the child area. Initially, it was required that students' research be focused on the multi-problem child. Most students were able to meet that requirement. However, in looking over the past three years of this program, a more flexible approach is necessary. The research problem that the student is interested in may or may not lend itself to investigation with this specialized child population. Empirical work with normal populations may be a necessary first step in a research program. A more realistic requirement is that the student's research be relevant to children with multiple problems.

Other useful experiences for students in the subspecialty have been attendance at one national conference a year and paricipation in specialty miniseminars (4-6 weeks) within the Psychology Department. These experiences expose students to a broad range of clinical and research issues relevant to a multi-problem child. A large number of clinical students not on the specialty tract also participated in the additional seminars and have become aware of the complexity of issues involved in working with these children.

In conclusion, it is possible to develop a specialized clinical child track within a general clinical child program which the student can complete in five years, with the internship in the fifth year. The goals spelled out in the previous section are realistic. Students who are now finishing their second and third year of the program "look different" than their general clinical child peers. They do have a more specialized knowledge base, are working effectively with multi-problem children, and have more specialized research projects. It will be important to do continual follow-up of their work after they complete their doctoral degrees to assess whether their clinical and research activities have indeed been affected by their specialized graduate training experience.

References

Baher, E., Hyman, C., Jones, C., Jones, R., Kerr, A., & Mitchell, R. (1976). *At risk: An account of the work of the NSPCC battered child research team.* Boston, MA: Routledge & Kegal Paul.

Drotar, D. (1975). Clinical psychology training in the pediatric hospital. *Journal of Clinical Child Psychology, 4,* 46-49.

Drotar, D. (1978). Training psychologists to consult with physicians: Problems and prospects. *Journal of Clinical Child Psychology, 1,* 57-61.

Drotar, D. (1981). Psychological perspectives in chronic childhood illness. *Journal of Psychology, 6,* 211-228.

Drotar, D. (1982). The child psychologist in the medical system. In P. Karaly & T.T. Steffen (Eds.), *Advances in child behavior analysis and therapy (vol. 3): Child health psychology* (pp. 1-21). Lexington, MA: Lexington Books.

Freedheim, D.K. (1973). The role of psychology in an interdisciplinary system. *Professional Psychology, 4,* 99-103.

Gelles, R.J., & Strauss, M.A. (1979). Violence in the American family. *Journal of Social Issues, 35,* 15-39.

Gil, D.G. (1975). Unravelling child abuse. *American Journal of Orthopsychiatry, 45,* 346-356.

Green, A.H. (1978). Psychopathology of abused children. *Journal of the American Academy of Child Psychiatry, 17,* 92-103.

Ho, C., Glanville, S., & Brave, J. (1980). Challenges in evaluating young developmental disabled children. *Journal of Clinical Child Psychology, 9,* 223-235.

Johnson, J.H., & Tuma, J.M. (1983). Training in clinical child psychology: A brief overview of selected issues. *Journal of Clinical Child Psychology, 12,* 365-368.

Kempe, C.H., Silverman, F.N., Steele, B.F., Droegemueller, W., & Silver, H.K. (1962). The battered child syndrome. *Journal of American Medical Association, 181,* 17-24.

Kinard, E.M. (1980). Emotional development in physically abused children. *American Journal of Orthopsychiatry, 50,* 686-695.

Martin, H., & Beezley, P. (1977). Behavioral observations of abused children. *Developmental Medicine and Child Neurology, 19,* 373-387.

National Institute of Mental Health. (1977). *Child abuse and neglect programs: Practice and theory.* Washington, DC: U.S. Government Printing Office.

Reidy, T. (1977). The aggressive characteristics of abused and neglected children. *Journal of Clinical Psychology, 33,* 1140-1145.

Reiss, S., Levitan, G., & McNally, R. (1982). Emotionally disturbed mentally retarded people: An underserved population. *American Psychologist, 37,* 361-367.

Russ, S. (1978). Teaching psychological assessment: Training issues and teaching approaches. *Journal of Personality Assessement, 42,* 452-456.

Russ, S. (1980). Graduate training in clinical psychology: Quality and beyond. (Comment). *American Psychologist, 35,* 766-767.

Russ, S. (1981, March). *Future directions in teaching child assessment.* Paper presented at the meeting of Society for Personality Assessment, San Diego, CA.

Stearns, A. (1982, August). *A survey of continuing education efforts in pediatric psychology.* Paper presented at the annual meeting of the American Psychological Association, Washington, DC.

Steele, B.F. (1977, February). *Phychological dimensions of child abuse.* Paper presented at the annual meeting of the American Academy for the Advancement of Science, Denver, CO.

Steele, B.F., & Pollack, C.B. (1974). A psychiatric study of parents who abuse infants and small children. In R.E. Helfer & C.E. Kempe (Eds.), *The battered child* (2nd. ed.) (pp. 103-147) Chicago, IL: University of Chicago Press.

Sweet, J.J., & Resnick, P.A. (1979). The maltreatment of children: A review of theories and reasearch. *Journal of Social Issues, 35,* 40-59.

Tuma, J.M., & Pratt, J.M. (1982). Clinical child psychology practice and training: A survey. *Journal of Clinical Child Psychology, 11,* 27-34.

Wohlford, P. (1977). Issues facing clinical child psychology. *Journal of Clinical Child Psychology, 6,* 4-5.

Clinical Child Psychology as an Applied Developmental Psychology: Toward a Redefinition of Mission and Training

Donald Wertlieb
Tufts University

As we grapple with the critical issue involved in the professional preparation of clinical child psychologists, it is imperative that we address the strengths and weaknesses of the traditional models of training and practice as well as integrate the current and anticipated pressures and progress in the field. This paper presents such an analysis and suggests a promising resolution which involves a reorientation of our mission and training — clinical child psychology as an applied developmental psychology. Accounts of the history of the field of clinical psychology emphasize the ebb and flow of the rapprochement between clinical psychology and developmental or child psychology as the discipline of clinical child psychology emerged. These convergences and divergences among the child guidance movement, child welfare institutes, child study movement, experimental child psychology, and clinical child or child clinical psychology are well described by Ross (1959, 1972) and Santostefano (1978), so they will not be repeated here.

Until very recently, the resolution has been only a partial one with some clinical psychologists specializing in research and service related to children and some developmental psychologists pursuing questions implicitly and explicitly focused upon understanding or helping atypical or problem children. Most recently, there is a growing awareness of the need for a new rapprochement, a marriage between clinical and developmental psychology under the umbrella of the applied developmental psychologies (Wertlieb, 1979, 1983b; Zigler, 1980). There is an emphasis upon the "synergistic relationship between basic and applied research" (Zigler, 1980; p. 1). There is renewed appreciation and recommitment to the "scientist-practitioner" ideal. Current and previous resolutions left clinical child psychology as somewhat of a stepchild to clinical psychology, and fostered a splintering of stepsiblings such as pediatric psychology, neuropsychology or forensic psychology. This new orientation promises a more integrated, solid and appropriate base for a discipline, clinical child psychology, along with its siblings, such as pediatric psychology, school psychology, education, child welfare — all attaining their most impressive, compelling and effective status as applied developmental psychology.

What is "applied developmental psychology?" Recent effort to articulate a definition include a symposium published in the *Journal of Applied Development Psychology* (Scholnick, 1983; Scott, 1983; Sigel, 1983; Wertlieb, 1983b) and the introductory chapter of the new edited series on *Applied Developmental Psychology* (Morrison, Lord & Keating, 1984). In the Symposium, I suggested that:

> "Applied developmental psychology is a superordinate discipline, an unbrella under which good clinical psychology, good educational psychology, good school psychology, etc., all progress as they organize as applications of the developmental psychology data-base. The assumptions, methods and data of developmental psychology guide the applied developmental psychologist in his or her professional work — be it research, theorizing, service or other forms of practice". (p. 349-350)

Morrison (1984) offer several elaborations in defining the field, as I have abstracted in my review of their book (Wertlieb, 1985): "In contrast to the by now traditional ivory-towerish priority of 'knowledge for knowledge's sake,' applied developmental psychology (ADP) is driven by a sense of responsibility for contributing to the solution of social problems. A second hallmark of ADP is its devotion to ecological validity, again in dissatisfaction with by now traditional laboratory methodology and assumptions. Morrison et al., note important convergence around four features of ADP, which include (1) an attraction to and acceptance of complex questions, (2) an appreciation of the necessity of multidisciplinary approaches, (3) a balance of 'basic' and 'applied' endeavors with enhanced positive feedback and cross-fertilization between the two, and (4) a sustained focus on real world issues and everyday life" (p. 503). The congeniality and fit with the world of the clinical child psychologist is unmistakeable. To reorient should not require a great deal of effort.

The need for this reorientation can be understood as a manifestation of interacting pressures within the mental health field, within psychology, and of the broader sociopolitical and economic context of our times. The President's Commission on Mental Health (HEW, 1979) appropriately emphasizes the need for more focused attention upon children and upon the social forces which create or maintain the health and mental health problems of children and families. There is, thus, a mandate for clinical child psychologists to recognize their responsibilities as social change agents with such social change being an appropriate route for servicing the needs of children and families. Both explicitly and between the lines, there is a call for broad-based social change. The individual, or family-oriented skills fostered by traditional clinical training, are but one part, albeit an important part, of the skills required to meet such a mandate. Traditional developmental training has provided important understandings of how children grow and learn and how these processes interact with the social forces of concern. Neither discipline, clinical nor developmental, has emphasized the application of its skills or knowledge base in the service of this mandated social change. The new clinical child psychologist, as an applied developmental psychologist, will be well attuned with the strategies of applied behavioral science and will be well-equipped to fulfill this portion of his or her mandate.

Even the more traditional and accepted mandate of clinical child psychologists (understanding and treating troubled or troubling children and their families) has come under fire from within and without. Even our most forward looking and promising evolutions in theory and practice can be subsumed under an analysis which portrays the field as preoccupied with the "medical model" or reactions to it. Albee (1978) has called for a "Fourth Revolution" in mental health, a revolution which might be spearheaded by the new clinical child psychologists. Albee calls for a genuine breaking away from the old medical model. This hardly precludes continued collaboration with medicine, but rather dictates that such alliances and collaborative arenas be within the "new medical model" (Engel, 1977), which recognizes health and illness as complex bio-psycho-social processes. The clinical psychologist, as an applied developmental psychologist, can do more than just the current lip-service to an interest, can even place a priority upon health and adaptation rather than illness or pathology. Bardon (1983), Fox (1982), Levy (1984), and Masterpasqua (1981) echo similar concerns.

Such a revolution might also provide for a needed reorganization of boundaries with allied applied developmental psychologies (school psychology, education, child welfare). Of course, such new alliances assume concurrent and complementary evolution in those disciplines. Given that many of the societal pressures are similar, it is likely that such evolution will occur. For example, as schools attempt to meet the challenges of Public Law 94-142 (Federal legislation requiring that they serve and educate all children, despite handicaps or special needs), the disciplines of school pyschology and education will necessarily seek channels of collaboration with clinical child psychology, especially in the context of an ideally shared common framework of "applied developmental psychology." Whereas traditional training in clinical child psychology has emphasized our role on the mental health team, collaborating with psychiatrists and social workers under the umbrella of the old medical model, the proposed reorientation broadens our alliances to include pediatricians and family practitioners, teachers, and school psychologists, with the emphasis upon enhancing children's development under the umbrella of applied developmental psychology.

Within psychology, on a more intramural basis, it is important to recognize current dilemmas, even crises, over the professionalization of psychology, a dilemma at the heart of clinical child psychology. Clinical psychology appears to be investing heavily in the professional model of training and practice, the PsyD model. Clinical child psychology must, and will, respond in a like manner. However, it is imperative that our evolution as the discipline of clinical child psychology also includes a recommitment to the "scientist- practitioner" model of PhD training. The clinical child psychologist as an applied developmental psychologist approaches the Boulder ideal. He or she is first and foremost a PhD psychologist, well versed in psychological theory and research. As important are his or her skills in translating this knowledge base in child development into individual, family, and social change. This proposed reorientation in the mission of clinical child psychology involves a number of new and old problems in training, a number of which are addressed by the more concrete proposals outlined below.

There are basically two general innovations in curriculum and internship training that would facilitate the reorientation of clinical child psychology called for above. One involves a shift and broadening of the academic curriculum. The other involves the integration of the internship and thesis experiences in a way more conducive to the professional and scientific responsibilities and opportunities of the practicing clinical child psychologist in our society. These changes redefine our discipline as an applied developmental psychology, better prepared to meet the challege and expectations we face in coming decades. Much of the discussion that follows borrows from my contribution to the above mentioned symposium addressing the definition of applied developmental pyschology (Wertlieb, 1983b).

Innovations in Curriculum

Recognizing that as clinical child psychologists our basic science is that of developmental psychology, changes are dictated in course content and focus in the academic training curriculum. Thus, the priority becomes an appreciation of both normal and atypical processes of cognitive, socioemotional, and family development. Skill courses in assessment and treatment strive to integrate theory, research, and practice within this framework of development (e.g., Santostefano, 1978). Within this framework, the clinical psychologist can contribute in a range of settings, including health care, mental health, education, human service, and public policy arenas. The focus on normal, as well as atypical development, provides for positive and preventive approaches rather than only remedial and illness -oriented ones which have been criticized in traditional clinical psychology.

As an example, recent work in developmental psychopathology can illustrate the promise and necessity of reorienting ourselves as applied developmental psychologists. To be very concrete with this example, take hold of the recent special issue of *Child Development,* edited by Dante Cicchetti (1984) on developmental psychopathology. The range and depth of the theoretical and empirical reports contained in that volume attest impressively to the current concerns and challenges we face as clinicians and academicians. The traditional problems of assessment and therapy that confront the clinical child psychologist on a day-to-day basis are given new perspectives when seen from the framework of applied developmental psychology. In an especially cogent and powerful paper in that volume, Kendall, Lerner, and Craighead (1984) conclude:

> "The synthesis between the study of human development and the practice of intervention has important implications for the advancement of both fields. Interventionists will come to understand better why their techniques do not have equipotentiality across life and how one portion of life circumscribes possibilities for change in succeeding ones. On the other hand, developmentists will come to recognize that the prototypic developmental course is more open to change than previously or generally thought and that, because of the plasticity of human developmental processes, the potential for substantial flexibility remains present for more of life than previously believed.
>
> Together, developmentalists and interventionists may contribute to clarifying a major issue in psychology today, the issue of constancy and change over the life course. From such collaboration we may come to know better the conditions under which we see and/or precipitate change, and we may learn how we can best balance these two ubiquitous features of life to improve the human conditions." (p. 79)

Clearly, an eloquent statement of a major agenda for clinical child psychology and a guidepost for the reorientation of our curriculum.

Equally compelling is the conclusion of Garmezy, Masten, and Tellegen's (1984) contribution to the volume:

> "The study of the etiology, symptom expression, course, and treatment of childhood disorders will remain a central one. But this more traditional orientation must be complemented by a "new look," one that emphasizes those adaptive and resilient individual and familial attributes whose neglect may have caused our predictions of disorder to go awry. This latter function is one in which developmentalist and psychopathologist can join together in research that will, in time, have significant implications for intervening to prevent or to ameliorate childhood disorders." (p. 109)

Equally compelling specific examples and broad generalizations could be lifted from other contributions to that volume, as well as a number of other recent important publications (e.g., Bobbit & Keating, 1983; Elkind, 1982; McMahon & De V. Peters, 1985; Selman & Yando, 1980).

A second innovation in curriculum involves strengthening the clinical child psychologist's knowledge and skill base in organizational and social change. As an applied behavioral scientist, the clinical child psychologist must be capable of understanding and altering the complex social systems and bureaucracies within which he or she functions. To provide family therapy for a child-abusing family is certainly a critical function of the clinical child psychologist. As important, or perhaps more so, is the understanding and skill necessary to influence the human service system (e.g., welfare, school, hospital, etc.) so that the family therapy can have meaningful impact. There is much to be learned from our colleagues in community psychology and organizational psychology (Masterpasqua, 1981). The clinical child psychology curriculm must address these needs via coursework and practicum experiences in consultation, program evaluation, and organizational behavior. As an applied developmental psychologist, the clinical child psychologist will be responsible for the diffusion of our understandings of normal and atypical development into the health care, human service, education, and public policy arenas. The guidelines for training developed by APA Division 37, Child, Youth and Family Services, are consistent with this view (Erickson, Roberts, & Tuma, 1983; Roberts, Erickson, & Tuma, 1985) (see Appendix E).

Integration of Internship and Thesis

When originally conceptualized, training in clinical psychology was to provide for mutual renewal, stimulation, and cross-fertilization between the academic community and real-world clinical settings. The internship was considered the trainee's opportunity to test out and develop the understanding and skills provided by the university faculty. Upon completion of the internship, the trainee was to have a better understanding of the research needs of the field and could return to the university to embark upon meaningful dissertation research (Shakow, 1978).

Since originally conceptualized, there has been much disappointment. The plan and promise have been unfulfilled. As a faculty member at a prestigious clinical child psychology internship program, I was repeatedly distressed during interview season at hearing of the fourth year students' experience and expectation of "Now that my thesis is out of the way, I want to get down to clinical training." Similarly, it is distressing to deprive or relieve the third year internship applicant of his or her hope "To get some work done on my thesis," as well as participate in the clinical training in assessment, treatment and consultation. The former problem is distressing in that it reflects a failure in implementing the originally conceptualized program and an early breakdown of the "scientist-practitioner" model. The latter is distressing in that it reflects unrealistic expectations and pressures upon the trainee, again leading to early breakdown of the "scientist-practitioner" model.

The clinical child psychology training program in the applied developmental psychology framework has a renewed commitment to the original goals of integrating theory and practice and producing "scientist-practitioners." The internship is extended to a two-year period during which both intensive clinical training and movement toward completion of the dissertation are accomplished. The dichotomization between clinical practice and dissertation research will be minimized. The viability of the scientist-practitioner model will be upheld via modeling and apprenticeship training. Of course, only highly specialized sites could provide such integrated training, sites which have functioning service and research components, a commitment to the scientist-practitioner model, and a staff or faculty of scientist-practitioners. Such settings do exist and, indeed, within the present conceptualization, these settings are the future of clinical child psychology.

Among the possible disadvantages of such combined clinical and research training is that there may be a greater impetus for a trainee joining an ongoing project for his or her dissertation, rather than pursuing more autonomous functioning. Further, research designs are likely to de-emphasize the more purely experimental or more purely basic research in favor of applied research and program evaluation. Examples of research domains would include instrument development, treatment process and outcome research, developmental studies, intervention studies, all with an explicit tie-in of the research and service implications for the clinical child psychologist. The trainee may be gaining clinical experience and training in cognitive-behavioral therapy and consultation to classroom teachers, while at the same time, evaluating a cognitive-behavioral curriculum being implemented in the laboratory school of the particular clinical setting. As an applied developmental psychologist, the clinical child psychologist achieves a new integration of the "scientist-practitioner" ideal.

Models for this type of training are already emerging. Doctoral programs in applied develomental psychology are beginning at several universities (Scholnick, 1983; Wertlieb, 1983a). The Bush Programs in Child Development and Public Policy at Yale and UCLA and the Center for the Study of Families and Children at Vanderbilt represent related emphases in preparation of a new kind of professional. Clinical settings such as Judge Baker Guidance Center are being revitalized as training and research centers committed to developmental frameworks for clinical child psychology. Clinical child psychology belongs at the forefront of this evolution.

Clinical child psychologists are being increasingly called upon to participate as social change agents and public policy advisors. A narrow mental health or psychiatric focus no longer meets the challenges we face as a profession and society. The advocated critical base in applied behavioral science and developmental psychology places the clinical child psychologist in an important position in many health care, education, human service, and public policy settings. We must acknowledge our role and potential contributions in such settings and reorient training accordingly. Clinical child psychology is first and foremost an applied developmental psychology in the best scientist-practitioner mold.

References

Albee, G.W. (1978). A manifesto for a fourth mental health revolution. *Contemporary Psychology, 23,* 549-551.

Bardon, J.I. (1983). Psychology applied to education: A specialty in search of an identity. *American Psychologist, 38,* 185-196.

Bobbit, B., & Keating, D. (1983). A cognitive-developmental perspective for clincial research and practice. In Philip Kendall (Ed.), *Advances in Cognitive-Behavioral Research and Therapy* (vol. 2, pp. 195-239) New York: Academic Press.

Cicchetti, D. (1984). The emergence of developmental psychopathology. *Child Development, 55,* 1-7.

Elkind, D. (1982). Piagetian psychology and the practice of child psychiatry. *Journal of the American Academy of Child Psychiatry, 21,* 435-445.

Engel, G.L. (1977). The need for a new medical model: A challenge for biomedicine. *Science, 196,* 129-136.

Erickson, M.T., Roberts, M.C., & Tuma, J.M. (1983). *Recommended minimal training criteria for psychologists working with children, youth and families.* Task force on training for Division of Children, Youth and Families, American Psychological Association.

Fox, R.E. (1982). The need for a reorientation of clinical psychology. *American Psychologist, 37,* 1051-1057.

Garmezy, N., Masten, A.S., & Tellegen, A. (1984). The Study of Stress and Competence in Children. A Building Block for Developmental Pyschopathology. *Child Development, 55,* 97-111.

HEW (1979). *Report of the President's Commission on Mental Health.* Washington, DC: Author.

Kendall, P.C., Lerner, R.M., & Craighead, W.E. (1984). Human development and intervention in childhood pyschopathology. *Child Development. 55,* 71-82.

Levy, L.H. (1984). The metamorphosis of clinical psychology: Toward a new charter as human services psychology. *American Psychologist, 39,* 486-494.

Masterpasqua, F. (1981). Toward a synergism of developmental and community psychology. *American Psychologist, 36,* 782-786.

McMahon, R., & De V. Peters, R. (Eds.). (1985). *Clinical disorders: Behavioral-developmental approaches.* New York: Brunner/Mazel.

Morrison, F.J., Lord, C., & Keating, D. (Eds). (1984). *Applied developmental psychology* (vol. 1). New York: Academic Press.

Roberts, M.C., Erickson, M.T., & Tuma, J.M. (1985). Addressing the needs: Guideline for training psychologists to work with children, youth, and families. *Journal of Clinical Child Psychology, 14,* 71-79.

Ross, A. (1959). *The practice of clinical child psychology.* New York: Grune & Stratton.

Ross, A. (1972). The clinical child psychologist. In Wolman, B. (Ed.), *Manual of child psychopthology* (pp. 1287-1296) New York: McGraw Hill.

Santostefano, S. (1978). *A biodevelopmental approach to clinical child psychology.* New York: Wiley.

Scholnick, E.K. (1983). Scrutinizing application: An agenda for applied developmental psychology. *Journal of Applied Developmental Psychology, 4,* 329-339.

Scott, K.G. (1983). Applied developmental Psychology. *Journal of Applied Developmental Psychology, 4,* 319-327.

Selman, R., & Yando, R. (Eds.). (1980). *Clinical-developmental psychology: New directions for child development* (vol. 7). San Francisco, CA: Jossey Bass.

Shakow, D. (1978). Clinical psychology seen some 50 years later. *American Psychologist, 33,* 148-158.

Sigel, I. (1983). Applied developmental psychology symposium. *Journal of Applied Developmental Psychology, 4,* 327-318.

Wertlieb, D. (1979). Applied developmental psychology: New directions. *APA Monitor, 10,* 10.

Wertlieb, D. (1983a, August). *Doctoral training in applied developmental psychology: Our emerging discipline's investment in itself.* Symposium presented at the annual meeting of the, American Psychological Association, Anaheim CA.

Wertlieb, D. (1983b). Some foundations and directions for applied developmental psychology. *Journal of Applied Developmental Psychology, 4,* 349-358.

Wertlieb, D. (1985). A discipline re-emerging: Applied developmental psychology. *Journal of Pediatric Psychology, 10,* 502-506.

Zigler, E. (1980). Welcoming a new journal. *Journal of Applied Developmental Psychology, 1,* 1-6.

Integrating Pediatric and Clinical Child Psychology: Perspectives in Clinical Training

Dennis Drotar
Case Western Reserve University School of Medicine

In recent years, the knowledge base and job opportunities in pediatric and clinical child psychology have increased dramatically. Moreover, the potential roles and responsibilities of pediatric psychologists are expanding more rapidly than can be accommodated within existing training programs (Tuma, 1977, 1980). Consequently, greater numbers of psychologists are currently working with children than have been adequately trained for this work. Such issues challenge us to consider a number of difficult questions in order to enhance the quality of our training programs: (1) What are the special roles and responsibilities of pediatric psychologists? (2) What are the key ingredients of training in pediatric psychology? (3) How does core training in clinical child psychology relate to pediatric psychology?

Although the recent advances in clinical and scientific knowledge in pediatric pyschology are a welcome sign of health, we must guard against counterproductive specialization (Sechrest, 1985; Staats, 1981). For this reason, consideration of integrating themes concerning pediatric and clinical child psychology will facilitate the development of creative training models that bring the best of what pediatric psychology has to offer to clinical child psychology and vice versa. To the extent that we select appropriate integrating themes, questions related to the precise boundaries of pediatric versus clinical child psychology will become secondary to such issues as the productivity of our graduates, how well they are equipped to work successfully with children and their families, whether they can compete in an ever-changing job market, and whether they are satisfied with their work.

There is substantial agreement that pediatric and clinical child psychologists share a specific interest and expertise with children and their families. However, pediatric psychologists can be differentiated from other clinical child psychologists by the settings in which they work, populations, and specific job functions. For example, pediatric psychologists work in an expanding array of settings such as pediatric ambulatory services in the public and private sector, community hospitals, tertiary care medical school settings, health maintenance organizations, and specialized developmental clinics, private practice, and academic settings. The populations relevant to the practice of pediatric psychology are more likely to involve very young children, children with chronic physical illness, and psychosomatic conditions, in the broad classification proposed by Wright (1977). Assessment techniques in pediatric psychology are not restricted to but are more likely to include specialized assessment with young children with specific physical and sensorimotor handicaps, behavioral, and observational methods. Interventions with pediatric populations are more likely to be concrete and pragmatic in character, to involve behavioral methods, and to be short-term (Roberts, Maddux, Wurtele & Wright, 1982).

In recent years, the pediatric setting has emerged as an important context for the training of clinical child psychologists. The present discussion, which has broad implications for clinical training, concerns integrating themes and their specific application in the training of psychologists to conduct clinical work and research with children. One major theme concerns the integration of psychology and biology as it pertains to children's health and development. The biopsychosocial model developed by a physician, Engel (1977), but recently considered by psychologists (e.g., Schwartz, 1982), underscores the interrelationship of biologic, psychologic, and environmental variables as they pertain to childrens' health and to intervention, especially preventive intervention with behavioral and developmental disorders in children. Key applications of this model include: (1) utilization of psychological research and theory, especially learning theory, in the management of health-related problems, and (2) research and practice concerning the interrelationships between physical health and mental health, encompassing such topics as physical illness and psychological adjustment, biologic risk factors and developmental disorders, and the interrelationship of family risk factors to the expression of physical symptoms. In this model, medical diagnosis and psychological assessment should be oriented to consider the interaction of biologic, psychological, and social factors in health and disease.

The biopsychosocial model also suggests a number of specific roles for psychologists, such as designing and implementing comprehensive research and interventions with specialized pediatric populations, assessment of psychosocial influences on health and illness, and interventions to enhance adapation and health in a variety of populations. Rather than being the province of a single profession, the body of knowledge on which a biopsychosocial model is based is interdisciplinary in scope and represents a significant alternative to training models which are based (either explicitly or implicitly) on psychological or psychiatric disease models. The emphasis on health maintenance and prevention inherent in this model is a significant development for clinical child psychology and one which is very much an antidote to the inherent limitations of a research knowledge base and clinical practice focused solely upon children with primary emotional disorders (Matarrazzo, 1980; Millon, 1982).

To enhance training efforts, it is important that this approach to human problems be illustrated through specific clinical and research experiences with pediatric populations. For example, psychological assessments of chronically ill children can increase trainees' understanding of the emotional stresses associated with chronic physical disease. Family-oriented diagnostic assessment can give students an illuminating look at important etiological factors in emotional disturbances of children with chronic physical diseases and psychosomatic disorders. To further enhance their knowledge, students can conduct interventions with children and adolescents whose psychological adjustment is stressed by hospitalization. Trainees' consultation with hospital staff can help coordinate support for hospitalized children and integrate the information from psychological evaluations into a plan of comprehensive care (Drotar, 1978). Other pediatric conditions, such as mental retardation, language deficits, hyperactivity, and learning problems, can also illustrate the biopsychosocial model in that they require pediatricians, neurologists, and psychologists to collaborate in their clinical management and research.

A second organizing theme that I would strongly advocate in the training of pediatric and clinical child psychologists is an emphasis on health and normal developmental processes as they relate to the origins and prevention of developmental deviations and mental disorders. Concepts of development provide a link to understand the relationship between biologic determinants and environmental variables (Eisenberg, 1980). In addition, familiarity with normative developmental transitions provides a foundation for the understanding of aberrations in development (Wenar, 1982). Moreover, to the extent that we develop a firm knowledge base concerning normative developmental outcomes, it will be easier to identify the factors that contribute to resilient outcomes in groups and individuals. On the other hand, gaps in understanding of basic developmental processes and transitions are a major impediment to advances in science and service delivery in clinical child psychology (Dusek, 1974).

Trainees require practical experiences to learn to utilize developmental perspectives in their clinical and research work. The following experiences have been helpful in implementing a developmental perspective in clinical training: (1) prospective observation of development, particularly early transactions between parents and their children; (2) assessment and intervention with infants, who are at high risk for emotional and cognitive disorders, and their families; (3) conducting clinical research with a child developmental focus.

One of the most important features of the pediatric setting is the prospective access to children and their families at key times in their development provided via well-child supervision and medical care of special populations, such as chronically ill children. As a consequence, clinical experiences in a pediatric setting gives students a unique opportunity to appreciate the value of observation, sequential pychological assessments, and prospective methodolgy, all of which are key ingredients in a developmental approach (Achenbach, 1978). Students' understanding of the origins and maintenance of behavioral deviations can be greatly facilitated by observing how young children behave in their family context and in the hospital setting. Moreover, an observational approach leads to novel ways of construing cause and effect in the development of behavior disorders. For example, the recognition that the child is not passively shaped by his/her transactions with parents, but is an active partner who influences the quality of parental response and the development of parent-child relationship has emerged from investigations based on observational methods. Moreover, variables, such as the specificity, duration, and quality of the child's attachment behavior, are emerging as predictors of competent management of emotion, problem solving, and peer relationships in later life (Ainsworth, Blehar, Waters, & Wall, 1978).

Although observation has long been recognized as an important element in clinical training (Shakow, 1972) in many training programs, observations are often relegated to a secondary place in favor of more traditional intellectual and personality assessments. For this reason, we have found that it is important to focus trainees' clinical experiences on certain pediatric populations in order to facilitate their learning of observational methods. For example, clinical experiences with infants and young children at risk are a productive way to illustrate the importance of both observational methods and developmental perspectives.

Successful implementation of a developmental perspective in child clinical training is based on students' access to settings in which infant developmental and emotional problems can be identified at an early age. Pediatric hospitals are an ideal setting for early recognition of infant problems for a variety of reasons. For example, pediatric well-child care takes place in a long-term, continuing relationship with the family which allows access to critical developmental transitions. Moreover, pediatric hospitals treat a variety of infants at risk owing to conditions such as physical illness and handicap, prematurity, and child abuse and neglect. Such clinical problems provide ample opportunities for observation of infants and their families, both in the hospital and at home, which can be supplemented by clinical experiences, such as parent interviewing, history taking, and formal assessment of infant cognitive development with instruments such as the Bayley Scale of Mental Development (Bayley, 1969).

Our students receive supervised experience in observing infants and their families in the home setting and in structured case conferences. In addition, students have clinical responsibilities for assessment and treatment planning for infants and young children with a range of problems, such as delayed cognitive or language development, child abuse, behavior problems, and environmentally based failure to thrive. An emphasis on home observations as a method of assessment not only encourages child oriented clinicians to become increasingly comfortable and skilled in making observations, but enhances their appreciation of the vital role observations can play in intervention planning. Students are also encouraged to accomplish prospective reassessment of children's developmental progress during their practicum training. In selected cases, students also conduct mental health interventions with infants and their families in which observations of parent-child transactions are used to give constructive feedback to parents and to gauge the progress of intervention.

Research experiences are another means to facilitate learning of the importance of a developmental approach to clinical problems as well as the unique relevance of applied research. To my mind, one of the reasons that it has been difficult for clinical psychologists to establish a productive track record in research activity is that they have not been provided with sufficient opportunities to conduct research on applied problems or exposed to mentors who are conducting applied research in a programmatic fashion. The pediatric setting has a number of special advantages for sensitizing student researchers to the conceptual and logistical problems involved in applied research. Populations and, hence, opportunities for applied research abound in pediatric settings (Routh, 1985). Moreover, pediatricians are generally supportive of student research, which they perceive not only as a means of enhancing their own knowledge but as providing a direct benefit to their patients.

Research experiences in applied developmental problems encountered in pediatric settings can enhance the development of clinical child psychologists in a number of ways. For example, conducting research with a developmental focus familiarizes students with relevant literature, methods, and research designs which are potentially applicable to clinical problems. In the process of conducting their research, students are often sensitized to the importance of a thorough knowledge of normal childhood development as a basis for understanding abnormal behavior. In addition, one of the most important advantages of research training in a pediatric setting is the opportunity for integration of clinical and research experiences. Our experience over a number of years suggests that students' clinical work with infants and young children can whet their appetite to learn more about the methods and paradigms employed in child developmental research. In turn, student research can enhance their enthusiasm for clinical topics. For example, in the course of her practicum training, one student, Lynn Singer, became quite interested in the clinical problem of failure to thrive, conducted an interesting application of infant recognition memory in her dissertation, and has subsequently followed the cognitive development of this population in a prospective study (Singer & Fagan, 1984). Other students' research contributions on such topics as the psychological aspects of chronic physical illness (diabetes, cystic fibrosis, and sickle cell anemia) stemmed in part from questions raised by their clinical experiences with such populations.

A final integrating theme involves the application of psychology to health settings. To maximize our potential as a professional discipline, we must train psychologists to be adept at assimilating a variety of professional cultures and translating this information so that it can be utilized by a variety of consumers, including practitioners and researchers in other professional disciplines (Bibace & Walsh, 1982; Stabler & Whitt, 1980). Training in pediatric settings can equip psychologists to function in difficult medical settings, to become aware of the impact of the health care context on children and their families, and to help members of other disciplines, especially physicians and nurses, function more effectively in their work environments. As Stabler & Whitt (1980) have described, trainees in pediatric settings face a formidable task in that they must learn specialized clinical knowledge at the same time that they are learning the medical setting, culture, and the rudiments of consultation with physicians. However, the excitement that is generated in students through their exposure to medical settings stimulates their interest in learning how to apply their knowledge in this setting.

We learned that it is important for students to have at least some prior clinical training in their home departments before they venture into pediatric settings, which are characterized by a fast pace and by a high level of work-related stress. The pediatric hospital environment can be an especially intimidating one for students because it lacks structures for psychosocial care. For this reason, our experience indicates that training is based most effectively in those areas in which senior psychology staff have achieved harmonious collaboration with medical and nursing staff. The psychologist-supervisor in the pediatric setting should have developed a sense of respect for psychology among his or her physician colleagues to allow students to have a proper context in which to develop their consultation skills.

To enhance student learning about consultation, it has been helpful for them to review each of their assessment and intervention cases from the standpoint of the communication that transpired between them and the physicians who made the referral. Group conferences in which physicians present cases from a psychological vantage point have also been useful to students, especially as a means of illuminating differences in medical versus psychological points of view and the potential contributions of psychology to medical management. Finally, students are strongly encouraged to conduct their psychological evaluations from the vantage point of an advocacy role in which they are taught to understand how the pressures on pediatric staff and on families affect their communication and relationships.

The journey between the integrating themes I've discussed and their application is a long one which is fraught with a number of obstacles which pertain to three major domains: (1) within the profession, (2) between professions, and (3) intrinsic forces. One set of obstacles involves disagreements among psychologists concerning orientation and methods which can limit the effectiveness of our efforts with physicians. For this reason, we must strive to resolve special interests in order to develop innovative training programs that integrate pediatric and clinical child psychology. Apart from the limitations of physical proximity between the medical setting and the psychology training program and program development in pediatric psychology, a key ingredient in the success of a pediatric psychology training program is the quality of communication between faculty in the different settings. In recent years, the quality of our training program in pediatric psychology has been enhanced by close communication between the director of clinical training and the major supervisor in the pediatric setting.

A second set of obstacles concern interdisciplinary collaboration. Effective training of psychologists in pediatric settings depends greatly upon collaborations with physicians which are hard to build and need to be fostered and renewed. In our setting, collaborations between pediatricians and psychologists have been built over a 14 year period. However, even with this history of collaboration, new collaborative relationships with physicians need to be developed in order to respond effectively to program changes within the setting. In addition, one can't expect that the course of interdisciplinary collaboration will always be a smooth one, especially given economic competition and differences in concepts of clinical practice between physicians and psychologists (Drotar, 1978; McNamara, 1981).

A final set of obstacles to the development of training programs involve intrinsic factors, such as increased pressures on pediatric psychology faculty for fee generation which make it more difficult for them to invest their energies in training activities. Finally, disease-centered patterns of insurance reimbursability function as incentives against the prevention-centered and developmentally focused models of clinical training advocated earlier.

References

Achenbach, T. (1978). *Research methods in developmental psychology.* NY: Free Press.

Ainsworth, M.D.S., Blehar, M., Waters, E., & Wall, M. (1978). *Patterns of attachment.* Hillsdale, NJ: Erlbaum.

Bayley, N. (1969). *Bayley Scale of Mental Development.* NY: Psychological Corp.

Bibace, R., & Walsh, M. (1982). Conflict of roles: On the difficulty of being both scientist and practitioners in one life. *Professional Psychology, 13,* 389-396.

Drotar, D. (1978). Problems and prospects in training psychologists to consult with physicians. *Journal of Clinical Child Psychology, 8,* 117-127.

Dusek, J.B. (1974). Implications of developmental theory for child mental health. *American Psychologist, 27,* 19-24.

Eisenberg, L. (1980). Development as a unifying concept in psychiatry. *Family and Child Health, 6,* 99-117.

Engel, G.L. (1977). The need for a new medical model: A challenge for biomedicine. *Science, 196,* 129-36.

Matarazzo, J.D. (1980). Behavioral health and behavior medicine. *American Psychologist, 33,* 23-29.

McNamara, J.R. (1981). Some unresolved challenges facing psychology's entrance into the health care field. *Professional Psychology, 12,* 391-399.

Millon, T. (1982). On the nature of clinical health psychology. In T. Millon, C.J. Green, & R.B. Meagher (Eds.) *Handbook of Clinical Health Psychology* (pp. 1-28). NY: Plenum.

Roberts, M.C., Maddux, J.E., Wurtele, S.K., & Wright, L. (1982). Pediatric psychology: Health care psychology for children. In T. Millon, C. Green & R. Meagher (Eds.) *Handbook of Clinical Health Psychology* (pp. 191-226). NY: Plenum.

Routh D.K. (1985). Psychology, child health and human develoment. In A.R. Zeiner, D. Bendell, & C.E. Walker (pp. 99-111). *Health Psychology.* NY: Plenum.

Schwartz, G.E. (1982). Testing the biopsychosocial model: The ultimate challenge facing behavioral medicine. *Journal of Counsulting and Clinical Psychology, 50,* 1040-1053.

Sechrest, L.N. (1985). Specialization? Who needs it? *Clinical Psychologist, 38,* 1-3.

Shakow, D. (1972). Education of the mental health researcher. *Archives of General Psychiatry, 27,* 15-25.

Singer, L.T., & Fagan, J.F. (1984). The cognitive development of the failure to thrive infant: A three year longitudinal study. *Journal of Pediatric Psychology, 9,* 363-384.

Staats, A.W. (1981). Paradigmatic behaviorism, unified theory, unified theory construction methods, and the zeitgeist of separation. *American Psychologist, 36,* 239-256.

Stabler, B., & Whitt, J.K. (1980). Pediatric psychology: Perspectives and training implications. *Journal of Pediatric Psychology, 5,* 245-251.

Tuma, J.M. (1977). Practicum, internship and postdoctoral training in pediatric psychology. *Journal of Pediatric Psychology, 2,* 9-12.

Tuma, J.M. (1980, August). *Redirecting training efforts to provide services to children, youth and families.* Paper presented at the annual meeting of the Amercian Psychological Association, Montreal, Canada.

Wenar, C. (1982). Developmental psychology: Its nature and models. *Journal of Clinical Child Psychology, 11,* 197-201.

Wright, L. (1977). Conceptualizing and defining psychosomatic disorders. *American Psychologist, 32,* 625-628.

Summary of Concurrent Small Groups on Roles and Responsibilities and Boundaries Issues Academic Level

Andrew S. Bradlyn
University of Florida

Consistent with many of today's plenary session speakers, this group adopted a system approach to organizing and discussing the roles and responsibilites of clinical child psychologists, whether that system(s) was the child, family, or community. The group's discussion focused on three primary areas: (1) child related training that should be a part of all clinical programs; (2) specific recommendation for clinical child training, in particular, and (3) a brief discussion of boundary issues with other professionals, and in particular, with applied developmental psychologists.

Regarding the first area (child related training which should be a part of all clinical programs), there was consensus among group members that all graduate students in clinical programs should receive certain minimum training which focused specifically on the assessment and treatment of children, youth, and families. This instruction could take place within the context of both didactic and practice settings. The intent of the group was not to mandate that all clinicians should be competent clinical child psychologists, but rather that there should be certain minimum levels of exposure to child assessment and treatment so that clinicians could have a standard of comparision to help in identifying limits of clinical competence, as described in the APA *Ethical Principles of Psychologists* (1981). Given the fact that a significant percentage of psychologists may provide services to children with little or no formal instruction and experience in child assessment and treatment, this was seen as a critical component for clinical training programs. There was no resolution as to precisely how many hours of such instruction and experience were necessary, however. Additionally, there was strong agreement among group members that there should be instruction in a lifespan developmental approach to clinical training.

Another area of discussion that cut across both general clinical psychology training and specialty training in clinical child psychology was an implicit emphasis on consultation as both an attitude to be instilled in students and a group of competencies or skills. Gaining competencies in consulation need not occur in the context of a course specifically devoted to that topic, but could be integrated as an integral part of current coursework and practice training.

Within clinical child specialty training, the group members agreed on the importance of students gaining consultation experience with schools, in particular, and with at least one other system, be that the child, his or her family, or the community. There was also general agreement concerning the perception of rural and pediatric emphasis as being subspecialty areas within clinical child psychology.

The final question addressed by the group involved boundary issues with other professionals, primarily with applied developmental psychologists. It was noted that there has been a great deal of trouble defining specifically which competencies were necessary for professionals working with children. Given this limitation, there was general consensus that the boundary or boundaries were best centered on the issue of service provision. The group adopted the definition of applied developmental psychologists as *not* providing services to children and being primarily involved in research and related activities.

Reference

American Psychological Association. (1981). *Ethical principles of psychologists*. Washington, DC: Author.

Summary of Concurrent Small Groups on Roles and Responsibilities and Boundary Issues
Internship Level

Lynne Doran
Yale Child Study Center

The first issue raised for group discussion involved not boundaries between specialties in psychology, but boundaries between academic training programs and clinical psychology internships. The question raised was "What is the *shared responsibility* between the academic training program and the internship program in assuring standards of competence?" There are currently no standard mechanisms for insuring that a student's internship experience will meet his/her specific training needs. Also, while some academic programs and internships have developed formal procedures for documenting and communicating about an intern's performance, there are not useful, uniform mechanisms for working with interns whose performance is not satisfactory. As long as there is lack of specification of competencies within the field, and as long as there is lack of clarity regarding the responsibilities of the academic program and the internship, insuring competence for all students will be difficult.

The group discussed a variety of models for facilitating coordinated training and evaluation of training. With some disagreement, the group generally concurred that the advantages of internship training outside the academic department outweigh the disadvantages. The group identified several principles and offered several suggestions toward the goal of clarifying responsibilities:

1. The internship should not be considered the final training experience. The field needs to establish appropriate and realistic expectations for postdoctoral supervised training that take into account issues, such as differences among state licensing law, the financial implications for students of requiring additional training, and the shortage of clinical child psychologists.
2. The internship is an essential component of clinical child psychology training that must be integrated with other predoctoral experiences, including didactic classes, clinical practica and research.
3. Internship and academic programs must share responsibility for insuring minimum competence upon completion of the doctoral degree. Development of more formal procedures for comunication between academic programs and internships will facilitate sharing this responsibility.

Suggestions for improving communication included:

1. Internships should specify prerequisite experiences, both didactic and practical, that are necessary for admission to the internship program.
2. Internship should specify the clinical competencies that will be achieved by the end of the internship year.
3. Consideration should be given to developing Individual Educational Plans (IEPs) for each student in clinical child psychology. These IEPs would specify competencies, training experiences, and methods for evaluating performance toward the goal of coordinating internship and academic training.

The second focus of group discussion was an attempt to specify those competencies that define clinical child psychology. This proved to be an extremely difficult task. When we looked at why we had difficulty with this discussion, a couple of concerns emerged. First, we were wary of reifying the concept of clinical child psychology. A major strength of the field is its breadth and diversity; specification of standards should not rob from this richness. Second, we realized that we were unclear about the purpose of defining the clinical child psychology specialty. Are we trying to exclude professionals without adequate training? Are we trying to protect children and families? Are we trying to advocate for children who are currently underserved?

Despite our difficulty with this discussion, a couple of recurrent themes emerged. There was general agreement that strengthening and enriching the developmental focus of generic clinical psychology programs is essential. Training that focuses on individual, family, and community development across the life cycle will improve service delivery and research with any population. Second, both implicitly and explicitly, our group acknowledged the importance of the clinical child psychology research base. An empirical approach to acquiring knowledge and clinical practice is a unique asset of the pyschologist that should be preserved.

Summary of Concurrent Small Group Discussions on Roles and Responsibilities and Boundary Issues Postdoctoral/Continuing Education Level

Sheila Eyberg
University of Florida

Roles and responsibilities of clinical child psychologists at the postdoctoral level of training are difficult to delineate without specifying first what training needs can be assumed to have been met at earlier levels of training. Generally, the group supported the idea that a basic core curriculum within general clinical psychology training programs include lifespan developmental psychology and family systems issues early in the training sequence. In addition, support was expressed for the development of a special set of competencies that should be included in the basic training of clinical child psychologists. The Division 37 guidelines for training psychologists to work with children, youth, and families provide a good basis from which to start. From there, areas of training specific to *clinical* child psychologists may best be determined by further deliberations from this training conference. Perhaps a task force within clinical child psychology will be useful to work on further concrete curriculum recommendations. Clearly, there is a burgeoning of new knowledge that is necessary in the field. It is difficult to delineate what knowledge is more specialized. Beyond a basic core for all clinical child psychology students, some individuals may best specialize at the postdoctoral level; these individuals can then serve as resource persons for others when special situations arise for them.

In order to determine at what level of training the various types of specialized knowledge should be taught, however, it seems necessary to first define the total dimension of training needed in the field. Regardless of content areas that will ultimately best be taught at the postdoctoral level, there was general consensus that all postdoctoral training should incorporate research training. As an example of how this might be implemented, the Oklahoma postdoctoral program in pediatric psychology in which research participation or grant writing is a requirement, was described.

A repeated theme was the difficulty of learning all of the specialized knowledge that will ultimately be needed by clinical child psychologists once they are in actual work settings. The issue of continuing education arises in this regard. The discussion group struggled with the issue. On the one hand, there is the question of how much we want to depend on continuing education to meet training needs because of the current proliferation of offerings with clearly less quality control than can be provided by accredited training sequences at the graduate and internship level. On the other hand, it is clear that there are, and will continue to be, new areas of knowledge arising that clinicians will need and will seek to learn after they have completed their formal training and have entered work situations.

Curriculum Issues

Introductory Comments: Curriculum

Thomas H. Ollendick, Chair

In recent years, it has become evident that the training of clinical child psychologists has not kept pace with the need. Further, it is clear that most existing training programs at the predoctoral, internship, and postdoctoral level are unable to provide the range of experiences necessary for working with children and adolescents. These developments and trends have resulted in the emergence of a number of programs purporting to offer clinical child specialty or subspecialty training. These programs have taken one of four basic forms: 1) programs which offer specialty training in clinical child psychology apart from the structure of general clinical training programs; 2) programs which offer clinical child training within the context of a developmental or school psychology program; 3) programs which offer clear and well-defined subspecialty training within the framework of general clinical training programs; and 4) programs which offer clinical child training in an unstructured way with no clear or well-defined specialization. These programs vary widely, with some offering training on an informal basis and others offering a much more structured and formal approach. The relative strengths and weaknesses of each are being examined and carefully evaluated.

In response to this situation, Diane Willis, then President of the section on Clinical Child Psychology (Section 1) established a National Training Committee in 1982. This committee was charged with the task of considering those curriculum and related issues relevant to specialty training in clinical child psychology. Similar factors led to Tuma's proposal that the National Training Conference be held.

In the papers that follow, curriculum issues related to assessment (Elbert), treatment (Johnson), consulation (Schroeder), prevention (Felner and Lorian), and continuing education (Ollendick) are examined. These reports are based largely on surveys of the membership of Section 1 and theoretical speculations of the presenters. They are intended to serve as a focus of subsequent discussion, debate, and deliberation. In effect, they are intended to identify important trends, needs, and directions in establishing curriculum needs related to clinical child psychology training.

General Program Related Issues in Clinical Child Specialty Training: Survey Input from Child Oriented Clinicians

James H. Johnson
University of Florida

In recent years, it has become apparent that there are far too few psychologists who are adequately trained to meet the mental health needs of children and that existing clinical programs often fail to provide the range of experiences necessary for working with younger age groups (Tuma, 1980). This realization has resulted in the development of a rapidly increasing number of graduate programs offering clinical child specialty or sub-specialty training (Mannarino & Fisher, 1982; Roberts, 1982). As these programs vary widely, with many offering such training on an informal-individualized basis and apart from the stucture of a formal clinical child curriculum (Mannarino & Fisher, 1982), questions have been raised regarding the nature of those training experiences that constitute adequate preparation for specialization in the clinical child area. Questions such as these led to the establishment, in 1982, of a Section 1 Training Committee charged with the task of considering the issue of specialty training and developing general training guidelines for programs offering specialty training in the clinical child area. Through a series of working meetings, this committee has attempted to develop preliminary recommendations regarding various aspects of the clinical child curriculum with the expectation that these would be discussed, debated, and refined within the context of this training conference.

To place the present paper in context, it may be noted that addressing the issue of clinical child specialty training requires a consideration of a broad range of issues (see Johnson & Tuma, 1983). At the most basic level, questions arise regarding just how specialized "specialty" training should be, as well as with regard to those training models and contexts within which specialty training can best be accomplished. For example, one might ask whether clinical child training is best conducted within a scientist-practitioner model of training or within the framework of some other model which places less emphasis on "scientific" issues. Related questions deal with the extent to which the curriculum should include training in basic psychology and in research. As those working in the child area frequently find themselves interacting not only with children but with parents and other adults, one might also ask to what degree training in the adult area should be a required part of the clinical child curriculum. Concerning the context for training, one might ask whether specialty or subspecialty training can be carried out most effectively within the organizational structure of a general clinical program or within specialty programs that have an organizational structure and requirements separate from the general clinical area.

There are other questions having to do with those training experiences in the broader clinical child area and in specific areas, such as child assessment, child treatment and consultation, that are seen as essential components of the clinical child curriculum. Related to these issues are questions concerning the form that these training experiences should take (didactic courses or seminars; applied clinical experiences) and the ways in which these experiences should be integrated within the total curriculum.

In the papers to follow, attention will be given to training in child assessment, child treatment, consultation, and to other specific curriculum-related issues. The focus of the present paper, however, is on more general programmatic issues relevant to training in the clinical child area. While the paper deals primarily with the predoctoral curriculum, certain of the issues to be discussed would also appear relevant to training at the internship and postdoctoral levels.

Survey of Child-Oriented Clinical Psychologists

In an attempt to address issues such as those outlined in the preceding section, an attempt was made to solicit input from psychologists actively involved in the clinical child area so that their views could be taken into account in training committee discussions. To obtain this input, a Clinical Child Training Survey was developed and sent to 100 psychologists who were either members of Section 1

The author wishes to thank the other members of the Section 1 Training Committe (Jean C. Elbert, Thomas H. Ollendick, Carolyn S. Schroeder, June M. Tuma, chair) for their contributions to the present paper.

or who were known to be actively involved in clinical child psychology training. The sample was non-random in that an attempt was made to survey psychologists who had distinguished themselves in the clinical child area as a result of their involvement in training, research and/or clinical activities. The purpose was to gain input from a variety of individuals, especially those able to comment on training issues by virtue of their experience.

The training questionnaire itself consisted of 15 sections with each being related to some aspect of clinical child psychology training. Questions dealt with appropriate training models, the roles of research, the importance of training in basic psychology, the role of training in working with adults, and with specific experiences in the areas of assessment, treatment, and consultation that were seen as desirable.

Of those surveyed, a total of 63 returned completed questionnaires. Respondents ranged from 1 year to 32 years of post degree experience, the average being approximately 12 years. While those with PhD degrees made up the bulk of the sample, several respondents held EdD degrees and one held a PsyD degree. Individuals working in both applied and academic settings were represented with 13 listing an applied clinical work situation and 43 listing academic settings. It should be noted that these figures are a bit misleading as many of those who listed an academic setting were employed by medical schools where they were actively involved in applied clinical work as well as academic and teaching activities. Of the total, 46 described themselves as clinical child psychologists and 8 labeled themselves as clinical psychologists with an interest in children. Several others referred to themselves by other labels; pediatric psychologist, school/clinical psychologist, developmental psychopathologist, and so forth.

This overview of respondent characteristics suggests that we were able to survey a diverse and highly experienced group of psychologist who were identified with the general clinical child area and who had backgrounds which should have enabled them to provide relevant information concerning various aspects of training. In the following sections, information will be presented regarding the responses of these psychologists to questionnaire items dealing with several more general issues related to clinical child specialty training.

Preferred Model(s) of Clinical Child Training

Regarding models of training, respondents were asked whether they thought clinical child training could be best accomplished within a program emphasizing a scientist-practitioner model of training (focusing on the equal development of research and clinical skills), a practitioner-scientist model of training (giving attention to both research and clinical skills, but with a distinct emphasis on clinical skills) or an applied-clinical model of training (with exclusive emphasis on the development of clinical skills). Of those responding there was overwhelming support for the traditional scientist-practitioner model. Approximately 76 per cent endorsed this model while only 21 and 3 per cent endorsed the practitioner-scientist and applied clinical models, respectively.

Training in Basic Psychology

Related to the issue of training models, respondents were questioned concerning the degree to which they felt clinical child psychologists should obtain a background in areas of basic psychology. Specifically, they were asked whether such training was desirable and were then asked to indicate which of the following courses or training experiences should be a required part of pre-internship training: social psychology, physiology psychology, learning, perception, motivation, cognitive psychology, experimental design, statistics, history and systems, and other.

Virtually all respondents endorsed the notion that training in basic psychology is an essential part of clinical child training. Courses suggested as requirements by at least 50% of the respondents included social psychology, physiological psychology, learning, cognitive psychology, experimental design and statistics. In terms of other courses, it should be noted that developmental psychology was not listed among the courses to choose from in this question but was considered in a larger portion of the survey dealing with general clinical child requirements. In this section over 80% of the respondents indicated that a course in normal child development should be a requirement and over 50% endorsed a specific course in personality and social development. Thus, developmental psychology is clearly seen as an additional area that is central to training in this area.

The Role of Research Training

Not unrelated to the question of training models, respondents were asked to indicate whether clinical child psychologists should be required to complete a formal research project or projects as part of their graduate training. Given a response in the affirmative, they were then asked to indicate which of the following should be required: masters thesis (or its equivalent); doctoral dissertation; other supervised research. Given the strong endorsement of the scientist-practitioner model, it is not suprising that the role of research training was heavily supported. Just over 90% of those completing the survey responded in the affirmative to this question. Seventy-three per cent suggested that a masters thesis should be required. Eighty-nine per cent indicated that a dissertation should be a requirement. Approximately 30% endorsed the importance of other supervised research experience. It may be noted that the total figures presented here sum to more than 100% as some respondents endorsed more than one type of research experience. It is clear from these responses that formal training in research is seen as important to the specialty training experience.

The Importance of Adult Related Training Experiences

As psychologists working with children must frequently work with adults in the context of their clinical child activities, questions arise concerning the degree to which training in the adult area should be a required part of the clinical child curriculum. To provide information regarding this issue, respondents were presented with several questions. One question simply asked whether they thought clinical child psychologists should receive training in general clinical/adult related areas of clinical psychology. A second question asked which of a number of adult related courses or training experiences they thought should be required as part of pre-internship training. These courses included personality theory, personality research, general psychopathology, assessment of adult intelligence, adult personality assessment, neuropsychological assessment (adult), methods of psychotherapy (adult), practicum in adult assessment, and practicum in adult treatment. A third question asked respondents to indicate what proportion of clinical courses and practica should be adult related and child related. (A similar question was also asked regarding the proportion of adult versus child related internship training experiences). While it was realized that it is sometimes difficult to break down training experiences in precisely this way, it was thought that the overall group responses would be useful in providing some general guidelines as to the degree of emphasis desirable with regard to the adult and child areas.

Ninety-five per cent of the respondents endorsed the importance of training in the adult area. Four adult related courses were suggested as necessary by at least 50% of those responding. These included personality theories, general psychopathology, methods of adult psychotherapy, and a practicum in adult treatment. In terms of the proportion of pre-internship courses which should be adult related versus child related, respondents indicated that, on the average, about 35% should be adult related and 65% child related. In terms of practicum experiences, the findings were similar. Here it was suggested that around 32% of the practicum should be devoted to adult work while 68% should focus on the child area. Parenthetically, the importance of adult related experiences at the internship level was also suggested by the fact that respondents, as a group, suggested that close to 30% of these clinical experiences should be adult related. To the extent that the experiences of these respondents has provided a basis for judging those training experiences necessary for adequately assuming the role of a clinical child psychologist, these results provide strong support for including certain adult related experiences as part of any specialty training curriculum.

The Context for Clinical Child Specialty Training

Finally, given the existence of several types of specialty training programs (see Roberts, 1982), we also sought to obtain information from our sample concerning what these child clinicians saw as the most appropriate context for training in the clinical child area. Specifically, respondents were asked whether they thought this training could best be accomplished within the context of a general clinical program (where students are admitted to the general program and then subspecialize), within a clinical child specialty program (where students are, from the beginning, involved in specialization separate from the requirements of the general clinical program) or whether context makes a difference given that the necessary training experiences are obtained.

Approximately 31% of those responding endorsed the idea of clinical child training within the more general clinical program. Twenty-six per cent endorsed the idea of a specialty training program which exists apart from the general clinical program. The majority (43%), however, indicated that the specific context makes little difference given that students are exposed to the necessary types of training. This varied response would suggest that there is more than one type of specialty or subspecialty program that is viewed as acceptable to a substantial number of those actively involved in the child area.

Discussion

The survey findings presented here seem to provide useful information concerning the views of experienced child-oriented psychologists regarding several important aspects of clinical child training. Although these respondents, as a group, support the notion that specialty training can take varying forms, their responses indicate rather definite views concerning certain other aspects of training. Relevant here is the strong endorsement of the scientist-practitioner model of training and the endorsement of formal research training, training in basic psychology, and the importance of gaining experiences in working with adults as well as children.

To the extent that it is appropriate to consider input from this survey in developing specialty training guidelines (and this would seem quite appropriate as those surveyed are in an excellent position to comment on the training experiences necessary for working within the clinical child area), these results suggest that any approach to specialty training should be characterized by some degree of breadth. Indeed, the broad range of experiences suggested as important by respondents cause one to question whether the term "subspecialty" training might be a more appropriate term than "specialty" training in characterizing the type of program which is being advocated.

Considering the emphasis placed on training in basic psychology, on research, on working with adults, and the degree of support given to the scientist-practitioner model, one might question whether the type of training endorsed by the respondents differs in any significant respect from that provided by existing general clinical programs.

Although it is obvious that our respondents favor retaining many features of general Boulder Model programs, there are ways in which clinical child training is seen as distinguishable from training in the general clinical area. These differences relate to a more restricted range of training experiences in certain non-child-related areas and the relative emphasis given to child versus adult related aspects of the clinical curriculum. To illustrate, one might consider the area of working with adults and the types of courses and training experiences seen as most important. Here, rather than endorsing the whole spectrum of adult related experiences, experiences emphasized were those related to developing an understanding of adult psychopathology and the treatment of adult disorders. While it is true that assessment is usually seen as a necessary prerequiste to treatment, emphasis on adult psychopathology and treatment is consistent with the fact that the most common involvement with adults is likely to be in the therapeutic modification of parental and family behaviors that may impact on the child, rather than in terms of a more general clinical involvement with an adult population. Thus, while training in working with adults is considered important, these training experiences are seen as being of a more restrictive nature than might be the case in a general clinical program. Differences between a clinical child specialty program of the type suggested here and general clinical programs are also reflected in the fact that respondents, as a group, recommended that approximately two-thirds of all clinical coursework and applied clinical experiences be within the child area. This clearly reflects a much greater emphasis on child related training than is characteristic of most existing clinical programs. The nature of the specific child related experiences suggested as essential components of the clinical child curriculum will be discussed in some detail in the papers to follow.

By way of summary, it would appear that many issues, both general and specific, must be addressed in attempting to develop guidelines for specialty (subspecialty?) training. In this regard, the views of those psychologists surveyed seem to provide a useful framework for considering a number of more general program-related issues that are central to training in the clinical child area.

References

Johnson, J.H., & Tuma, J.M. (1983). Training in clinical child psychology: A brief overview of selected issues (Editorial). *Journal of Clinical Child Psychology, 11,* 365-368.

Mannarino, A.P., & Fischer, C. (1982). Survey of graduate training in clinical child psychology. *Journal of Clinical Child Psychology, 11,* 22-26.

Roberts, M.C. (1982). Clinical child psychology programs: Where and what are they? *Journal of Clinical Child Psychology, 11,* 13-21.

Tuma, J.M. (1980, August). *Redirecting training efforts to provide services to children, youth and families.* Paper presented at the annual meeting of the American Psychological Association, Montreal, Canada.

Current Trends and Future Needs in the Training of Child Diagnostic Assessment

Jean C. Elbert
Child Study Center
University of Oklahoma Health Sciences Center

Because no comprehensive standards currently exist for training of clinical psychologists who provide direct clinical services to children, the relative emphasis devoted to the specialized diagnostic assessment of children apparently varies widely across both graduate programs and clinical internship settings. While traditionally assessment, intervention, and professional consultation have been regarded as solid components in the training of clinical child psychologists, there has perhaps been more diversity of opinion regarding the relative impurtance of assessment in recent years. Several issues relate to this diversity of opinion. (1) While some would acknowledge the potential usefulness of formal assessment, they would argue that this is not a priority in doctoral level training, but a service more appropriately performed by Masters' level psychological assistants or technicians. (2) Others view psychological assessment as a distinct subspecialty (e.g., cognitive neuropsychology, developmental assessment) and advocate that referral be made to those specializing in the area of assessment. (3) Some programs reflect a more general trend toward the deemphasis of assessment among clinical psychologists, generally.

Over the past 15 years, several accounts have reported a decline in the once traditional psychodiagnostic and psychometric models of assessment, both in professional practice as well as in university training programs (Cleveland, 1976; Korchin & Schuldberg, 1981). Such a shift in emphasis has been attributed to several factors, among them: (1) the increased emphasis on applied behavioral analysis and cognitive behavioral techniques which rely more on objectively observable behavioral assessment; (2) a rigorous scientific model which has let to disappointing research results when the technical qualities of some assessment measures have been evaluated; (3) the amount of time necessary for administration, scoring, interpretation, and reporting of test results, which may not be cost effective in an economy characterized by rising professional fees (Korchin & Schuldberg, 1981; Lewandowski & Saccuzzo, 1976).

In contrast to the reported decline in more traditional assessment, however, a trend in the direction of specific skills assessment, neuropsychological assessment, and behavioral and environmental assessment appears to be emerging (Glaser, 1981). Some reports have described a shift toward "narrow band instruments" such as objective personality measures of anxiety, depression, ego strength, self concept, skills deficits, and specific symptoms. With regard to children, strong arguments have been made for broadening the procedures for assessment and classification of children to include evaluation of such areas as motivation, problem-solving strategies, social competence, creativity, family and environmental impact on child behavior, and for making assessment directly relevant to the development and implementation of intervention strategies (Reschley, 1981; Scarr, 1981).

The current diversity of child populations and clinical problems with which clinical child psychologists are involved professionally has created a break with traditional specialty boundaries. In 1981, APA developed specialty guidelines for the delivery of services by clinical psychologists. The practice of assessment was defined by the Committee on Professional Standards as "...directed toward diagnosing the nature and causes, and predicting the effects of subjective distress; of personal, social and work dysfunction; and of the psychological and emotional factors involved in, and consequent to, physical disease and disability." (American Psychological Association, Committee on Professional Standards, 1981, p. 642). While these guidelines are not addressed to a subspecialty area of clinical child psychology, the definition appears insufficient and/or restrictive when applied to clinical child psychologists who are currently providing clinical services to a broad spectrum of exceptional children. For example, in the past, school

The Section 1 Training Committee was composed of June M. Tuma, Chair, Jean C. Elbert, James H. Johnson, Annette LaGreca, Thomas H. Ollendick, and Carolyn S. Schroeder.

psychologists have traditionally served as the professionals primarily involved in the assessment of educational or school-related problems in children. However, federal legislation providing for an independent evaluation of children being considered for special education services (Public Law 94-142), as well as reduced funding resulting in numbers of children being inappropriately served in the schools, have generated increased involvement by clinical child psychologists acting as independent advocates for children. This has necessitated assessment, intervention, and consultation with a more clinically diverse population of children than clinical child psychologists may have served in the past. There is a growing need for both comprehensive and specialized assessment of multiple levels of competence in children of varying ages and handicapping conditions. This suggests a careful examination of current practices in training in clinical child psychology and how training might be strengthened to meet the changing needs for assessing broad areas of competence in children.

Current Practices in Assessment Training

With respect to current training relating to child assessment, data have been collected by the Section 1 Training Committee from several sources: (1) a survey of the members of Section 1 regarding their attitudes toward specialty training in clinical child psychology, (2) a survey of predoctoral graduate programs (Elbert, 1984), (3) a survey of clinical internship sites now in progress. A clinical child training questionnaire endorsed by a sample ($n = 52$) of the Section 1 membership has provided views regarding proposed needs for specialty training in child assessment (see Tables 1 and 2).

Table 1. *Percentage of Respondents Advocating* ***Required*** *Predoctoral (Pre-internship Training in Child Assessment)*

	Area of Curriculum			
Type of Assessment	Separate Course	Course Topic	Separate Practicum	Practicum Area
Developmental Assessment	26*	54	17	57
Child Intellectual Assessment	52	13	44	44
Achievement Testing	2	81	0	58
Visual-Motor Assessment	2	79	6	67
Child Personality Assessment	50	33	25	48
Child Neuropsychological Assessment	11	67	15	54
Child Behavioral Assessment	23	63	23	50
Parent/Child Interviewing	11	75	15	65
Assessment of the Handicapped Child	13	65	15	54
General Practicum in Child Assessment	26	2	60	17

*Numbers indicate percentage of respondents. $N = 52$.

Table 2. *Percentage of Respondents Advocating* ***Required*** *Clinical Internship Training in Child Assessment*

	Area of Curriculum		
Type of Assessment	Separate Seminar	Seminar Topic	Clinical Experience
Developmental Assessment	20*	22	70
Child Intellectual Assessment	19	19	83
Achievement Testing	0	33	56
Visual-Motor Assessment	0	33	59
Child Personality Assessment	14	23	66
Child Neuropsychological Assessment	9	28	56
Child Behavioral Assessment	6	34	72
Parent/Child Interviewing	6	26	80
Assessment of Handicapped Child	6	31	69

*Numbers indicate percentage of respondents. $N = 52$.

At the predoctoral (pre-internship) level, there was collective agreement by at least 75% of respondents that didactic coursework (either a separate course or a course topic) should be provided in the following areas: developmental assessment, achievement testing, visual-motor assessment, child personality assessment, child neuropsychological assessment, child behavioral assessment, parent-child interviewing, and assessment of the handicapped child. The percentage of individuals favoring separate coursework for the various areas of child assessment (52% and 50% endorsing a need for separate courses in child intellectual assessment and child personality assessment, respectively) might seem to reflect the need for a general course in child ability assessment which includes a variety of areas and types of assessment. At least one-half of respondents taken collectively endorsed a practicum experience in child assessment in all of the areas assessed.

At the level of internship training in clinical child psychology, respondents gave stronger endorsement to the need for clinical experience in assessment. When asked what proportion of an intern's time should relate to child assessment, the mean response was 31.09% (SD = 11.66). At least 50% of respondents believed a clinical child intern should have clinical experience in all areas of child assessment listed in the survey. Those areas receiving endorsement by 70% or more of the respondents were Child Intellectual Assessment (83%), Parent-Child Interviewing (80%), Child Behavioral Assessment (72%) and Developmental Assessment (70%). Less agreement was obtained regarding the proposed need for didactic seminar(s) in child assessment; when taken collectively, at least one-third of the respondents perceived a need for either a separate seminar or seminar topic in all of the areas of child assessment surveyed.

Beyond the documentation of need for specialty training in child assessment, data are available regarding training in child assessment at the predoctoral level, and a survey of internship training in assessment is underway. A questionnaire to clinical psychology graduate programs surveyed the level of coursework exposure and experience in test administration which graduate students receive on a broad array of assessment instruments, both traditional and specialized (Elbert, 1984). Respondents from 30 of the 36 programs previously listed as having formal programs in clinical child psychology (Mannarino & Fischer, 1982), were asked to report on child-related coursework offered in their programs (see Table 3).

Table 3. *Percentage of Programs Offering Coursework Relevant to Clinical Child Psychology.*

Course	Required	Recommended or Elective	Not Offered
Child Intellectual Assessment	77	6	17
Child Psychopathology	63	18	19
General Child Assessment	50	34	16
Survey of Child Psychotherapy	53	27	20
Child Behavior Management	43	37	20
Child Personality Assessment	43	27	30
Family Psychotherapy	30	57	13
Parent Counseling	27	36	37
Mental Retardation	17	26	57
Consultation	17	50	33
Assessment of Learning Disabilities	13	26	61
Theory of Learning Disabilities	10	26	64
Exceptional Children	10	50	40
Child Neuropsychological Assessment	7	53	40

Note: $N = 30$

(Table reprinted from Elbert, J.C. (1984). Training in child diagnostic assessment: A survey of clinical psychology graduate programs. *Journal of Clinical Child Psychology, 13,* 122-133).

A majority (77%) of these programs apparently require a course in child intellectual assessment, while general courses in child assessment and in child personality assessment are required in 53% and 43% of programs, respectively. From responses to the issue of training in specialized child assessment, it appeared that detailed training in the traditional measures of intelligence (WAIS-R, WISC-R, Stanford-Binet) and personality functioning (MMPI, Rorschach, TAT) occurred in at least 50% of programs. However, training in the more specialized assessment of specific skill areas and in narrow band instruments was not apparent, despite the reported trends toward this type of assessment (Korchin & Schuldberg, 1981).

At the internship level, a survey of internship and postdoctoral training programs in pediatric and clinical child psychology found that "psychodiagnostics" was rated as the second most important training priority in approximately 40% of 60 programs offering clinical internship training (Tuma & Grabert, 1983). Training in intelligence testing and projective assessment techniques was stressed by approximately 70% of the programs responding. However, data regarding the type and extent of this assessment training was not available.

Finally, preliminary data from a survey of assessment training at the clinical internship level are currently being analyzed (Elbert & Holden, 1985). As a follow-up to the survey of predoctoral graduate programs, directors of internships were asked to rate the amount and type of training their interns receive in child diagnostic assessment. To date, surveys have been received from 24 child specialty internships and 42 general clinical internships, all of which have APA approval. In addition, surveys from 30 additional non-APA approved internship programs have been received, resulting in a total of 96 internship programs. Of the child internship programs, directors reported that their interns spent approximately 85% of their time in child-related experiences, and 15% in adult-related experiences. By contrast, directors of general clinical programs reported that their interns spent approximately 60% of their time in adult-related experience and 40% in child related experience. Interns in child related programs were reported to spend approximately 27% of their clinical child experience involved in child assessment, 46% in child treatment and 25% in child-related consultation. It is of note that the relative proportion of internship time devoted to child assessment closely approximates the mean proportion of time Section 1 members endorsed as being important.

Proposed Guidelines for Child Assessment Training

Efforts to establish minimal standards for training child psychologists have been made by APA's Division 37 (Division of Child, Youth and Family Services). A task force of this division has proposed recommendations for minimal training criteria for psychologists who provide clinical service to children (Erickson, Roberts, & Tuma, 1983; see Appendix E).

This group stressed that competent assessment of children and families requires specialized training experiences. Included is the recommendation that assessment training should extend beyond the more traditional intelligence testing to include advanced and specialized techniques, and that basic assessment skills should be extended to include developmental assessment, behavioral and ecological methods, assessment of personality, achievement, hyperactivity, and learning disabilities. The recognition that psychologists now provide clinical services to a broad spectrum of children is underscored by this Task Force's recommendation that training in specialized assessment should extend to special populations of handicapped children.

Similar views regarding minimal training standards for clinical child psychologists are shared by the Section 1 Training Committee, and several general goals for training competence in assessment have been discussed. First, it was felt that training in assessment should extend to specialized populations of children, including the gifted, mentally retarded and/or developmentally disabled, visual and/or hearing impaired, speech and/or language impaired, learning disabled, chronically physically ill, and neurologically/physically impaired, in addition to those children presenting with emotional or behavioral disorders. Secondly, it was felt to be important that assessment training should optimally emphasize competence in the broad, comprehensive process of assessment, including referral clarification, selection of assessment based on a planful, theoretically-based rationale and a subsequent systematic hypothesis-testing approach. Third, the student clinician should be trained in the use of a wide variety of measurement instruments designed to assess broad levels of functioning, including specialized techniques appropriate for the various types of exceptional children. Competence in assessment involves an understanding of the complex interrlationships among cognitive, language, perceptual-motor, and affective systems in the child. The intent of expanded training is not to promote excessively narrow technical specialists, but to train competent diagnosticians who have sufficient breadth and fundamental knowledge of the range and effects of potentially handicapping conditions in children. Fourth, the training committee felt that assessment training for child clinicians should optimally cover the broad developmental age span — including infancy, preschool, school-age, and adolescence — with minimal levels of competence in the use of diagnostic procedures and test instruments appropriate for each developmental age level.

Finally, increasing specialization in the area of the child assessment raises the important issue of the role of the clinical child psychologist vis-a-vis other child specialists within psychology (e.g., school psychology, applied developmental psychology, pediatric psychology, child neuropsychology) as well as within related disciplines (e.g., speech and language pathology, special education, early childhood education, pediatric neurology, pediatrics, child psychiatry). As Johnson and Tuma (1983) suggest, this is a major question requiring discussion and input from training agencies.

With the above considerations and general goals, the Training Committee outlined minimal guidelines for training at the preinternship and internship levels. With respect to training at the university level, there was strong support for a minimum of two formal courses and one practicum in child assessment. Based on input from the clinicians surveyed, one course in *Assessment of Children's Abilities* would ideally cover a variety of areas, including basic assessment of intelligence, developmental assessment, assessment of auditory-verbal abilities, visual processing and visual-motor skills, achievement, and the specialized assessment of handicapped children. Recommended as ideal is a comprehensive approach to the assessment of intelligence which moves away from the traditional function of classifying and placing children (Reschley, 1981) and toward and integrative approach to the whole child (Scarr, 1981). Attention to the complexity of cognitive functioning, including current concepts regarding creativity, individual differences in cognitive style, problem-solving strategies, and motivational/emotional variables, is seen as being an ideal component in the training of competent child diagnosticians. Such training at the predoctoral level would ideally extend beyond the traditional exposure to Weschler and Stanford-Binet measures, should provide coverage of the assessment of infant and preschool abilities, and should at least provide exposure to the cognitive assessment of specialized populations of children, including competence in nonverbal measures for deaf, language impaired, or linguistically different children. Prerequisites for such a basic assessment course would ideally include course work in child development and in the psychology of exceptional children.

A second proposed course in *Child Behavior and Personality Assessment* would ideally cover such areas as parent and child interviewing, methods of child behavioral and environmental assessment, assessment of social skills and adaptive behavior, specialized techniques in family assessment, and various approaches to child personality assessment. Although the committee recognizes the need for maximum flexibility in such training, it was felt that a student clinician should be exposed to varying theoretical perspectives and their relationship to assessment methods, including objective and projective techniques. Attention to the narrow band instruments, such as objective personality measures of anxiety, depression, ego strength, and self concept (Glaser, 1981), would be appropriate for such a course. With this course too, prerequisite understanding of developmental issues and child psychopathology would seem to be desirable.

A third proposed university-based experience

would be a *Practicum in Child Assessment.* Such a practicum would ideally include experience with a range of children and clinical problems and would expose students to as many as possible of the types of assessment taught in the didactic courses. Beyond supervised administration, scoring, and interpretation of tests, such a practicum would provide the initial clinical experience in integrating and applying knowledge of assessment gained from coursework training. It should be noted that the breadth of practical experience in assessment at this level may vary considerably accordingly to both individual faculty expertise and clinical populations available in practicum sites. The need for maximum flexibility is therefore, essential.

The experiences described were viewed as being minimal training for those students wishing to pursue specialty training in clinical child psychology. The Training Committee felt that it would be desirable for university programs to provide additional seminars, mini-workshops, or elective courses for those wishing to pursue additional training in child assessment. In view of the rapid growth and specialization in the field of child assessment, discussion was given to how training might be extended to populations of handicapped children. Since competent assessment of these children presumes a basic understanding of the exceptionality, it was felt that supplementary lectures or seminars by interdisciplinary faculty (e.g., special education, communicative disorders) may be informative and useful. An additional area of training, considered to be important by at least 50% of respondents to the training questionnaire, is the area of child neuropsychological assessment. This is considered to be a highly specialized area of child assessment with prerequisite foundations in both neuroscience and general child assessment. Since training guidelines are being developed in this field (Noonberg & Page, 1982; International Neuropsychological Society Task Force, 1981), it will be important to seek input from professionals in this area regarding entry-level training.

The second primary level of training occurs at the internship level. The training committee generally viewed this training period as the opportunity to refine and extend basic skills obtained at the university level and to fill in the gaps in an individual's clinical experience. The clinical child psychology internship would ideally provide greater breadth and depth of experience in assessment training than was possible during pre-internship practice. The internship would ideally expose clinicians to assessment of children who are at varying developmental levels, who present with a variety of handicapping conditions and referral problems, and who are in diverse settings (including schools, hospitals, pediatric practice, and inpatient or residential setting where possible). Greater depth might be gained in mastery of specialized techniques for a particular type of child by reading literature pertinent to the child's particular syndrome or behavioral pattern, and by relating assessment to design of relevant treatment or programming goals and strategies. Competent assessment at the internship level also presumes experience with both family and environmental assessment. Support was also given to internship level didactic and/or case-related seminars in assessment of children. Such a seminar might ideally be designed to integrate both theoretical models and empirical findings with current clinical case material. Based on input from respondents to the training questionnaire, topics considered as being important for such seminar(s) were: (1) specialized assessment of perceptual, memory, and motor skills involved in learning, (2) psychoeducational assessment, including academic achievement, (3) assessment of varying types of skill deficits in handicapped children. Exposure to other disciplines and consultation with professionals having expertise in specialized assessment of children might be introduced through lectures, mini-workshops, or in combination with seminar content.

Finally, the Training Committee felt it important to underscore the need for maximum flexibility within and among training programs, while maintaining minimal standards of competency for those who intend to pursue a clinical child specialty. Variation in both program emphasis and individual clinician's interest in assessment can be expected to occur. However, it also would be expected that the prospective clinical child psychologist has an adequate level of competence in assessing a broad range of children. The important point is that if child clinicians are to be skilled and competent professionals, their training should reflect the greatly expanded knowledge base concerning infants, children, and families. The Training Committee also recognized that basic entry level skills discussed here may be insufficient for psychologists in service delivery; greater breadth and depth in all areas of training, including assessment may be neccessary. A series of workshops directed by individuals with expertise in certain areas of assessment has been suggested as one means of supplementing formal training and providing continuing education.

References

American Psychological Association (Committee on Professional Standards). (1981). Specialty guidelines for the delivery of services by clinical psychologists. *American Psychologist, 36,* 640-651.

Cleveland, S.E. (1976). Reflections on the rise and fall of psychodiagnosis. *Professional Psychology, 1,* 309-318

Elbert, J.C. (1985). Training in child diagnostic assessment: A survey of clinical psychology graduate programs. *Journal of Clinical Child Psychology, 13,* 122-133.

Elbert, J.C., & Holden, W. (1985). *Child assessment-training: A survey of clinical psychology internship programs,* work in progress.

Erickson, M., Roberts, M.C., & Tuma, J.M. (1983). *Recommended Minimal Training Criteria for Psychologists Working With Children, Youth and Families.* Prepared by Task Force on Training for APA Division 37: Division of Child, Youth and Families.

Glaser, R. (1981). The future of testing: A research agenda for cognitive psychology and psychometrics. *American Psychologist, 36,* 923-936.

International Neuropsychological Society Task Force. (1981, February). *Report of the task force on education, accreditation, and credentialing of the International Neuropsychological Society.* Atlanta, GA: Board of Governors of the International Neuropsychological Society.

Johnson, J.H., & Tuma, J.M. (1983). Training in clinical child psychology: A brief overview of selected issues. *Journal of Clinical Child Psychology, 12,* 356-368.

Korchin, S.J., & Schuldberg, D. (1981). The future of clinical assessment. *American Psychologist, 36,* 1147-1158.

Lewandowski, D.G., & Saccuzzo, D.P. (1976). The decline of psychological testing. *Professional Psychology, 7,* 177-184.

Mannarino, A.P., & Fischer, C. (1982). Survey of graduate training in clinical child psychology. *Journal of Clinical Child Psychology, 11,* 22-26.

Noonberg, A.R., & Page, H.A. (1982). Graduate neuropsycholgy training: A later look. *Professional Psychology, 13,* 252-257.

Reschley, D.J. (1981). Psychological testing in educational classification and placement. *American Psychologist, 36,* 1094-1102.

Scarr, S. (1981). Testing for children: Assessments of the many determinants of intellectual competence. *American Psychologist, 36,* 1159-1166.

Tuma, J.M., & Grabert, J. (1983). Internship and postdoctoral training in pediatric and clinical child psychology: A survey. *Journal of Pediatric Psychology, 8,* 245-260.

Providing Training Experiences in Child Treatment: Recommendations for the Clinical Child Psychology Specialty Curriculum

James H. Johnson
University of Florida

While a case can be made for including a range of courses and clinical experiences as part of the clinical child curriculum, none of these is more important than those related to child treatment, as it is primarily through the application of effective treatment methods that the mental health needs of troubled children are met. While not minimizing the importance of training in other areas, it could be argued that a *knowledge* of developmental psychology, child psychopathology, child assessment and the like, is of primary importance because of its relevance for treatment planning. And, well-developed treatment *skills* are essential if the clinician is to translate these treatment plans into action. Training in child treatment would thus seem to represent a vital aspect of the total clinical child curriculum.

While most child clinicians would agree that it is important to provide training in child treatment, differences of opinion are likely to arise regarding those training experiences most essential to the clincial child curriculum. Differences of opinion are especially likely when one considers the wide range of approaches that have been used with children (e.g., child behavior therapies, play therapies, family therapies, group therapies, drug therapies, residential treatments, school-based interventions, parent training), how these approaches are used with different populations (e.g., adolescents, chronically ill children), the level at which specific types of training should occur (pre-internship or internship level) and the degree to which this training should take the form of didactic courses, clinical practica or other applied experiences.

The present paper represents a summary of the Section 1 Training Committees views regarding those treatment related experiences seen as important aspects of clinical child specialty training. These views have evolved over a period of two to three years as a result of extensive Training Committee deliberations dealing with various curriculum related issues. In these discussions, a deliberate attempt was made to incorporate the views of a broader group of child-oriented psychologists by considering data obtained from responses to a number of treatment related items included as part of the Clinical Child Training Questionnaire, described earlier (Johnson, 1985). It should be noted that the recommendations made here are presented simply as a working proposal designed to stimulate further discussion that may lead to the development of more formal guidelines for training in this area.

Pre-Internship Training

In terms of training at the pre-internship level it was felt that there should be at least two basic child treatment requirements. One of these would be a basic survey course in *Approaches to Child Treatment,* a requirement which was endorsed by almost two thirds of those responding to the training survey. We would see this course as one which would serve as an initial introduction to a range of child treatment methods and cover a variety of topics such as child behavior therapy, play therapy, family therapy, parent training, residential treatment, school intervention, pharmacological approaches, and adolescent psychotherapy (each of which was suggested as an essential topic for coverage by at least 50% of those responding to the training questionnaire). It is felt that such a course should consider research findings related to the effectiveness of child treatments, ethical issues related to treatment, and serve to convey an empirical-scientific approach to the treatment of the individual child. It is also felt that an emphasis should be given to the way in which assessment information may be used to determine the optimal approach to treatment, in guiding the course of therapy, and in evaluating the effects of treatment. Essential prerequisites for such a course would include coursework in developmental psychology, child psychopathology, and child assessment.

The second requirement would be a *Practicum in Child Treatment* (a requirement endorsed by over 75% of all training questionnaire respondents). It

The author wishes to acknowledge the important role of other members of the original Section 1 Training Committee (Jean C. Elbert, Thomas J. Ollendick, Carolyn S. Schroeder, June M. Tuma, Chair) in formulating the views expressed in the present paper.

is felt that this practicum should provide the trainee with closely supervised experiences in treating children displaying differing types of problems and who vary in age. Likewise, it seems important that the student be exposed to as wide a variety of treatment approaches as is practical and consistent with the strengths of the faculty. Here it may be noted that play therapy, child behavior therapy, family therapy, parent training, adolescent psychotherapy, and school-based interventions were endorsed as important areas for practicum training by at least half of those responding to the training questionnaire. While it is probably unrealistic to believe that all programs will be able to provide experiences with each of these treatment methods for all students within a single practicum experience, the fact that each of these approaches was endorsed as an important area for practicum training suggests that providing clinical training in the use of multiple treatment techniques is seen as highly desirable.

Before beginning the treatment practicum, students should have completed certain prerequsites to prepare themselves for this clinical involvement. In addition to having completed predoctoral core courses it would seem important for students to have also completed a course such as the one just described *(Approaches to Child Treatment),* the prerequisites for this course, as well as having either prior or concurrent clinical practicum experience with child assessment methods. If the treatment practicum is to include contact with children displaying physical, as well as psychological problems (and this is seen as desirable), then the curriculum should provide prior didactic training in the area of pediatric psychology. As respondents to the training survey endorsed the view that clinical child training should also involve experiences in the treatment of adults, and, specifically, that trainees be required to take a survey course in adult treatment methods and an adult treatment practicum, it would seem desirable that these also be included within the specialty curriculum.

It should be noted that these experiences are seen by the committee as providing *minimal* training in the area of treatment. It would seem highly desirable that programs offer additional elective courses, seminars, and/or practicum experiences dealing with family therapy (which many respondents thought should be required as a separate course) and other child treatment approaches, as well as seminars dealing with issues such as the treatment of special populations (e.g., abused children, children with medical disorders, adolescents). The intent here is that doctoral students be given didactic exposure to a range of child treatment approaches and be given an opportunity, within the context of a comprehensive practicum experience, to begin developing treatment skills in working with a broad range of children (and their parents) from a variety of perspectives.

Internship Training

While pre-internship experiences in child treatment are seen as providing introductory didactic and clinical experiences, the internship is seen as an opportunity for gaining experiences of greater depth and variety. These experiences should build on those obtained earlier in training and provide the intern with opportunities to develop general compentencies in the treatment of children (and adults) and perhaps special skills in the application of specific treatment methods and/or in working with specific treatment populations. Specific to the area of treatment, it would seem that the internship should provide experiences of several types and in several areas.

One aspect of internship training viewed by the committee as important relates to seminar offerings. While there was some sentiment on the part of the committee for not overwhelming the intern with a large number of seminars, it was felt that at least two treatment related seminars would be desirable. It was suggested that one of these (which was strongly supported by responses to the training questionnaire) deal with approaches to child treatment such as those considered in the pre-internship treatment course. At this level, however, treatment approaches and other treatment related issues might be dealt with in greater detail and in a more clinically relevant way than was possible at the predoctoral level. In the case of interns who have not had this sort of predoctoral treatment course, the seminar, perhaps supplemented by additional reading materials and the like, could serve as an important and extensive introduction to the area.

A second specialty seminar seen as desirable by the committee would deal with the general area of case management. Rather than considering treatment methods per se, such a seminar might focus on the range of activities clinician's engage in and the various roles they assume when working with children or adolescents in treatment; consulting with parents regarding child treatment; consulting with the school (e.g., to facilitate appropriate placement; to assist the teacher in dealing with behavior problems); making referrals to other professionals (e.g., to physicians for health related concerns or for medication consults); making referrals to service agencies (e.g., Vocational Rehabilitation); being a child advocate (e.g., dealing with suspected child abuse). It would also seem desirable that the seminar deal with the interrelated nature of assessment, treatment, and consultation, as these activities relate to working with the individual child.

While certain types of information can best be dealt with through well-organized seminars, there was general agreement on the part of the committee that the bulk of the internship should be of an applied clinical nature where the intern gets intensive hands-on supervised experience with clinical cases. While making specific recommendations here is more difficult, it was the view of the committee that these experiences should be designed, first of all, to develop and enhance the trainee's general child treatment skills. It is thought that this can be best accomplished through working with children of different ages, displaying different types of difficulties, while obtaining supervision from clinicians with diverse theoretical orientations. In addition to the development of these general treatment skills, it would seem desirable that the intern also have the opportunity to gain more extensive clinical treatment experience in areas of special interest or in areas that represent unique strengths of a given internship setting. These opportunities might involve obtaining additional treatment experience with specialized treatment populations (e.g., depressed children, children with chronic illness, autistic children) or in the use of particular treatment methods (e.g., family therapy, nondirective play therapy, parent training, residential treatment).

It would seem that some flexibility is necessary in the way these training experiences are provided. Trainees interested in the child area are likely to come to the internship with varying backgrounds. Some may have extensive didactic and clinical experience in child treatment while others, unfortunately, may have little prior exposure to this area. Internship settings may also be expected to vary in terms of available treatment populations and in the treatment approaches emphasized by those involved in training. While certain core experiences, such as those alluded to here, should be provided as a basic part of internship training, the internship may be seen as a time when existing deficiencies in training can be remedied and where trainees are given the opportunity to enhance existing skills and develop special competencies. As long as some breadth of training is provided, internship settings should be encourged to maximize those child treatment related experiences that they may be uniquely qualified to offer. The important point would seem to be that by the end of the internship the clinical child trainee should have skills in the treatment of children experiencing a range of problems, in interacting with the significant adults in their environment (as well as other professionals), and they should be prepared to deal with the complex array of child and family problems that are seen in clinical practice. It would also be hoped that in the process of gaining these clinical experiences and through integrating what is learned with the available child treatment literature, that relevant questions regarding child treatment approaches will be raised and that some trainees will be motivated to contribute to what we know in this important area.

References

Johnson, J.H. (1985, May). *General program-related issues in clinical child specialty training: Survey input from child oriented clinicians.* Paper presented at the Conference on Training Clinical Child Psychologists, Hilton Head, South Carolina.

Clinical Child Psychology and Prevention: Toward a Workable and Satisfying Marriage

Robert D. Felner
University of Illinois

Raymond P. Lorion[1]
University of Maryland

Over the past decade, it has been said repeatedly that prevention is an idea that now has gained widespread acceptance (Felner, Jason, Moritsugu, & Farber, 1983), that prevention is an "in term" and a valued term, "an appealing movement that many people would like to join" (Cowen, 1982, p. 240) and that, for clinical child psychology in particular, a preventive perspective not only offers an attractive alternative direction but is an important element to include as part of the core of clinical child psychology (Felner, Gillespie, & Smith, 1985; Long, 1979; Peterson, Gelfand, & Hartmann, 1980; Wohlford, 1978). Consistent with these arguments, it is the stance of the authors of this paper that training in preventive approaches to emotional and physical disorders should be a required part of training in clinical child psychology for all students. That this position is clearly held more broadly as well, and is one with which those involved in the training of child clinicians must be concerned is well illustrated by several recent examples. During the past year, the authors of this paper received two requests for proposals for clinical training grants from the National Institute of Mental Health. The first of these sought applications for grants targeted at specific populations, with one of these being child mental health. Among the special award criteria listed for grants in this area was one we found particularly relevant to this paper; that is, those "programs that address the needs of the target groups (children) from the standpoint of prevention" (p. 11, ADAMHA Announcement MH-85-02) were to receive increased priority. A short time later, another request for proposals (Announcement MH-85-08) arrived in which it was stated that, "The intent of this initiative is to support the development, evaluation, and dissemination of didactic and experience-based model programs for use in training graduate students in the core mental health disciplines in the applicability of prevention research findings to clinical education." (p. 1)

The Need for Integration of Perspectives

The reason for these efforts to increase the emphasis accorded preventive approaches, particularly within clinical training, are myriad. Early interest was fueled by a recognition that both our approaches to service delivery and our available professional and economic resources were not sufficient to effectively treat those in need of service or to reduce the incidence or severity of new cases of disorder (Felner et al., 1983). Even the most conservative estimates indicate that 10-20% of all children may be in need of intensive mental health services (President's Commission on Mental Health, 1978) and that, as recently as 1970, 85% of these children were not receiving needed services (Peterson et al., 1980). Further, recent estimates are that 50% or more of all children may be at heightened risk for the development of emotional or physical disorders due either to genetic factors or exposure to environmental pathogens (e.g., stress, environmental disorganization and life changes, emotional or material deprivation) (Felner et al., 1985). Thus, it is clear that if child mental health professionals are to have a substantial impact on the emotional or physical well-being of children, more traditional approaches to these problems will not suffice. However, despite the widespread recognition of these issues, prevention has continued to be, as was noted in the second of the NIMH announcements discussed above, "a substantive area . . . . which customarily receives little attention in clinical training programs." (p. 2)

A further examination of the difference between the rhetoric in favor of prevention and the degree to which it has actually been integrated into training programs for clinicians may be particularly instructive for our purposes. That is, before embarking on a discussion of how training for prevention may be integrated into clinical child psychology, it may be helpful to briefly consider why this has not already occurred to a greater extent than it has currently. In addressing this issue, Felner et al. (1983) have noted that one of the primary factors which has impeded the development of prevention more generally is that issues of "turf" may have, however

[1]Order of authorship does not imply relative contributions as both authors contributed equally.

unintentionally, inhibited the growth of an integrated body of knowledge to inform prevention. One of the strengths of prevention is the breadth and diversity of paradigms that contribute to current perspectives. These paradigms often draw from a number of what have traditionally been somewhat discrete subdisciplines of psychology (e.g., developmental, social, health, pediatric) (Cowen, 1983; Felner et al., 1983). While this diversity is in many ways a virtue, it may also have had a limiting effect. Individuals from many of the areas involved often did not identify what they were doing as prevention or relevant for it and, even when they did, regularities that support and foster the distinctions between sub-disciplines (e.g., journals, etc.) more often than not lead to insufficient cross-fertilization among research efforts. These sub-disciplinary differences had implications not only for the ways in which investigators viewed the questions being asked but for the ways they viewed prevention more generally. One particularly important example may clarify this issue here. Over the past several decades, there has been a great deal of debate between "clinical" and "community" psychology about the relative merits of a "traditional" pyschopathology emphasis versus a focus on prevention and enhancement. This debate may have now become as dysfunctional as it is outdated. Both perspectives appear to be here to stay. Recent work has shown that efforts to integrate these views may be far more helpful, both heuristically and practically, than is continued debate focused on the merits of one in the interest of excluding the other. As has been noted elsewhere, "Although continued debate about the relative merits of each may serve to make both sides refine their positions and better articulate ways in which they may each contribute to understanding adaptive and maladaptive behavior, it is time to go beyond this debate to explore ways in which the combination of these perspectives may act synergistically to expand our knowledge of human adaptation" (Felner et al., 1985, p. 3) and, thus, to enhance the effectiveness of our intervention efforts.

Accomplishment of this integration may require the modification of basic paradigms that clinicians have typically relied upon for viewing adaptation and pathology as well as the processes which underlie them. A focus not only on pathology and its absence as evidence of health, but which includes a concern with positive adaptation and development, represents for us the opportunity to effect a stable and mutually beneficial marriage between prevention and clinical psychology. The pursuit of answers to such important questions as "what factors are key to understanding vulnerability to disorder in childhood?" and "how to reduce this vulnerability?" (Felner et al., 1985) are to our minds, best served by such shifts in our guiding frameworks. Indeed, given the forces which may act on preventive efforts to fragment them and, thus, impede the further development of a sound knowledge base for effective "next generation" interventions, an integrating framework is necessary for prevention, not only to facilitate its integration into clinical training, but also to enhance the more general growth of the emergent sub-disciplinary specialty that has come to be called "Preventive Psychology" (Felner et al., 1983). That these efforts may be particularly relevant to clinical child psychology can be seen clearly from an examination of the topics being discussed at this conference. A significant portion of the papers are devoted either to *boundary* concerns, the emergent roles of clinical child psychologists in a number of alternative settings and problem arenas and the problems of articulating the uniqueness of clinical child psychology, while at the same time not making these boundaries so rigid as to interfere with the further growth and development of diverse roles for clinical child psychologists. We feel that the clear acceptance of preventive approaches into this area will significantly contribute to our ability to affect a satisfactory balance in addressing these issues, while at the same time moving us toward conceptual frameworks which allow for the integration of the overlap that exists among concerns that are being explored in the so-called boundary areas and the concerns of clinical child psychologists.

A Prevention Model for Training in Clinical Child Psychology

This is perhaps a good time to pause briefly to consider what we mean by prevention and preventive psychology. There has been much debate about what constitutes *true* preventive efforts (c.f. Albee, 1982, 1983; Cowen, 1983). The nuances of these issues, while important, are far beyond the scope of this paper. There does seem to be general agreement, however, on two essential components of a preventive approach. First, there is a focus on the enhancement of competencies and the facilitation of optimal development, particularly when environmental or constitutional risk factors may be present. Second, there is both an emphasis on the reduction of the incidence of onset of new disorder, as well as the reduction of the prevalence of disorder by limiting its duration to its incipient stages (c.f. Cowen, 1982, 1983; Felner et al., 1983). This perspective, then, encompasses what have been labelled as primary and early secondary prevention strategies (Caplan, 1964; Cowen, 1983). Primary prevention refers to those interventions which seek to alter precursors to disorder or enhance the factors which make one resistant to disorder. Secondary preventive strategies rely heavily upon early detection procedures to identify individuals manifesting initial signs of disorder and seek to interrupt the further development of these problems, thus reducing the duration and severity of the disorder. Further, it should be noted that much of psychology's early emphasis on prevention was exclusively concerned with the prevention of mental health problems (e.g., Cowen, 1983). Our perspective, however, is that, given the growth and change the field has experienced in its views of the interrelationship of psychosocial functioning and the development and course of physical disorders (c.f. Albino, 1983; Peterson et al., 1980), statements of preventive concerns must now also allow for a focus on these relationships by preventively-oriented psychologists (Felner et al., 1983).

Given the issues raised thus far, it is now time to turn to the questions of how we train for prevention and, in particular, how we train clinical child psychologists in prevention without being plagued by issues of turf and fragmentation of knowledge, perspectives, and approaches. The answers to these questions are complex and incomplete. If the broad base that has been so critical to the growth of preventive perspectives is not to be lost, we may not want to overspecify a best approach or set of solutions. However, if this diversity is not to remain a limitation, then we need to provide unifying models to allow for the evaluation and integration of conceptual, empirical, and programatic contributions from diverse sources. Further, it is insufficient to say to our students that a shift in the way clinicians view dysfunction is necessary if we do not provide them with a new direction in which to go. A model which we feel meets both these needs and that, in light of much of what has been considered elsewhere in this conference (e.g., developmental training for clinical child), offers much to clinical child psychology, is one developed by Lorion (c.f. Lorion, Cowen, & Krauss, 1974; Lorion, 1974; Lorion, 1983; Lorion & Loundsbury, 1981). This model defines preventive interventions within a developmental paradigm. Within this framework, a preventive intervention involves the systematic alteration and modification of processes related to the development of adaptation and well-being or disorder with the goals of increasing or decreasing, respectively, the rate or level at which these patterns of functioning occur in the general population or some part thereof. The rationale of emphasizing processes is that, by definition, preventive efforts are directed to the avoidance of disorder and the enhancement of development and, hence, should focus on the mechanisms from which these outcomes result.

Given a developmental perspective for prevention that seeks to understand the processes underlying the evolution of disorder and the nature of these across stages in the life-span, a model of development that is transactional in nature, such as that of Sameroff and Chandler (1975) which emphasizes the necessity of fully understanding the ecological context in which the child grows (Bronfenbrenner, 1979), may be particularly well suited to the needs of prevention training in clinical child psychology. Such a transactional/ecological perspective emphasizes that dynamic transactions between constitutional and environmental factors lead to the development of health disorder. Sarason and Doris (1979) explain the model this way: "From the transactional perspective, heredity and environment are never dichotomous . . . . The transactional approach is always a two-way street. There is nothing in a transactional formulation that denies the existence and influence of genetic processes or the existence of a socially structured context . . . (p.25)

A training model and philosophy based on this perspective that may best serve efforts to integrate a prevention perspective into clinical child training, then, is one that emphasizes a broad base of coursework and field experiences that will provide the student with an understanding of: (1) those organismic factors that influence and shape development; (2) the nature of the social systems in which the child develops and how these systems and contexts may change over time; (3) the reciprocal influences that each set of factors may have on the other and, particularly, the ways in which alterations in one sphere may influence the other as well as the child's overall development; and (4) the ways in which intervention efforts to accomplish preventive goals may be developed, implemented, and evaluated. Further, given the preventive "action" emphasis when making decisions about how best to provide the student with this knowledge base and set of skills, programs may be well advised to pay particular attention to the roles that a graduate of the program might occupy (Havelock & Havelock, 1973; Price, 1983). That is, for example, while the basic issues to be addressed across clinical child psychology programs are similar, those who put greater emphasis on the training of their students for preventive work in the context of pediatric settings (Felner, 1983) may wish to deal with a somewhat different set of specific issues and experiences than those who train their students primarily for work in school or other traditional clinical and community contexts.

Curriculum Issues

To train clinical child/preventive psychologists who are able to conceptualize emotional and somatic disorders that are influenced by psychosocial factors within a transactional developmental perspective and who are then able to translate that understanding into viable preventive interventions requires both didactic and experiential/practicum elements. At the didactic level, there are several content domains which seem of particular importance and should be required in one form or another. These include: (1) prevention concepts and methods; (2) normal development; (3) developmental psychopathology; (4) the assessment of risk, strengths, and competencies; (5) community psychology, with a particular emphasis on the nature and analysis of social systems and social environments; and (6) strategies for needs assessment and program evaluation. Additional, highly recommended, although not necessarily required coursework, would address issues specific to contexts in which prevention efforts might be carried out (e.g., educational, pediatric, or legal settings), as well as such issues as consultation (to be a required part of practicum training — see below), social policy for children, educational psychology, stress, coping and life changes, epidemiology and pediatric/health issues.

Practicum training for prevention also has a number of key elements, many of which are complimentary to the didactic courses. Cowen (1983) has argued that a critical feature of preventive efforts is their importance, not only for the specific target problem, but for adding to the "executive" knowledge base of prevention. Thus, a key element of practicum experiences for clinical child students receiving training in prevention is the development of attitudes and techniques that see the applied and research enterprise as inextricably interwoven. Practicum work needs to emphasize both program development and program evaluation. Further, given the transactional-developmental model espoused in this paper, consultative, program development, and evaluation activities all need to be planned with particular sensitivity to the necessity of considering the multiple levels of the systems involved that may be impacted, regardless of the actual level of intervention. Training for consultation, particularly interdisciplinary consultation or collaboration, is also essential since preventive activities frequently require that the clinical child psychologist be able to intervene with systems that are important contributors to shaping the child's development. Adding further shape to these practicum experiences will be the particular setting/target group that the intervention seeks to address.

Concluding Comments

Eight years ago, Wohlford (1978), who was then president of the Section on Clinical Child Psychology, echoed Albee and argued that "clinical psychology, if it is to survive (and, thereby, clinical child psychology, as well) cannot complacently continue its traditional practices, methods, and training models." (p. 89) Since then, as witness, for example, the tremendous growth of pediatric psychology and community interventions, our field has certainly undergone rapid change in its practices. Most striking has been the degree to which clinical child psychologists now engage in activities where the children being seen have not been referred for treatment of serious emotional disorder. Rather, because of a variety of reasons, ranging from poverty and serious debilitating physical illness to parental divorce, remarriage, school changes and/or birth of a sibling, the child may be identified as "at risk" and, hence, in need of services of some type. Indeed, with increasing frequency, child clinicians may be called upon to work with children or the systems with which they are involved when neither the children nor the system is at any discernible immediate risk and no disorder is present (e.g., well-baby clinics, preschool consultation activities).

Our methods and particularly our training models have sadly not fully kept pace with these changes in practices and roles. It is easy to see from the preceding examples, however, that the methods and models of prevention have much to offer to clinical child psychologists in their new roles. Perhaps most importantly, they offer a direction for reorientation that is consistent with the changes in demands and opportunities we now confront, while, at the same time, providing a unifying framework for integrating the diverse knowledge base that clinicians working with children must have to meet these challenges. Cowen (1983) has noted the knowledge bases and skills needed for prevention "as a group differ from the things that mental health professionals are trained to do, know best, and are most comfortable with. It is not that such skills differ absolutely from ones already known to psychology and other social sciences; rather they require significant recombinations of existing patterns of training, knowledge and technology." (p. 21) If we are to maintain a viable clinical child psychology, which more accurately reflects the full range of what it is we now concern ourselves with, then it is important that we make progress toward recombining and integrating our traditional ways of operating and thinking with those of preventive psychology.

References

Albee, G.W. (1982). Preventing psychopathology and promoting human potential. *American Psychologist, 37,* 1043-1052.

Albee, G.W. (1983). The argument for primary prevention. In

H.A. Marlowe, Jr., & R.B. Weinberg (Eds.) *Primary prevention: Fact or fallacy?* Tampa, FL: University of South Florida Press.

Albino, J.E. (1983). Health psychology and primary prevention: Natural allies. In R.D. Felner, L.A. Jason, J.N. Moritsugu, & S.S. Farber (Eds.), *Preventive psychology: Theory, research, and practice* (pp. 221-233). New York: Pergamon.

Bronfenbrenner, U. (1979). *The ecology of human development: Experiments by nature and design.* Cambridge, MA: Harvard University Press.

Caplan, G. (1964). *Principles of preventive psychology.* New York: Basic Books.

Cowen, E.L. (1982). The special number: A complete roadmap. American *Journal of Community Psychology, 10,* 239-250.

Cowen, E.L. (1983). Primary prevention in mental health: Past, present, and future. In R.D. Felner, L.A. Jason, J.N. Moritsugu, S.S. Farber (Eds.), *Preventive psychology: Theory, research and practice* (pp. 11-25). New York: Pergamon.

Felner, R.D., Gillespie, J.F., & Smith, R. (1985). Risk and vulnerability in childhood: A reappraisal. *Journal of Clinical Child Psychology, 14,* 2-4.

Felner, R.D., Jason, L.A., Moritsugu, J.N., & Farber, S.S. (1983). Preventive psychology: Evolution and current status. In R.D. Felner, L.A. Jason, J.N. Moritsugu, & S.S. Farber (Eds.), *Preventive psychology: Theory, research, and practice* (pp. 3-10). New York: Pergamon.

Havelock, R.G., & Havelock, M.C. (1973). *Training for change agents: A guide to the design of training programs in education and other fields.* Ann Arbor: Center for Research on the Utilization of Scientific Knowledge, Institute for Social Research, University of Michigan.

Long, B.E. (1979). Primary prevention and the feminine principle. *Journal of Clinical Child Psychology, 8,* 78-79.

Lorion, R.P. (1974, May). *The evaluation of school adjustment.* Paper presented at the NICHHD Conference on the Measurement of Outcome in the Care of Children with Chronic Illness, Fogarty International Center, NIH, Washington, DC. Reprinted in B. Pless & G. Graves, (Eds.). (1976). *Measurement of Outcome.* Washington, DC: Government Printing Office.

Lorion, R.P. (1983). *Evaluating preventive interventions: Guidelines for the serious social change agent.* In R.D. Felner, L.A. Jason, Moritsugu, & S.S. Farber, (Eds.), *Preventive Psychology: Theory, research, and practice.* New York: Pergamon.

Lorion, R.P., Cowen, R.P., & Krauss, R.M. (1974). Some hidden regularities in a school mental health program and their relation to intended outcomes. *Journal of Consulting and Clinical Psychology, 42,* 346-352.

Lorion, R.P., & Loundsbury, J.W. (1981). Conceptual and methodological considerations in evaluating preventive interventions. In W.R. Tash & G. Stahler (Eds.), *Innovative approaches to mental health evaluation.* New York: Academic Press.

Peterson, L., Hartman, D.P., & Gelfand, D.M. (1980). Prevention of child behavior disorders: A lifestyle change for child psychologists. P.O. Davidson & S.M. Davidson (Eds.), *Behavioral medicine: Changing health lifestyles* (pp. 195-221). New York: Brunner/Mazel.

Price, R.H. (1983). The education of a prevention psychologist. In R.D. Felner, L.A. Jason, J.N. Moritsugu, & S.S. Farber (Eds.), *Preventive psychology: Theory, research, and practice.* New York: Pergamon.

President's Commission on Mental Health. (1978). (Stock No. 040-000-00391-6, Vol. II, Appendix). Washington, DC: US Government Printing Office.

Sameroff, A.J., & Chandler, M.J. (1975). Reproductive risks and the continuum of care-taking causality. In F.D. Horiwitz, M. Hetherington, S. Scarr-Salapatek, & G. Stiegal (Eds.), *Review of child development research.* Chicago: University of Chicago Press.

Sarason, S.B., & Doris, J. (1979). *Educational handicap, public policy and social history: A broadened perspective on mental retardation.* New York: Free Press.

Wohlford, P. (1978). A challenge to clinical psychology: Better training to serve children. *Journal of Clinical Child Psychology, 7,* 89-90.

Training in Clinical Child Psychology: A Proposal for the Role of Continuing Education

Thomas H. Ollendick
Virginia Polytechnic Institute
and State University

In recent years, the *training* of clinical child psychologists has received increased attention. Whereas the field of clinical child psychology has a long and rich tradition (cf Ross, 1959), the development of philosophies for clinical child psychologists has not benefitted fully from recent developments in the fields of child psychology and clinical psychology. In part, the belief of most mental health professionals that children are best viewed as miniature adults has been responsible for this state of affairs. As such, special training programs have not been deemed necessary and what little *specialized* training existed was distilled from general clinical training programs. Resurgence of interest in the training of clinical child psychologists is undoubtedly related to our increased awareness that children must be understood, assessed, and treated *as children,* not as little adults (Knopf, 1979; Ollendick & Cerny, 1981; Schwartz & Johnson, 1981; Wenar, 1982). Further, it is now abundantly clear that too few psychologists have been trained adequately to meet the specific mental health needs of children and adolescents (Tuma, 1982).

Most recent efforts directed toward the training of clinical child psychologists have focused their sights on predoctoral, university-based training programs. In general, as noted by Roberts (1982), four basic models of training have been described: (1) programs which offer specialty training in clinical child psychology apart from the structure of general clinical training programs; (2) programs which offer clinical child training within the context of a developmental or school psychology programs; (3) programs which offer clear and well-defined subspecialty training within the framework of general clinical training programs; and (4) programs which offer clinical child training on an informal basis with no clear or well-defined specialization. The relative strengths and weaknesses of these models are currently being examined and carefully evaluated, with professionals in the field aligning themselves within specific camps (see 1982 issue of the *Journal of Clinical Child Psychology).* While firm conclusions regarding the relative merits of these diverse training models are not yet available, it seems obvious that some degree of specialization at the predoctoral level is both desirable and necessary. It was this recognition that led Diane Willis, President of the Section on Clinical Child Psychology (APA Division 12, Section 1), to establish a National Training Committee in 1982. This Committee, from which this report evolved, was charged with the task of considering those issues relevant to specialty training in clinical child psychology. Similar factors led to Tuma's (1982) proposal that a national conference on clinical child training be held.

As part of this growing awareness, the current report is designed to explore the role of continuing education in the training of clinical child psychologists. Fortunately, the field of clinical child psychology no longer makes the assumption that predoctoral graduate training (whatever its form) and an internship in a clinical setting provide the requisite knowledge or skills for a lifelong career. Increasingly, emphases are being placed on specialized postdoctoral training and on *continuing education* (the network of courses, in-service training, conferences, and workshops beyond graduate school and professional preparation). In this context, training in clinical child psychology is best viewed as a developmental process in which predoctoral, postdoctoral, and continuing education opportunities combine interactively to produce highly knowledgable and competent professionals. Given the veritable explosion of knowledge in the area of clinical child psychology, such postdoctoral and continuing education experiences appear mandatory if clinical child psychologists are to keep abreast of the many developments in their field of study. If such is not the case, professional obsolescence will rule. In this vein, Dubin (1972) pointed out that obsolescence rates for psychology, as well as other professions, are on the rise. He estimated the half-life of a psychologist's expertise to be 10-12 years, and that was 12 years ago! Given rapid advances, we might project the half-life of newly trained psychologists to be considerably less. Keeping abreast of current developments in psychology, let alone the rather narrow area of clinical child psychology, is no easy feat for most of us.

The Role of Continuing Education

For a variety of reasons, continuing education has been the subject of considerable interest and debate in recent years. From a positive standpoint, there is the conviction that continuing education can lead to increased knowledge, ability, and skill, which, in turn, can lead to enhanced professional competence. A very important, but as yet untested, side effect of such "training" is that it is also thought to assist professionals in maintaining a fresh and current outlook on their work and to result in increased self-efficacy and mastery expectations related to the work setting. On the negative side, criticisms of continuing education have been abundant. Critics are fast to point out that no direct relationship between continuing education and improved professional practice has been demonstrated. Further, they also argue that programs delivered to the front-line professionals rarely are integrated into a coherent sequence, and that the academicians and researchers who develop such programs possess little understanding, let alone appreciation, of the problems professionals face in their day-to-day practice. Finally, as noted by Jones (1975), professional competence itself is an elusive concept. Certainly, it is something that cannot be met solely by additional coursework. In the least, all of the hands-on learning and all of the maturing that occur in professional practice must be considered, as well as knowlege of new techniques and new scientific findings, in determining professional competence.

At the same time, professionals themselves increasingly are being subjected to a rising tide of criticism. The consumer movement of recent years has left few professionals unscathed. Accusing professionals of exorbitant fees and incompetence, the public no longer automatically assumes professional competency (Olesen, 1979). Instead, people are demanding that professionals be held accountable for their actions. Whether professional competency has *really* declined over the years is irrelevant, the public perception cannot be dismissed readily.

The problem of developing and delivering high quality continuing education and of ensuring professional competency are intertwined closely. Competence in practice is the idea on which continuing education must rest. Competence, however, is a multifaceted concept (Dubin, 1972, 1974). The delivery of competent services depends upon several factors, including organizational climate, adequate equipment and facilities, and qualified professionals. Granted that these elements, as well as others, are important, the primary contribution to competent services, however, must be the individual professional practitioner. Without a competent practitioner, other factors are less salient.

Rosenfeld and Thornton (1978) suggest that professional competence consists of two essential ingredients: possession of requisite knowledge, abilities, and skills, *and* the ability to apply that knowledge, ability, and skill to particular problems faced in real-life practice. To date, our continuing education efforts have been directed primarily to the former ingredients; we have neglected the latter. Certainly, knowledge, abilities, and skills are prerequisites for appropriate application in practice, but they are not substitutes for it. Furthermore, the latter cannot be inferred from the former. To avoid the trap of equating the possession of knowledge, abilities, and skills with professional competence, concerted attention must be given to relating learning and assessment processes to the practice setting more closely, and to the factors that contribute to adequate *performance* (Houle, 1980).

The concern with developing continuing professional education programs to assist clinical child psychologists in remaining (or becoming) competent necessitates a specification of their practice-related educational needs. A need can be defined as a gap that exists between actual or current practices and satisfactory or desired ones (Pennington, 1980). Needs assessments are intended to be systematic ways of identifying deficiencies or discrepancies that inhibit, in the case of professional practice, competent performance. A number of needs assessment techniques have been developed, including the use of self-perceived needs surveys, objective tests of knowledge, and expert panels (Dubin, 1972). Criticisms of these techniques indicate that self-determined surveys oftentimes result in the identification of *wants* rather than what is *needed* for competent performance, that objective tests of knowledge ignore the actual problem of how knowledge is applied, and that expert panels rely too heavily on *armchair theory* rather than empirical data related to day-to-day practice.

As this discussion illustrates, professional competence and needs assessments are closely related. A competent practicing clinical child psychologist is the desired end and needs assessments are the means to identify the education that should be provided to assist in the maintenance of competence. It should be clear that both require a careful understanding of what is demanded of a professional in practice: namely, to assess competence, a knowledge of the professional's roles and practices is necessary, and to determine needs, criteria against which to judge performance must exist. The provision of relevant and quality continuing education, thus, must rest on knowledge of the practitioner's roles and responsibilities. Without such knowledge-base, continuing education efforts must be necessarily shortsighted, ill-informed, and unsystematic.

The precise articulation of the roles and responsibilities of clinical child psychologists is presently incomplete; however, strides are being made and it is anticipated that this training conference will likely contribute substantially to this end. It should be evident that clarification of our role and function is a critical antecedent to the development of systematic continuing education efforts. A variety of techniques could be used to determine these roles and functions: interviews with practitioners, direct observation, expert panels, job diaries, open-ended questionnaires, behavior event analyses, and survey checklists of responsibilities. While strengths and weaknesses exist with each of these procedures (Pottinger, 1979), a clear consensus exists on one point: namely, that determination of professional roles and practices must be empirically derived rather than simply defined by experts who do not venture into the field. We would do well to adhere to this admonition in our training conference.

Outlines of responsibilities and tasks specify what the clinical child psychologist does. This is not enough, however. If competency is the final goal, criteria defining how well the task and responsibilities must be performed are also needed. These are *standards of practice.* Standards of practice address such matters as the frequency, accuracy, and timeliness with which each task and responsibility must be accomplished (Rosenfeld & Thornton, 1978). In the final analysis, it is these standards that define competency for a profession.

Efforts to help clinical child psychologists maintain their competence rest squarely on our ability to define competence *and* to assess it. Our major consideration must be to identify deficiencies in practice; too many assessment efforts have failed to address how individuals function in actual practice. Rather, past assessment procedures have simply asked individuals to recall information rather than how to apply it. Several strategies allow for assessment of professionals under practice-like conditions, including use of criterion-referenced tests (e.g., McClelland & Bojatzis, 1980), linear and branching simulation models (e.g., Pottinger, 1980), and patient-management centers, as well as simulated role-playing activities as used in behavioral studies. Assessment procedures that can identify deficiencies in practice set the stage for the development of relevant continuing education programs. Continuing education programs no longer need to be developed randomly; rather, they can be developed and presented in a systematic, coherent approach.

The articulation of the practices needs of clinical child psychologists is not an easy task, however. The above discussion indicates that it will require input from various sources. It is for this reason that the final useful element in developing systematic continuing education programs is collaboration. For too long, groups concerned with helping professionals maintain their competence have worked independently and without collaborative benefit. The barriers erected between professionals and academician/researchers have been particularly detrimental (Olesen, 1979). Given the complexity of the task, various types of expertise are needed. Continuing education professionals are experienced in the delivery of programs, university faculty members work on the development of knowledge and are experienced in program development, practicing professionals are in the closest touch with real professional needs, and professional associations possess the organizational expertise to "put it all together." Because each has something valuable to contribute, collaborative efforts can yield a better product than that produced by any one group alone.

A Proposed Continuing Education Model

Based on the foregoing comments, the following proposal for the role of continuing education in the training of clinical child psychologists is put forth. It should be noted that this proposal is specifically designed to address issues of providing practice-oriented continuing education for competency maintenance in practicing child clinicians. In the past, most decisions about the continuing education needs of practitioners was based on self-perception surveys which asked respondents to select from a list of topics those which they felt best fitted their educational needs. In most instances, this list of topics was determined by faculty members who felt they knew what practitioners needed to know. These procedures often resulted in offerings which were irrelevant to most practitioners.

The proposed model, based on that used in other professions like pharmacy and medicine (cf Queeney, 1981) involves identifying what practicing professionals actually do in practice and addresses the individual practitioner's ability to use knowledge and skills in handling everyday situations. In order to obtain agreement about what *ought* to be done, specification of the basic roles and functions of the profession need to be addressed first. Clearly, unless there is an understanding and agreement about what professionals do, or are *supposed* to do, there will be no foundation on which to proceed with assessment.

Once measures to compare performance with suggested acceptable practices are available, the next step is to identify items for inclusion in the assessment procedure. This is achieved by bringing together knowledgeable practitioners and other key professionals. Once the assessment is conducted and deficits are identified, the deficits can be aggregated and the data can be used as the basis for making decisions about specific educational offerings. Various methods, procedures, and formats of delivering the continuing education can be evaluated and, finally, the efficacy of the continuing education in fostering and maintaining competence can be carefully evaluated.

In sum, a systematic continuing education package might include the following steps:

1. **Organization of a Professional Team:** This team would be faculty members, professional association representatives, continuing education professionals, and practitioners. This team would guide the *systematic* development of a continuing education program.

2. **Identification of Practice Standards/Professional Competencies:** This component will require the definition of the scope of the profession of clinical child psychology, including its roles and responsibilites. The purpose of such a definition is to lend clarity to just what is meant by a "competent" professional.

3. **Construction of Needs Assessment Materials:** Whatever the form of such materials, they must allow for the assessment of content (specific topics) and performance (how the activity is performed in practice situations). Such materials should identify the practice-related educational needs of clinical child psychologists.

4. **Planning and Developing a Continuing Education Program:** A number of important issues must be addressed, including program content, format, instructors, instructional techniques, delivery mechanisms, and program promotional materials. Obviously, program content should be derived from the needs assessment and instructional techniques should facilitate the application of program content to the professional's work site.

5. **Implementing and Evaluating the Program:** Evaluations should attempt to discover whether programs contribute to the improvement of the professional's practice behavior, for that is the primary purpose of continuing education programs.

Conclusions

In sum, the initiation, development, and delivery of a *systematic* continuing education program for clinical child psychologists represent a complex, but worthwhile, undertaking. While a systematic model for achieving this goal has been proposed, it is readily acknowledged that other models exist and that some of the armchair speculations might not be related directly to the practice needs of the professional. Further, this model may not represent the most productive way to go. At this point in time, however, our efforts in the continuing education arena are truly in their infancy and must be viewed as rudimentary at best. We must start somewhere. Suggestions, recommendations, and assistance are most welcome.

References

Dubin, S.G. (1972). Obsolescence or lifelong education: A choice for the professional. *American Psychologist, 27,* 486-498.

Dubin, S.G. (1974). The psychology of lifelong learning: New developments in the profession. *International Review of Applied Psychology, 23,* 147-154.

Houle, C.O. (1980). *Continuing learning in the professions.* San Francisco: Jossey-Bass.

Jones, N.F. (1975). Continuing education: A new challenge for psychology. *American Psychologist, 30,* 842-847.

Knopf, I.J. (1979). *Childhood psychopathology: A developmental approach.* Englewood Cliffs, NJ: Prentice-Hall, Inc.

McClellan, D.C., & Bojatzis, R.E. (1980). Opportunities for counselors from the competency assessment movement. *The Personnel and Guidance Journal, 35,* 842-847.

Olesen, V. (1979). Employing competence-based education for the reform of professional practice. In G. Grant (Ed.), *On competence.* San Francisco:Jossey-Bass.

Ollendick, T.H., & Cerny, J.A. (1981). *Clinical behavior therapy with children.* New York: Plenum.

Pennington, F.C. (1980). Needs assessment: Concepts, models, and characteristics. In F.C. Pennington (Eds.), *New directions for continuing education: Assessing educational needs for adults.* San Francisco: Jossey-Bass.

Pottinger, P.S. (1979). Competence assessment: Comments on current practice. In P.S. Pottinger & J. Goldsmith (Eds.), *New directions for experimental learning: Defining and measuring competence.* San Francisco: Jossey-Bass.

Queeney, D.S. (Ed.) (1981). *The practice audit model.* Unpublished manuscript. Pennsylvania State University.

Roberts, M.C. (1982). Clinical child psychology programs: Where and what are they? *Journal of Clinical Child Psychology, 11,* 13-21.

Rosenfeld, M., & Thornton, R. (1978). *A national study of the practice of pharmacy.* Unpublished manuscript. Educational Testing Service.

Ross, A.O. (1959). *The practice of clinical child psychology.* New York: Grune & Stratton.

Schwartz, S., & Johnson, J.H. (1981). *Psychopathology of childhood: A clinical-experimental approach.* New York: Pergamon.

Tuma, J.M. (1982). Proposal for a National Conference on professional preparation of clinical child psychologists. *Journal of Clinical Child Psychology, 11,* 3-7.

Wenar, C. (1982). *Psychopathology from infancy through adolescence: A developmental approach.* New York: Random House.

Summary of Concurrent Small Group Discussions on Curriculum Issues Academic Level

Annette M. LaGreca
University of Miami

The sentiment of this group was to indicate important areas for inclusion in graduate level training programs; however, the emphasis was on general guidelines rather than specific course and practicum requirements.

The first issue of emphasis was the *importance of integrating experiences with children in "normal settings" into graduate training programs.* There was strong concensus on this issue. Although the explicit mechanism for accomplishing this goal was not delineated, the clear intention was that such experiences supercede coursework, and be more practical in focus. An additional suggestion was that some attempt be made to expose students to children from different ethnic groups and socioeconomic backgrounds.

A second main topic was *prevention.* Prevention was viewed as an attitude as well as a specific set of skills. Discussion ensued on: (a) the importance of prevention activities on both systems and individual/group levels, and (b) the value of stressing individual strengths and positive coping skills in prevention settings. A clear recommendation was formulated to *advocate that prevention concepts and experiences be integrated into graduate level training.* There was clear concensus that this be done, at the very least, for clinical child programs and also some strong sentiment that prevention activities be promoted in *all* clinical training programs.

Graduate level *assessment* constituted the third and most lengthy area of discussion. The group recognized the impossibility of providing students with hands-on experience with *every* test, instrument, or assessment approach, particularly in the face of an ever expanding armamentarium of tool and techniques. Rather, the group advocated that assessment be viewed as a process that requires *psychological understanding* of the child and the systems that affect the child (e.g., school, family, etc.). An empirical, hypothesis generating approach was stressed and clearly differentiated from a technician or *cookbook* approach to assessment. The following points represent the group's recommendations for *"minimal" considerations that should be integrated into graduate-level assessment training:*

1. Students should be familiarized with assessment instruments that exist for children of different ages (0 -18 years).
2. Students should be familiarized with multiple and varied methods of assessment (e.g., interviews, observations, standardized tests, etc.).
3. An appreciation of the special considerations involved in assessing children of minority backgrounds should be provided.
4. A thorough understanding and appreciation of psychometric theory should be provided, so that trainees can critically evaluate existing assessment instruments, and new measures as they are developed.
5. The importance of integrating information obtained from various sources should be recognized.
6. An awareness of the systems within which the child functions, and how these systems interact with the assessment process, should be provided (e.g., sensitivity in terms of what information *to obtain* on a child, and with whom the information may be *shared*). Related to this is an appreciation of the special ethical considerations one faces in the child assessment area.

The last main area of discussion was *treatment/consultation.* The group recognized that treatment and consultation were related (but require different areas of expertise) and felt that both were critical to graduate level training. Areas that were stressed included the importance of integrating assessment and treatment (each should impact upon the other) and that treatment should also consider the child's social system.

Perhaps the most general observation that was made regarding training students in the assessment and therapy areas was that we really wish to promote a critical attitude in students, so that they may independently evaluate the validity and utility of various assessment procedures and treatment approaches. This, in many ways, strongly supports the strength and utility of the scientist-practitioner model.

Summary of Concurrent Small Group Discussions on Curriculum Issues Internship Level

A.J. Finch, Jr.
Medical University of South Carolina

The Friday morning discussion of internship training in clinical child psychology focused on two broad and elementary areas. The first of these had to do with what constitutes an internship. The group felt that an internship should offer a broad based group of experiences in the general areas of assessment, treatment, and consultation. In addition, client populations should include both adults and children. In fact, one recommendation from this group was that *all* interns receive experiences with both adults and children. Once this minimal experience is obtained, the individual would be free to specialize with either population.

An internship should generally take place in a multidisciplinary setting which provides the intern with the opportunity to receive supervision from, and interact with, a wide variety of disciplines, thus, increasing the intern's ability to interact successfully with other professionals.

Internships should be developmental in nature, initially, the intern's work should be closely supervised and gradually the amount of freedom and responsibility should be increased. To facilitate this developmental sequence, each intern should be provided a primary supervisor to track his/her development during the internship with other supervision being provided by others with various areas of expertise.

Internships should be individually tailored to meet the needs of each incoming intern, but should have the flexibility and freedom to emphasize those aspects of the program that are unique. Thus, an individualized training plan will need to be developed for each intern.

Internships have the unique opportunity of bringing together individuals from a wide number of university backgrounds. In order to increase the learning opportunities for the intern, internships should facilitate the development of a sense of cohesive group cooperation among the interns.

Each internship should provide a number of core experiences in the area of assessment, treatment, and consultation. However, the exact nature of these experiences could not be determined by this group due to time consideration; this group again recommends the establishment of a task force to determine curriculum and other training issues in clinical child psychology internship programs.

The second major group of items discussed centered around *who* is an intern. Minimum preparation for an internship was discussed again without complete resolution. However, certain requirements were seen as necessary; (1) all interns should be from regionally accredited coherent doctoral programs in psychology; and, (2) in addition, the internship program should be considered a post clerkship, post practicum and post externship level training program. The group again discussed the minimum number of hours of practicum and supervised experience necessary for entry into an internship, but consensus could not be reached.

Some additional discussion centered around the issue of what to call an intern. The problems with the term *intern* in a medical settings were discussed with a suggestion that the individual be called a *resident*. Again, no specific recommendations were made in this area.

In conclusion, the following recommendations from this discussion group are as follow:

1. All psychology interns should receive experience in both adult and child treatment, assessment, and consulation.
2. All interns should be from regionally accredited coherent programs in psychology.
3. A task force should be formed to establish the nature of the clinical child psychology internship training.

Summary of Concurrent Small Group Discussion of Curriculum Issues Postdoctoral/Continuing Education Level

Diane J. Willis
Oklahoma Health Sciences Center

As we focused on the topics of continuing education and postdoctoral training following the position papers on curriculum issues, we quickly concurred on several points.

Since many states do not have continuing education requirements for continued licensure in psychology, we endorse the following resolutions:

1. Whereas, there is a wide range of backgrounds of preparation for people functioning as child psychologists and, whereas, there continues to be burgeoning knowledge in the field of significant relevance to clinical child psychologists, we recommend that continuing education be considered an ethical responsibility of all clinical child psychologists. In particular, assessment, treatment, consultation, and prevention are areas needing ongoing professional renewal.
2. We urge that all states adopt some minimum requirement for continuing education as a prerequisite to licensure and professional practice in clinical child psychology.

Since the content, relevance, and practicality of the multiplicity of continuing education workshops advertised in the APA *Monitor* are unknown, we offer the following resolution:

3. We recommend that the Section 1 form a task force to establish and publish criteria for endorsement of continuing education offerings in areas relevant to clinical child psychology.

It was suggested that the *Journal of Clinical Child Psychology* advertise continuing education workshops that meet the above criteria. Additionally, Section 1 might routinely offer a preconvention institute-workshop at APA. We suggest that the Section 1 survey topics of interest to clinical child psychologists (via the *Journal*). However, we suggest that the institute program address such topics as assessment, treatment, consultation, prevention, and family-school-community issues as they relate to children, youth, and families (the Divisions and Sections in APA interested in children might work out a cooperative arrangement in planning these institutes).

In regard to postdoctoral training, we proposed the following resolutions:

4. We recommend that the Section 1 establish a task force and conduct a survey of current postgraduate programming in clinical child psychology and establish guidelines for postdoctoral programming. These guidelines should include specification of levels and types of supervision.

Recognizing that the Hilton Head conferees will propose several recommendations and resolutions, we discussed implementation ideas. We felt it to be imperative to have appropriate representation in the governance structure of APA so that our ideas and suggestions have a chance of being implemented. Therefore, we propose:

5. That the Section 1 Executive Committee exert effort to gain representation for clinical child psychologists on the APA Education and Training Board and subcommittees dealing with continuing education.

While we punted on specific recommendations relevant to postdoctoral training, we did agree that clinical child psychologists ought to engage in at least one year of appropriate postdoctoral programming; thus, we purpose resolution 6:

6. We strongly suggest that clinical child psychologists engage in at least one year of appropriate postdoctoral programming.

Models of Training

Models of Clinical Child Psychology Training
Introduction

James H. Johnson[1]
University of Florida

While a major purpose of the present conference is to delineate necessary guidelines for programs offering training in the clinical child area (Tuma, 1982), it is important to note that there are existing programs with established track records in training psychologists to work with children. As these programs differ both in terms of specific program requirements and the context within which clinical child psychology training is offered, much can be learned from the experiences of those actively involved in such training.

At the predoctoral level, Roberts (1982) has identified four basic models of clinical child training. The most common of these involves subspecialty training within the structure of a general clinical psychology program where students specialize in the child area only after completing coursework in basic psychology and receiving the general clinical training required of all clinical students. Examples of such programs include those at the University of Alabama, Auburn, University of Florida, University of Miami (Florida), Michigan State University, University of Minnesota, Purdue University, Southern Illinois University, and Virginia Commonwealth University, among others. The three other models that Roberts has described are represented by the program offered within the Institute of Clinical Psychology at the University of Virginia (which historically has been identified with training in the combined areas of clinical child and school psychology), the program at the University of Washington (specialty training apart from the structure of the general clinical program), and the program at Ohio State, (specialty training within a program based in the developmental area). In the present session, we will consider each of these four models of training in detail as each would appear to represent a viable program structure through which curriculum related recommendations of the conference might be implemented.

We are fortunate to have with us four individuals who have been closely identified with the development of these training models. These include Dr. Marilyn T. Erickson of Virginia Commonwealth University, who will consider clinical child training within the general clinical psychology program, Dr. Richard R. Abidin, who is director of the program at the University of Virginia, Dr. Martha A. Perry, developer of the program at the University of Washington, and Dr. Felicisima C. Serafica, who, along with Dr. Charles Wenar, has been instrumental in the development of the clinical child psychology program at The Ohio State University.

Each of these participants will describe the nature of their training program, comment on the philosophy of training that led to the development of their particular program, discuss issues involved in implementing and conducting the program, and, where possible, provide information regarding students graduating from the program. This information should provide a foundation for considering the commonalities among these programs and the unique advantages of each in the small group sessions to follow this presentation.

[1]Chair of section Models of Clinical Child Training

References

Roberts, M.C. (1982). Clinical-child psychology programs: Where and what are they? *Journal of Clinical Child Psychology, 11,* 13-21.

Tuma, J.M. (1982). Proposal for a national conference on professional preparation of clinical child psychologists. *Journal of Clinical Child Psychology, 11,* 3-7.

Clinical Child Psychology Training in the Context of a General Clinical Psychology Program

Marilyn T. Erickson
Virginia Commonwealth University

Children have repeatedly been designated as an underserved population as far as mental health services are concerned (National Institute of Mental Health, 1983). There are two principal ways that children are underserved. One is that there are inadequate numbers of clinical psychologists to provide the necessary services, and the other is that there are clinical psychologists who provide services that are inadequate and/or of poor quality. Thus, our training programs should have at least two goals. One is to offer appropriate predoctoral training to adequate numbers of clinical psychologists who wish to offer services to children, youth, and families, and the other is to do a better job of protecting children and families from inadequately trained practitioners by communicating our concerns to the APA accreditation committee and to state licensing Boards and by creating training opportunities for inadequately trained psychologists to acquire the necessary skills.

As is obvious from the various training models being presented in this symposium, clinical psychology has no tradition for providing training for those who will deliver services to children, youth, and families. In comparison, about 25 years ago, psychiatry adopted a model that involves two years of training with adults followed by two years of training with children and families. Our lack of training standards has not gone unnoticed (Cass, 1974), and several proposals for programs have been presented (Carboy & Curley, 1976; Routh, 1977; Wohlford, 1978). Until recently, however, no plan for training standards in clinical child psychology has been adopted. Several years ago, Division 37 formed a committee to examine this issue, and a set of guidelines for training psychologists to work with children, youth, and families, was developed and adopted by Division 37 (Roberts, Erickson, & Tuma, 1985) (see Appendix E). These guidelines have been circulated to other relevant APA Divisions for critical review and are being presented during this Conference.

APA accreditation guidelines give the impression that training throughout the developmental range is the norm, but my experiences as a site visitor indicate that training in normal and abnormal lifespan development is a rare exception rather than the rule. Only about half of the APA approved programs in clinical psychology have any didactic requirements related to children, youth, and families.

We have probably not provided appropriate training for clinical child psychologists for a broad range of reasons. Our society has tended to depreciate the importance of children and, mirroring society, APA has, until recently, shown a lack of commitment to children as evidenced by the lack of attention to children in the accreditation criteria and no standing committee devoted to children, youth, and families, within APA's administrative structure. I would like to insert parenthetically here that I have just completed a three year term on APA's Board of Social and Ethical Responsibility (BSERP), and during that time served on the Task Force for Children, Youth, and Families. The Task Force recommended that APA create a standing committee on children, youth, and families, under BSERP. The other APA boards and committees have been divided in their support; the principal reasons against support for the standing committees are that children are not APA members and that APA doesn't have enough money. The recommendation for an APA standing committee on children, youth, and families will appear on the agenda of the APA Council of Representatives in August, 1985. This committee could have a significant role in implementing the recommendations that we make at this conference. (Council approved the Committee on Children, Youth and Families in August, 1985.)

In a number of ways, training in clinical child psychology is where adult clinical psychology was a generation or two ago. There are probably still a significant number of APA approved clinical psychology programs that offer virtually no didactic courses related to children, youth, and families, and whose students are still advised to get their children, youth, and family experience in practicum and internship sites. At the other end of the continuum, we also have more than a few programs that provide exemplary training. In between these two ex-

Table 1. *Four Year Curriculum of the Clinical Psychology Program Including the Child Track Course*

Fall		Spring		Summer		Credits
		Year 1				
*Statistics	3	*Research Design	3	**Practicum	2	
**Principles Psychological Assessment	1	**Introduction Practicum	3	*Learning	3	
**Assessment Human Intelligence	2	***Child Assessment	3			
**Introduction Clinical Psychology	3	***Child Psychopathology	3			
**Psychopathology (Adult)	3					
	12		12		5	29
		Year 2				
**Theories of Counselling and Psychotherapy	3	*Ethics and Professional Issues	2	**Practicum	2	
				*Biological Basis	3	
***Child Behavior Therapy	3	**Assessment Personality				
**Thesis	3	**Personality theory	3			
**Practicum	2	*Thesis	3			
		**Practicum	2			
	11		13		5	29
		Year 3				
*Social Psychology	3	***Family Therapy	3			
***Developmental Processes	3	Elective	3			
***Child Psychotherapy	3	Elective	3			
**Practicum	2	**Practicum	2			
	11		11			22
		Year 4				
*Dissertation	6	*Dissertation	6			
***Pediatric Psychology	3	Elective	3			
Elective	3	Elective	3			
	12		12			24
						104

* = Department requirement
** = Clinical core requirement
*** = Child Track requirement

tremes are most of our programs; they are primarily adult-oriented and have only one or a few clinical child faculty members.

During the past twenty-four years, I have been training clinical child psychologists in the context of general, or adult-oriented, clinical psychology programs. I would like to share with you the structure of our current program at Virginia Commonwealth University, some of the problems that have arisen during the development of the training program, and some ideas that I would like to suggest for the improvement of clinical psychology training.

Our clinical psychology program can be conceptualized as having three levels. The first, or foundation level, includes the basic areas of psychology as described in the APA accreditation criteria: statistics and research design, ethics, history, biological basic, learning, social, and individual differences. The second level is the clinical psychology core and includes courses in introduction to clinical psychology, introduction to practicum, tests and measurements, intelligence and personality assessment, personality theory, psychopathology (adult), and a survey course on counseling and psychotherapy. The third level includes the child track courses which are developmental processes, child assessment, child psychopathology, child psychotherapy, child behavior therapy, pediatric psychology (our most recent addition), and family therapy. Table 1 presents the four year curriculum of the clinical psychology program including the child track courses.

One important factor to note in Table 1 is that we have placed two child track courses in the first year. This placement has at least two goals. One is to provide minimal skills for starting child practicum at the end of the first year, and the other is to get the students affiliated with the track early in their graduate education. In our program, the first year of practicum is spent in our own Center for Psychological Services and Development and is supervised by our own faculty. The second year is spent in one or two commnunity placements that are chosen on the basis of the students' interests and training needs. Of the two years or six blocks of practicum, approximately half are devoted to clinical child activity and half to adult clinical activity.

The child track was developed with two core faculty members; we have recently been able to add a third one. In any one year, including the summer, we teach a total of three child track graduate courses, and three practicum courses. Two of the child track courses (child assessment and child psychopathology) are offered every year. The three therapy/intervention courses (child psychotherapy, child behavior therapy, and pediatric psychology) are offered sequentially every three years. Each of the three faculty members, thus, has a half-time formal teaching commitment to the child track. The remainder of our teaching is focused on undergraduate courses or other graduate courses. With three faculty members, we are able to cover child practicum both semesters and the summer. The developmental processes course is taught by one of our general experimental psychology faculty members and the family therapy course is taught by a clinical psychologist on our counseling psychology faculty.

Our clinical program admits approximately 12 students per year; during the admission process we attempt to select 4 of the 12 students as being strongly interested in the child track. There is, thus, some control of numbers during the admissions process. In practice, however, that number has ranged from 3 to 6 by the second semester of the first year. A small number of *advanced* non-child track students take the child assessment and child psychopathology courses prior to internship. The child therapy/intervention courses are offered only to students who have had the child assessment and child psychopathology courses. While the child assessment course is offered only to graduate students in the APA-approved clinical or counseling psychology programs, the child psychopathology course is available to any graduate student.

Interestingly, the child track has not produced clinical PhD's who are homogeneous with respect to their interests and activities. About a quarter of them are pursuing academic careers; the remainder are delivering services to children, adolescents, families, or schools, in community agencies. In recent years, an increasing number have become interested in children with medical and developmental problems.

The success of the child track within the clinical program has created some problems. In comparison with the other tracks in the program, the child track has attracted the most attention, probably because students generally join it early and have continuous involvement with it through courses and/or practicum and/or research throughout the four years. The students have tended to develop strong affiliations with the track and among themselves; younger students frequently obtain assistance and mentoring from the more advanced students. This cohesion and identity are not always viewed positively. In addition, there have been some attempts to withdraw the already minimal exposure to child issues in the core clinical curriculum. For example, when the course in child assessment was put into the curriculum, it was initially seen as an opportunity to decrease attention to children in the intelligence testing course. Also, when the course in child psychopathology was added, the professor teaching the required psychopathology course wanted to delete the material related to children in his course.

As I review my experiences in several doctoral programs and an internship setting, I have become convinced that PhD clinical psychology programs should be required to provide at least some training across the entire lifespan. Regardless of one's professional speciality, adult or child, there are frequent occasions when the therapist's knowledge of other age groups may be critical. Many adults have children in their lives, and, of course, children always have one or more adults in their lives. Knowledge of lifespan development would seem to be especially important when family therapy is the chosen intervention, and yet there are many practicing family therapists who have had no training with children. Internships are continuing to provide clinical child experiences to students who have no or minimal didactic background in the child area. These practices are a disservice to children, and we should be able to correct them.

There are really two major training issues that I have addressed. The first is "What should be the content of a doctoral program that plans to train clinical child psychologists?" I have discussed that question in the context of our own training program. The second is "What should be the content of a doctoral program that trains "generic" clinical psychologists?" My recommendation is that all clinical psychology programs should be required to provide training in normal development, assessment, and psychopathology across the lifespan. In other words, I believe that all clinical psychologists ought to be able to make a valid judgment about the psychological normality or abnormality of persons of any age. I view specialization as being related to treatment or intervention with particular developmental groups, such as children, adolescents, adults, and the elderly. Most community programs are already set up along developmental lines, and private practitioners often identify themselves as having a developmental specialty. I believe that this model of training may well be one that is optimally cost effective for our clients.

References

Cass, L. (1974). The training of clinical child psychologists. In G.J. Williams & S. Gordon (Eds.), *Clinical child psychology: Current practices and future perspectives* (pp. 463-482). New York: Behavioral Publications.

Carboy, J.J., & Curley, J.F. (1976). A new training model: Professional child psychology. *Psychology in the Schools, 13,* 153-156.

National Institute of Mental Health. (1983). *Announcement: Mental health clinical training in child mental health, geriatric mental health, and support for minority and disadvantaged students for fiscal year 1984.* Washington, DC: author.

Roberts, M., Erickson, M.T., & Tuma, J.M. (1985). Addressing the needs: Guidelines for training psychologists to work with children, youth, and families. *Journal of Clinical Child Psychology, 14,* 70-79.

Routh, D.K. (1977). What is a clinical child psychologist? *The Clinical Psychologist, 30,* 23-25.

Wohlford, P. (1978). A challenge to clinical psychology: Better training to serve children. *Journal of Clinical Child Psychology, 7,* 89-90.

A Speciality Program for Clinical Child Psychology Training: The Washington Model

Martha A. Perry, Ph.D.

In recent years, there has been a growing interest in clinical child psychology and this interest has led to considerable review and discussion of training for the field. This conference, in fact, came from the recognition that clinical child psychology training is unique and merits careful consideration. Stimulated, in part, by increased national interest in children, this growing concern also derives from the expanded role of psychologists in traditional child treatment settings and the expansion of psychologists' roles into new settings. Young people entering the field, besides being interested in and committed to work with children, are emphasizing the conviction that the formative years in a child's life are crucial to successful intervention and they are requesting graduate training programs that combine child or developmental psychology and the clinician's interest in pathology and knowledge of behavior change.

There are, as we have reviewed throughout this conference and are emphasizing in this panel today, a number of models of clinical child psychology training. These models are all of importance and may serve different needs in the field. The model which I will discuss is one that we use at the University of Washington. Our approach trains students in clinical child psychology as a specialty at the predoctoral level. Developed in 1972, we now have a twelve year history to evaluate.

Our choice to go with a program of early specialization was based on several premises. First, there are so many aspects of a child's functioning and such a multiplicity of child problems that must be understood by the professional treating the child, that one must start early to get a complete background. In addition, a truly child-oriented approach necessitates an approach that is different from that taken toward adults. A developmental approach to problems is unique and not simply a downward extention of adult pathology and psychotherapy. The treatment of children involves not just the child's problem, but a more complete understanding of the family and other child milieus than is usually considered necessary for adult treatment. The issues of rights, ethics, responsibilities, and values are also critical in this field. It is important to begin early with the philosophy, approaches, and content that form the basis of the field.

Undergraduates preparing for graduate school are increasingly sophisticated about the professional options open to them, and many have already had extensive field experience in working with children. They are prepared to make knowledgeable career decisions and are ready to begin to work toward their goals upon entering graduate school. If their undergraduate and graduate programs also provide strong basic psychology training, then a clinical child psychology speciality may be very appropriate for students who can state early in their careers their interest in specializing in work with children.

Philosophy and Issues

Several philosophical stances have guided the program's development. First, we are strongly committed to a model emphasizing both developmental and clinical foundations. Specifically, the belief is that work with children will be effective and theoretical knowledge will advance only if (a) the development of the child and family within their various contexts is throughly understood, and (b) a unique clinical approach is adopted that incorporates this understanding of development. These tenets led us to include coursework in the curriculum from both the developmental and clinical psychology course offerings and to develop new courses specifically directed toward assessment and treatment of children and families.

A second commitment is to a scientist-practioner model, consistent with the department's general clinical training program. For this model to really work, it must be actively taught and modeled. Too often, students are given clinical and research experiences that are never integrated and they fail to view clinical work as an inquiry process analogous to experimental inquiry. Thus, course work was developed to teach a scientist-practitioner philosophy and to provide an opportunity for students to integrate their clinical and research experiences.

Another basic stance is that the clinical child psychologist's role is no longer limited to dealing with the child's intelligence and emotional adjustment. Many new roles are recognized for professionals in the field. Thus, in our program, we have sought to introduce the variety of work settings and their professional opportunities, as well as to offer courses that expand students' views about children and their problems. We have not offered further specialization, such as pediatric psychology, developmental disabilities, or others. Rather, we seek to expose students to these possibilities and offer optional courses and experiences, as well as direct them to appropriate internships should they seek to specialize further.

Finally, we have grounded the program philosophy in an ecological model (Bronfenbrenner, Garbarino, & others) in which there is a focused examination of the multiple levels of impact that affect both the child and the family. Such a model encourages us to take the broader look at the family and community as well as to attend to preventions and early intervention.

Organization of the Program

The clinical child psychology program is recognized by the Department of Psychology at the University of Washington as a specialty, closely allied, however, the general clinical psychology training program. This independent status is in part a result of the development of the program as a joint effort of the clinical and developmental psychology programs. The clinical child program functions in many ways quite autonomously. Graduate student application and selection is handled by the speciality area, as is curriculum development and student practicum placement. Faculty members are clearly identified as clinical child, although in all cases, the faculty participate in other programs as well (clinical, developmental, community psychology). Students, likewise, are clearly identified and efforts are made, both formally and informally, to offer a close community atmosphere in order to provide support and identity. We are not an exclusive club, however. Our curriculum takes advantage of the breadth of clinical courses, as well as general departmental offerings. Further, not only are the child core and seminar courses available to any clinical student who wishes to take them, but many are taken by students from other departments, such as education and nursing.

As an outgrowth of our focus on understanding development, our ties with developmental psychology have been strong. We have required our clinical child students to minor in developmental psychology, and nearly all students have a developmental psychologist as a member of their supervisory committee of their general examination and their dissertation. Over the years, several developmental faculty have been closely associated with the clinical child psychology program. In fact, currently a developmental psychologist is coordinating the program.

Embedded within our program has been another model of training, one which I might add, has been somewhat controversial. We have offered a unique program for developmental psychology students: a minor in clinical child psychology. The focus of this program has been on the theoretical core and on the applied area of assessment. A number of these students have taken essentially a double major at the university, while some have expanded their training at the post-doctoral level. A few developmental students have not specifically used their clinical training, but perhaps bring a broader understanding of children to the work that they do. This dual approach I feel has been successful but has raised some particular issues. One issue has to do with selection of students and "backdoor" entry. Another has to do with second class citizen status as perceived by these students. One graduate, responding to an evaluation questionnaire, noted that after her second year of post-doctoral internship and now that she has a job, she has finally escaped the stigma of being "developmental." Finally, there have been some practical issues of developmental students overloading the system, since we cannot predict or control the number of students needing supervision at one time.

The Program

Over the course of twelve years, a program goes through a process of development, a period of maturation, and gradual evolution. In 1978, I published an article in *Professional Psychology* describing our development and detailing the program. Reading that article now, I recognize the changes, not so much in philosophy, but in the specific curriculum to carry out the philosophy. This is a function of experience and feedback from students (which is regularly solicited) and of changes in number and orientations of faculty members who are associated with the program. The program started with one faculty member. At one point, there were six faculty (three child clinical, one clinical, and two developmental) associated with the program. Currently, there are four with a fifth to be hired.

Originally, the curriculum offerings were small, limited to a few core courses, and we relied heavily on courses from other areas to supplement the program. There was emphasis on flexibility, small group discussions, and group support, as well as extensive supervision and faculty contact for individual projects and interests.

A core course which we have always considered essential is one which is simply labeled Child Clinical Psychology and which students take in their first quarter. The purpose of this course might be characterized as orientation and philosophical. It is not a content course, but rather seeks to set a scene, to deal with issues, ethics, and values, to explore implications of a scientist-practitioner model, to present an ecological model. I feel it is one of the most significant courses in the curriculum. In evaluative feedback with an open-ended question of which four courses were most important in training, graduates typically do not mention this course, but I feel that their attitudes have become so incorporated in their way of thinking that graduates no longer identify the course *per se* as the source of those attitudes.

As the program has grown we have, of necessity, become a bit more formal, although we try to retain flexibility and group support. In the past several years, we have put considerable effort into a thoughtful coordination of the curriculum and as a result of extensive discussion, have moved toward an explicit competency-based model of training. This has involved a specification of the knowledge, clinical, and research competencies needed by the clinical child psychologist of the 1980's and the establishment of specific means for students to acquire and demonstrate those competencies. Accordingly, curricular elements have been grouped under the broad general competency areas of ethical and professional issues, child psychopathology, assessment, treatment, systems, development, and research. Necessary general clinical competencies, as well as general psychological competencies, have also been outlined. Core courses ensure that students will aquire general competencies that are deemed essential. Beyond this, there is considerable flexibility which allows students to tailor their training to their own individual goals and interests. For example, students interested in pediatric psychology can choose to take a heavier load of biologically based courses, can take seminars relevant to pediatric psychology, and can select practicum placements in medical/pediatric settings. A student interested in family work can take a heavier course load of family-oriented courses, can select family cases in the clinical methods course, and can choose a clinical practicum in a family setting.

Record of Achievement

With a twelve year history, we can now look at our program and evaluate it, not on how conceptually neat the package looks, but on how well it has done its job. I recently surveyed the graduates and can speak from that viewpoint. The clinical child program awarded its first doctorate in 1976 and has awarded a total of 17 PhD's. In addition, thirteen developmental students have graduated with minors in clinical child psychology. All but two of the 24 graduated and current majors who have taken internships have chosen primarily child-oriented internships. Ten of the thirteen minors have taken either pre-doctoral or post-doctoral internships, all of which have been primarily child-oriented. The first jobs for thirteen of the majors have been child-oriented: the first jobs for all minors were child-oriented. Clearly, these students have predominantly chosen to follow their specialty. Two of the majors did change their orientation during the time of their training, and they, more than the others, commented in evaluation that the program did not place enough emphasis on adult pathology and treatment. One student, from the beginning, made a point of preparing to work with both children and adults, and, in fact, currently has a half-time child research position and a half-time adult mental health position.

The students' experience in getting internships has been very good, with most students receiving an offer from either their first or second choice. Formal and informal feedback received from agencies at which our students have interned has been uniformly good to excellent. Our students are seen as theoretically and conceptually sophisticated, well-trained clinically, and personally mature. Students and trainers, alike, recognize our program's strengths in assessment, research, and professional and ethical issues. We also recognize our relative weaknesses in breadth of theorethical approaches and treatment experiences. These weak areas have been supplemented by the internships, and we are addressing them within our program as well.

Our goal of providing a scientist-practitioner model can be assessed by looking at the types of jobs that students have taken. One graduate has an academic position in a psychology department, six have academic positions in medical departments, five have clinical research positions, seven have clinical positions in public or private agencies. Two of the majors and six of the minors have taken post-doctoral training. All of the graduates who responded to the questionnaire report that they felt adequately prepared for their first job.

Issues

I would like to underscore a number of issues that we have faced in program development. One has been the tendency to want to do everything. This may come from faculty who have vested interests in their pet approaches and/or research areas and who wish to require yet another course. It may also come from students, who, even if not all courses are required, overload their plates in the appealing smorgasboard provided by a rich set of offerings. An outgrowth of this is that students may take an inordinate amount of time to complete their degrees.

Another issue has to do with the coordination and/or integration of the clinical child psychology program with the general clinical program. In our program, the clinical child faculty have sought to maintain autonomy for specific functions, in particular for curriculum development, graduate student selection, and student guidance regarding their own course schedules and practicum experiences. Beyond these areas, we seek to coordinate wherever possible. The amount of coordination varies depending on the administrative structure and the particular emphasis and requirements of the general clinical program at any point in time. Considerable discussion is necessary to work out these issues.

Finally, I repeat the issue of the training of developmental students in clinical child psychology foundations. Beyond the problems of stigma noted earlier are problems of certification. It is increasing difficult for these students to find appropriate internships and post-doctoral experiences because they have not had "certified" pre-doctoral training. Because these students have been handicapped in their professional development, our program is moving away from encouraging developmental psychology graduate students to supplement their programs with clinical training.

Despite some of the growing pains that the evolving clinical child psychology program at the University of Washington has experienced, we feel satisfied that the program has more than satisfactorily served the needs of most of its students of the past twelve years. A few quotes from the graduates' evaluations provide a summary: "Given the diversity of job possibilities for a clinical child PhD, no program would include *all* training necessities." It is "rich with opportunities and flexible enough to allow one to make use of the most personally relevant opportunities." "While there are many aspects of the field of clinical psychology as a mental health profession that I feel dissatisfied and frustrated about, I feel positive about the UW program in particular and know of no program that I would rather have attended."

The Virginia Model of Combined School Clinical Child Psychology Training

Richard R. Abidin
University of Virginia

For 15 years, the University of Virginia has been educating school/clinical child psychologists in a combined program. In 1976, our program was accredited by the American Psychological Association in the category of Combined Scientific Professional Psychology. This accreditation, according to the APA Accreditation Committee, recognizes that our program educates psychologists to serve as school psychologists and clinical child psychologists. While our graduates have a child focus, they are generically trained clinical psychologists. We start with the premise that we are educating psychologists so that they will possess a generic core of both psychological knowledge and clinical skills. Further, it is our belief that many of these skills are held in common with all other types of psychologists dedicated to service delivery and to research in professional psychological practice. I have, for many years, personally expressed a concern, which I am sure is shared by many others, namely, that, all too often, psychology interest groups, licensing boards, and other sanctioners of psychological practice, focus on the titles or differences in the education of psychologists versus the commonality of generic skills and knowledge. This focus, all too often, creates unnecessary barriers to the delivery of clinical services to the public. All too often, the *True Believers* work to protect titles and erect barriers with no evidence to support their claim that only psychologists educated in a given program with a given title can do certain work. Before I continue, I must acknowledge one of my own prejudices, or if you will, *True Beliefs;* that is, when I speak of a psychologist I mean a doctorally educated individual.

Our focus on the generic core, we believe, ensures that our students will be competent to serve as psychologists in a variety of settings with a minimum of additional experience and supervision. The reality of the service delivery market place is such that no program or graduate student can predict the exact nature of the problems, populations, and skills which the graduate clinical psychologist will face. The wide diversity of initial position which our graduates fill will be described later.

Given the history of professional psychology during the past 30 years, it is clear that professional education and practice is in a continual state of change. New labels are constantly being created to describe new interest groups, specialties, subspecialties, and microspecialties. The problem of barriers has been exacerbated by, and is in part the result of, the American Psychological Association's (APA) system of specialty level versus generic psychology accreditation (American Psychological Association, 1983). Thus, clinical psychology must be viewed as a specialty when compared to industrial organizational psychology, and clinical child psychology, logically, may be viewed as a subspecialty. Clinical Child Psychologists interested in the area of neuropsychology then become microspecialists. Despite APA's focus on specialty accreditation, it is clear that graduates of a variety of accredited programs migrate from one specialty area to the next (VandenBos, Stapp, & Kilburg, 1981). These migrations from one specialty field to another appear to take place without any adverse affect upon the public (Schneider, 1981, in a follow-up report of NIMH-supported graduates from a variety of APA accredited clinical, counseling, and school programs). He concluded that these individuals seem to possess valuable knowledge and skills which were useful in a wide range of settings, such as mental health clinics, hospital facilities, and educational systems. It appears that it may now be time to challenge the belief that only individuals from psychology programs with a given label are suitable practitioners of professional practice in a given setting. It may be time for us to ask the following question: *How much difference is there among well-educated psychologists who hold the title clinical child psychologist, pediatric psychologist, school psychologist, or developmental psychologist?*

During my 10 years of experience on the Virginia Board of Psychology, I had the opportunity to review the transcripts, internships, vitae, examination results, and to participate in the personal interviews of psychologists from PhD programs across the nation. From this experience I have concluded that among APA accredited programs the within-program variance is just as great as the between-program variance on matters of courses, practica, supervision, internship, and the intellectual and professional competence of students. While there are some differences in the way psychologists practice in different settings, and there are certain domains of knowledge which are more useful in one setting over another, these differences are relatively minor when compared to the commonality of knowledge and skills which all well educated professional psychologists possess.

Given that no one has defined the generic knowledge and clinical skills of a professional psychologists in any but the grossest manner, we must, therefore, acknowledge the fact that it is difficult to define the *unique knowledge and skill* needed for any given specialty training. If we are concerned with adequate preparation to function as a clinical child psychologist, we must define the unique knowledge, skills, and experiences which are not part of generic training in counseling, clinical, school, or developmental psychology. It appears logical therefore, that we must devote at least some of our thinking and energy to defining the generic core. How else will we know what is unique? In this regard we may want to consider the results of the 1983 ETS study *Job Analysis of Licensed Psychologists in the United States and Canada* (Rosenfeld, Shimberg, & Thornton), which examined the responsibilities, knowledge, and techniques which were used by clinical, school, and counseling psychologists. It was not surprising to me that there was extensive overlap in terms of the amount of time spent in the same basic procedures and the perceived importance of the activities to the various *types* of psychologists. The clinical psychologist, IO psychologist or school psychologist all must interview people, review records, formulate hypotheses, select assessment strategies and instruments. These are all generic psychology skills relative to the process of defining problems and developing psychological understandings. Likewise, in terms of intervention one might ask how unique are the knowledge and skills required to perform a given service. For example, how much difference is there in the process of consulting with physicians, teachers, parents, or employers? Certainly, there is some situation specific information; however, given the intelligence and interest of students, this can be acquired by independent reading, while on practica, and on internship. Further, the generic research skills of psychologists are defined by knowledge of statistics, design, and by practice in reasoning out relationships and hypotheses. I would suggest that it doesn't matter for competent performance if the variables relate to school performance, job performance, or social skills.

It also appears reasonable, while we are defining the different components which make up generic clinical knowledge and skill versus subspecialty knowledge and skills, that we recognize that these components, of themselves, do not imply a heirarchical arrangement of levels of training experiences such that all subspecialty knowledge and skills are acquired at the internship or post-doctoral levels. It would also appear reasonable to recognize that students' interest, practica, and internship experience will shape the students' development in relation to any specialization throughout their education.

Acknowledging the above issues as a context for considering the endeavor of training clinical psychologists, and in the absence of any operationally defined national standards pertaining to specific generic knowledge and skills, the University of Virginia, like other institutions, has attempted to define the needed generic knowledge and clinical skill base of a clinical psychologist. The following section of this paper will attempt to describe our five-year full time program of study in combined school/clinical child psychology which we view as an integration of generic profession psychology with "specialty" training. The following description is divided into two parts, the first being our assumption, and the second, an overview of the core curriculum. In providing this description, it is hoped that others will see ways in which we can improve our program, and, hopefully, see the merit of integrating both generic and specialty training during the course of a student's graduate education.

Assumptions

1. Professional practice is built upon an equal foundation of generic psychological knowledge and generic clinical skill. The failure to attend adequately to either area will create a deficiency in the student's ultimate level of functioning.
2. Psychology is an empirical data-oriented science and profession, and therefore, knowledge of methods of research and research experiences are essential to all psychologists in order for them to conduct research, consume research, and function as scientifically-based practitioners.
3. Clinical skills, like wisdom, accrues over time and, therefore, students must begin *learning about, observing,* and *practicing* clinical skills from the first week they begin their graduate studies. The internship is not the time to learn clinical skills and knowledge, but to refine them to a level which will insure competent, independent practice, which in most states is permitted at the end of the internship experience, or shortly thereafter.

4. Clinical psychologists must be skilled in developing *psychological understanding*. Problem definition, diagnosis, assessment, and evaluation are but some of the terms used when psychologists try to develop a psychological understanding of an individual, situation, or social system. Psychological assessment and evaluation, using a broad range of methods and techniques, must be seen as a foundational clinical skill.
5. Clinical psychologists must possess a wide range of problem-solving skills (intervention techniques and therapeutic approaches), but, most importantly, they must recognize the role of invention and flexibility when faced with the uniqueness of a given individual and of a given situation.
6. Graduate programs in clinical psychology should educate *psychologists,* not behavioral therapists, rationale emotive therapists, family therapists, etc., nor should they educate neuropsychologists, clinical child psychologists, pediatric school psychologists, etc. The fact is that clinical *psychologists* will use different techniques and serve different populations in different settings.

Curriculum

I. *Practica and Research*

(a) All students must be involved in a minimum of eight hours of research activity and eight hours of clinical practice every week for the first four years of their program. All practica are supervised by either full-time faculty or part-time institute faculty who monitor the student's skill development. Typically, students will exceed these levels of involvement, particularly during their fourth year.

(b) All students must complete a masters project and a doctoral dissertation. While not working on their own projects, they work as part of a research team which is focused on a clinical problem or population.

(c) *Pre-internship Clinical Practica* (A Typical Four-Year Practica Sequence): *First year* — public school setting, working with a school psychologist. *Second year* — Children's Rehabilitation Center, working with a pediatric psychologist. *Third year* — Center for Clinical Psychology Services at the Institute of Clinical Psychology, working with a clinical child psychologist. *Fourth year* — Community Mental Health Center or hospital setting, working with clinical psychologist.

II. *Quality Control*

The heart of a good educational program is quality control. Most programs use written examinations to insure mastery of generic knowledge and facts. Quality control in the *clinical area* requires a variety of assessment strategies, most of which are labor-intensive and, unfortunately, few programs are capable of rigorous quality control in this area. Further, quality control over rapport-building, recognizing opportunities to facilitate clients' self-understanding, and other clinical interactions is much more subjective and stressful upon the student-teacher relationship.

All students in our program must maintain a continuous daily log of their *clinical activities, observations,* and *supervision* throughout their education, including internship. The clinical log during the first four years is monitored by their advisor and during the internship by the internship coordinator. Regardless of the location of the practicum placement each student has in a given year, they must do periodic assessments and interventions under the supervision of the institute faculty in the Institute's Center for Clinical Psychology Services. Supervision for these quality control checks are done either live or with video tape. Any significant skill or knowledge deficit, as defined by the student's supervisors, leads to remedial action. Remedial action occurs even when the student is on internship (e.g., students may have their internship downgraded to a practicum and be required to take another internship).

III. *Formal Coursework*

All school clinical child psychology students must complete a minimum of 63 formal course hours:

First Year:

Fall Course	**Spring Course**
Cognitive Assessment	Seminar on Professional Psychology
Developmental Psychology	Psychopathology
Statistics-Research Methods	Personality/Social Development

Summer Coursework

Special Education-Curriculum
Learning and Motivation

Second Year:

Fall Coursework	**Spring Coursework**
Principles of Psychotherapy I	Principles of Psychotherapy II
Personality Assessment I	Psychological Assessment II
Physiological/Neuropsychology	Social/Community
Family Theory and Therapy	School Intervention

Table 2. *Initial Positions of UVA Graduates during the last five years (N=44)*

Setting	Populations served	Number
Community Mental Health Center	Adults, children, families	6
Universities	Teaching graduate students and residents	6
School System	Children, teachers	5
Private Psychiatric Hospitals	Adults, children, families	4
Children's Hospitals	Child, families, handicapped	3
Dept. Beh.Medicine Medical School	Adult, children, families, Teaching residents and medical students	3
HMO	Adult, children, families	3
Res. Treatment Centers	Emotional & physical handicapped children	3
General Hospitals	Adults, children, families (Physical illness acute and chronic)	2
VA Hospitals	Adults and families	2
U.S. Air Force Hosp.	Adult, children, families	2
Private Practice		2
Post-Doctoral Program	Adult (1), Child (2)	3

Third Year:

Fall Coursework	Spring Coursework
Elective Individual Therapy	Elective Special Therapy
Elective Non-Individual Intervention	Elective Non-Individual Intervention
Non-Clinical Elective	Non-Clinical Elective

Fourth Year:

Fall Coursework	Spring Coursework
Specialization Electives (e.g., Pediatric Psychology)	Specialization Electives (e.g, Forensic Psychology)

IV. *Comprehensive Examinations*

(a) *Masters Examination.* A one-day examination reviewing the first year curricula. (b) *Doctoral Comprehensive Examination.* Two days of doctoral examinations are taken typically in the fall of the fourth year. Two-thirds of the examination is designed to cover the generic core of clinical knowledge and skills, with one-third focusing on specialty knowledge and skills.

V. *Internship*

All students are required to complete a one-year clinical internship. Students are guided in their selection of internships by the internship coordinator to ensure that students undertake an internship for which they are qualified and which provides them with specialty experiences which they are seeking.

One indication of whether a progam is educating *psychologists* who can function generically as clinical psychologists is whether its graduates are acceptable to the service delivery marketplace. During the past five years our combined program at Virginia has graduated approximately nine PhD's each year (total = 44). Table 2 describes our recent graduates' initial job placement.

Our experience leads me to believe that psychology as a profession is not sufficiently well developed and defined for it to move toward subspecialty standards in any area, without a clearer definition of generic clinical skills. For the present, professional ethics, peer pressure and advisory standards are the most which should be sought in seeking to define the subspecialty of clinical child psychology. Advisory standards, if developed, need to be made available to students, interns, and programs as general guidelines, and nothing more.

References

American Psychological Association. (1983). *Accreditation Handbook.* Washington, DC: Author.

Rosenfeld, M., Shimberg, B., & Thornton, R.F. (1983). *Job Analysis of Licensed Psychologists in the United States and Canada.* Educational Testing Service, Princeton, NJ:

Schneider, S.F. (1981). Where have all the students gone? Positions of Psychologists trained in Clinical Service Programs. *American Psychologist, 36,* 1427-1449.

VandenBos, G.R., Strapp, J., & Kilburg, R.R. (1981). Health Service Providers in Psychology: Results of the 1978 APA Human Resouces Survey. *American Psychologist, 36,* 1395-1418

A Developmental Perspective on Training Clinical Child Psychologists The Ohio State University Clinical Child Psychology Program

Felicisima C. Serafica and Charles Wenar
The Ohio State University

The relationship between child psychology, from which developmental psychology evolved, and clinical psychology is an old one, dating back to 1896 and the beginning of clinical psychology in the United States with the establishment at the University of Pennsylvania of a clinic for children with psychoeducational difficulties by Witmer (Fernberger, 1931). Like other relationships, it has had its ups and downs and fluctuations in degree of closeness (Ross, 1972).

In recent years, the clinical relevance of developmental psychology has been reaffirmed by clinicians such as Ross (1972) and Cass (1974). The former recommended developmental psychology as a source of principles and methods that can be applied to the clinical situation. The latter proposed that the concept of development be the core of theoretical knowledge, the common denominator in clinical child psychology and, ideally, for all clinical psychology. Both suggested that treatment and prevention of psychological disorders are more appropriately construed as problems of development, so a knowledge of how behavioral systems evolve is necessary for the proper assessment and treatment of psychological disorders and the prevention of their occurrence. The Clinical Child Psychology Program at The Ohio State University was founded on this premise that developmental psychology should constitute the theoretical and empirical core of a clinical child psychology curriculum. In this paper, we will describe briefly the program's philosophy, goals, structure, and curriculum, then report some observed outcomes.

Before addressing these topics, however, it seems necessary to establish some important distinctions. According to Rie (1967), who was one of the architects of the program and played a major role in its first decade, clinical child psychology is not exclusively clinical psychology nor exclusively developmental psychology though it draws heavily on both. It differs from clinical psychology in its particular focus on infants, children, and youth. It differs from developmental psychology in its particular focus on psychological problems and its emphasis on treatment and prevention. To these comments we would add that clinical child psychology also differs from applied developmental psychology in its narrower focus on the application of developmental theory and research solely to mental health issues and only as they arise during the first three major periods of the life span. The program about to be described is a clinical child psychology program.

Philosophy

The OSU Clinical Child Psychology Program was founded on two major premises. The first is that clinical child psychology is distinct from clinical psychology applied to adults. Its distinctiveness arises from the following conditions: (1) the relatively more rapid rate of change during the pre-adult versus the post-adolescence years; (2) the qualitative differences between immature and mature individuals' psychophysiological, cognitive, linguistic, social, and affective functioning; and (3) the uniquely dependent and reactive status of infants, children, and adolescents. These conditions imply that psychopathology during the pre-adult years must be conceptualized differently from adult psychopathology. They also indicate that the clinical child psychologist will need communicative, interactive, assessment, and treatment skills which will differ in important ways from those used with adults. Furthermore, they underscore the necessity for viewing the client in relation to his or her environment, particularly the family, peer group, and school. Finally, they suggest that the clinical child psychologist is in a more effective position to engage in the prevention of psychological disorders. In sum, clinical child psychology is sufficiently distinct from adult clinical psychology that it merits being taught programmatically in its own right.

The second major premise is that developmental theory and research constitute an appropriate substratum for clinical child psychology practice. During the period of rapid growth from infancy through adolescence, psychopathology is more appropriately viewed as *normal development gone awry* (Wenar, 1982). Phenomena which are viewed as deviant at one age are quite typical at another and behavior which is indicative of adult disorder may be a characteristic signpost of childhood development. Further complicating the picture and underscoring their distinctiveness from adult psychological disorders, many childhood disturbances (e.g., early infantile autism) have little or no counterpart in adulthood. Moreover, psychopathology during these early years is sometimes expressed in an atypical pattern of development among functions, with normality alternating with regressive and precocious behaviors. Thus, providers of psychological services to minors must learn to distingish behavior which is normal at different stages of development and is likely to be "outgrown" (i.e., replaced by more mature patterns) from deviant behavior with little likelihood of being outgrown. This distinction is a shifting, complex one, and the result of longitudinal studies suggest that even the experts have sometimes been seriously mistaken in regard to prognosis. Thus, it is critical for clinical child psychologists to be familiar with the rate and emergence of various functions and of their maturation and integration. It is equally important for them to be aware of the environmental and intraorganismic factors which either facilitate or impede development so that the client may be understood in his or her totality. The possible consequences of failure to acquire such knowledge were aptly described by Rie (1975) when he said, "Ignorance of these issues can and does lead to grossly unsuitable interventions, failure to intervene when necessary, avoidable distress, or unwarranted hope."

A corollary of the second major premise is that the required developmental knowledge base now exists. The unprecedented growth of research during the 1960s resulted in considerable advances in our understanding about perceptual, cognitive, and language development, as well as learning, during infancy and childhood (e.g., Mussen, 1970). Scientific progress in these fields continued during the subsequent decade which also saw significant advances in our understanding of social development (e.g., Maccoby, 1980). In this decade of the 1980s, the study of cognitive and social development continue to flourish, augmented by increased attention to emotional development and the study of early adolescence. Additionally, there is a growing fund of scientific information about individual differences in development, particularly as a function of gender, ethnicity, or socioeconomic status (e.g., Yando, Seitz, & Zigler, 1979). We have also learned a great deal about the development of high risk and other clinical populations (Kopp & Krakow, 1983). New insights about traditional concepts and techniques are emerging (Chandler, Paget, & Koch, 1978). Last, the formulation of developmentally-based assessment and therapeutic techniques also has received attention from researchers (Uzgiris & Hunt, 1975; Gibbs, Arnold, Ahlborn, & Cheesman, 1984).

Other clinical child psychology programs also acknowledge the usefulness of a developmental psychology knowledge base. What perhaps sets the OSU Clinical Child Psychology Program apart is the depth of its commitment to this view and the thoroughness of its attempt at implementation.

While advocating the centrality of developmental theory and research to clinical child psychology, philosophically, the program also favors exposing students to diverse theoretical orientations, methods, and research, so that students may judge for themselves the validity and usefulness of these theories, and assess how different theories can complement one another.

The Program is also firmly committed to the scholar-practitioner model of training (Hoch, Ross, & Winder, 1966). It is predicated on the notion that the role of the clinical child psychologist is not only to provide psychological services, but also to contribute to the growth of scientific knowledge in these specific domains.

Finally, the program's philosophy includes the view that clinical child psychology training should build on a broad-based background in psychology. The clinical child psychologist is first and foremost a psychologist and should be familiar with the history of psychology as a science, and with basic research on the biological, cognitive, perceptual, affective, and social bases of behavior, as well as learning and individual differences.

Structure

When the Clinical Child Psychology Program at OSU was established in 1967, under the direction of Charles Wenar, it was a joint enterprise of the developmental psychology area, which at that time included school psychology, and the clinical psychology area, with close ties to the Department of Psychology at Children's Hospital of Columbus, then headed by Herbert Rie. Subsequently, due to reorganizations and personnel changes within the OSU Department of Psychology, the affiliations with school psychology and clinical psychology weakened and today, the program is completely in the developmental psychology area of the OSU Department of Psychology, while maintaining its traditionally close relationship with the Psychology Department at Columbus Children's Hospital.

The core faculty consists of two members of the Department of Psychology, one of whom has a joint appointment in the Department of Pediatrics; two whose primary appointments are in the Department of Pediatrics, but have joint appointments in the Department of Psychology; and two who hold adjunct appointments in the Department of Psychology. From time to time, local psychologists without formal faculty status have augmented the core faculty through supervision of advanced practicum. Developmental and clinical psychology faculty are often members of students' masters thesis, general exams or dissertation committees.

Goals

The overall goal of the program is to produce PhD level clinical child psychologists who are scientist-practitioners with a predominantly developmental perspective on diagnosis, assessment, remediation and prevention of psychological disorders during infancy, childhood, and adolescence. More specifically, the program seeks to turn out highly competent clinicians and researchers who will continue to explicate the developmental approach to clinical child psychology through creative and critical application of clinical techniques, through teaching, through systematic research, theoretical essays, research reviews, case studies, or, in part, through all of these.

Curriculum

Table 1. *Core Curriculum of the OSU Clinical Child Psychology Program*

Theoretical and Empirical Background

- History & Systems of Psychology
- Developmental Psychology (6 courses): Nature & Direction of Human Development, Psychoanalytic & Social Learning Theories, Structural Theories of Cognitive Development, Infancy, Child Development, Adolescence.
- Personality Theories
- Psychopathology (3 courses): Concepts of Childhood Psychopathology, Psychological Disturbances of Childhood, Adult Psychopathology
- Assessment (2 courses): Concepts & Techniques of Assessment, Survey Course on Tests for Infants, Children, & Adolescence
- Therapy (2 courses): Child Psychotherapies, Child behavior and Therapy
- Neuropsychology (3 courses)
- Social Psychology
- Seminar on Ethical, Professional, & Legal Issues

Clinical Training

- Intellectual assessment
- Personality assessment
- Interviewing and Behavioral Observation
- Clinical methods- placement in psychology department clinic
- Clinical methods- placement in a community setting
- Clinical internship

Research Training

- Research apprenticeship for first year students (3 quarters)
- Methodological Problems in Developmental Psychology
- Statistics (3 courses): Descriptive Statistics in Psychology, Analysis of Variance, Correlational Analysis
- Research for master's thesis and dissertation

Table 1 shows the current core curriculum or set of required courses and experiences. In addition to the core, there are also courses on neuropsychological assessment, pediatric psychology, and family therapy. Typically, students take additional courses in general developmental psychology such as cognitive styles, language development, sociomoral developmental, or adulthood and aging; courses in the developmental disabilities program such as adaptive behavior, projective testing, or play therapy for the developmentally delayed; courses in other areas of psychology such as clinical and counseling; and courses in other departments of the university such as social work, sociology, anthropology, law, and family relations and human development. The curriculum is tailored to the individual student's style: some like to stay close to home, some like to venture out.

The curriculum was designed so as to have a continual interplay between clinical child and general developmental courses, as well as between academic and applied courses. The three first year courses on human development form the background for the courses on psychopathology and psychotherapy, both of which are taught from a developmental perspective. While the first psychopathology course is addressed to general issues in conceptualizing and diagnosing childhood disturbances, the advanced course is for in-depth exploration and critique of the theoretical and research literature concerning a specific psychopathology. In the first year while the student is learning how to give inteligence tests, he or she is taking a course on assessment focusing on measurement theory. The practicum on personaltiy testing is complemented by an assessment course which surveys and evaluates tests frequently used by clinical child psychologists. Likewise, the practicum on interviewing and behavioral observations co-occurs with a course on child behavior assessment and therapy taught from a behavioral perspective. In the second year, while the student is taking courses on infancy, childhood, and adolescence, the practicum provides more intensive training in the assessment and treatment of psychological disorders manifested by infants, children, and adolescents. Students also work with parents and families, drawing from the courses on parenting, adult psychopathology, and family therapy. In addition, they provide psychological consultation to health and school personnel. The setting for this practicum is the department psychological clinic where the relationship of theory and research is constantly emphasized. Beyond the second year, students may take practicum in settings outside the university. The advanced practicum is designed to provide supervised experience in specialized techniques (e.g., neuropsychological evaluation), assessment and therapy with special populations (such as adolescents), or in special settings (such as an emergency clinic or a milieu oriented treatment center). Although this practicum is optional, almost all students take it prior to going on internships.

Research training begins in the first year when the student undergoes a research apprenticeship, usually with his or her adviser, and takes the three-course statistics sequence. In the second year, all students take the required course on research methods in developmental psychology. A few take a fourth statistics course, usually in the third or fourth year. All students are required to do a master's thesis and doctoral dissertation, usually on a topic of the student's choosing. In addition, they often get involved in faculty research projects. As part of their professional socialization, students are encouraged to submit papers for presentation at professional meetings and publication in research journals. In 1984-85, our students gave 7 paper presentation and published 4 articles.

The close affiliation between the Clinical Child Psychology Programs and the Department of Pediatrics and Columbus Children's Hospital enhances the students' clinical and research training. Because of this relationship, students have access to a large and diverse population of disturbed children while being able to obtain training in specialized techniques. Children's Hospital is also the setting for research; clinical child students work as graduate research assistants or conduct their own masters and dissertation studies, using the hospital's population. The Children's Mental Health Centers of Columbus have recently been aquired by Children's Hospital. We anticipate that this will lead to an expansion of clinical and research training opportunities.

Training and professional socialization also take place through periodic meetings of the Clinical Child Psychology Club for the purpose of socializing and discussing, informally, topics of local and national interest in regard to clinical child psychology. There is a colloquium series on professional topics (ethics, legal aspects of clinical child psychology, legislation, APA accreditation) and relevant research being conducted in the university and in the community.

Outcomes

When the Clinical Child Psychology Program at OSU became a subspecialty within developmental psychology, the faculty were not entirely without some misgivings. Yet, subsequent experience has shown that teaching clinical child psychology within the context of general developmental psychology is a workable concept. The feedback that we have received about students on internship and alumni has been very positive. The most recent survey of our alumni showed that, of those about whom information was available, 16% held full-time academic positions, 18% had combined clinical-academic appointments, and 66% were doing full-time clinical work. Among the latter, only two were engaged full-time in private practice. Many are still doing research and publishing.

The program also seems to be succeeding in its objective of encouraging clinically relevant developmental studies. An examination of masters theses and doctoral dissertations completed between 1967 and 1982 showed that 79% investigated the sequence, correlates or determinants of development in clinical or normal populations. The remainer (21%) dealt with child psychopathology or assessment. Currently, students are encouraged to do research on development of clinical populations, developmentally-based assessment and treatment techniques, or the relationship of developmental variables to efficacy of nondevelopmental approaches to treatment.

In sum, while providing a broad-based training in psychology, the Clinical-Child Psychology Program at OSU is especially designed to train psychologists whose specialty is the assessment and treatment of psychological problems from a developmental perspective. Such psychologists are equally knowledgeable about normal and deviant development (and prepared to do research on these topics) and on the construction, as well as validation, of developmentally-based assessment and treatment methods. They are equally prepared to hold positions in academic, clinical, and research settings.

The major issue confronting the Program is APA accreditation. Because the Program is a part of the OSU Developmental rather than its Clinical Psychology Area, it is not eligible for accreditation under the current guidelines. We have been monitoring with a great deal of interest the movement to have clinical child psychology designated as a specialty area by the American Psychological Association and hope to learn more about it at this conference.

References

Cass, L.K. (1974). The training of clinical child psychologists. In G.J. Williams & S. Gordon (Eds.), *Clinical child psychology* (pp. 463-482). New York: Behavioral Publications.

Chandler, M.J., Paget, K.F., & Koch, D.A. (1978). The child's demystification of psychological defense mechanisms: A structural and developmental analysis. *Developmental Psychology, 14,* 197-205.

Fernberger, S.W. (1931). The history of the psychological clinic. In R.A. Brotmarkle (Ed.), *Clinical psychology: Studies in honor of Lightner Witmer to commemorate the thirty-fifth anniversary of the founding of the first psychological clinic* (pp. 10-36). Philadelphia PA: University of Pennsylvania Press.

Gibbs, J.C., Arnold, K.D., Ahlborn, H.H., & Cheesman, F.L. (1984). Facilitation of sociomoral reasoning in delinquents. *Journal of Consulting and Clinical Psychology, 52,* 37-45.

Hoch, E.L., Ross, A.O., & Winder, C.L. (1966). Conference on the professional preparation of clinical psychologists. *American Psychologist, 21,* 42-51.

Kopp, C.B., & Krakow, J.B. (1983). The developmentalist and the study of behavioral risk: A view of the past with an eye toward the future. *Child Development, 54,* 1086-1108.

Maccoby, E.E. (1980). *Social development.* New York: Harcourt Brace Janovich.

Mussen, P. (Ed.) (1970). *Carmichael's manual of psychology (vol. 1).* New York: Wiley.

Rie, H.E. (1967). *A tentative proposal for administration of the OSU Clinical Child Psychology Doctoral Program.* Unpublished manuscript.

Rie, H.E. (1975). *Clinical child psychology program accreditation.* Unpublished manuscript.

Ross, A.O. (1972). The clinical child psychologists. In B.B. Wolman (Ed.). *Manual of clinical child psychology* (pp. 1287-1296). New York: McGraw-Hill.

Uzgiris, I.C., & Hunt, J. McV. (1975). *Assessment in infancy.* Urbana: University of Illinois Press.

Wenar, C. (1982). *Psychopathology from infancy through adolescence.* New York: Random House.

Yando, R., Seitz, V., & Zigler, E. (1979). *Intellectual and personality characteristics of children: Social class and ethnic group differences.* New York: Erlbaum.

Credentialing and Licensing

Introduction: Credentialing and Licensing Issues

June M. Tuma
Louisiana State University

One of the primary goals of this Conference was to evaluate the need to pursue specialty status for clinical child psychology. Even though there are advantages as well as disadvantages in obtaining such status, one of the major implications of achieving it would be the credentialing and licensing aspects. Just as the major specialty areas recognized by APA (clinical, counseling, school, industrial/organizational psychology) are defined by training guidelines, they also require special considerations for certification, licensure, and accreditation of programs offering such training. Should clinical child psychology ever be considered a specialty area, alterations in the conceptualization of the present structure of specialties in psychology would be required.

A number of psychologists expert in the area of licensure, accreditation, and certification by ABBP agreed to present some considerations for the conferees to assist in determination of the advisability of pursuing specialty status at this time. Thus, Patricia Aletky presented the current APA stance and progress in developing specialty criteria.[1] In her presentation the difficulties inherent in any area pursuing specialty status became clear. The major hurdle for any area to meet current guidelines is to show that the area is distinct from any other. Joe Weaver presented issues related to licensing. He outlines the relationship between licensing and training standards and applies them to clinical child psychology. In the course of his discussion, he presents some illuminating facts about the history of licensure in this country, the development of the national licensing examination, and how licensing boards typically look at competency in specialty areas. Taking note of the same difficulties Patricia Aletky presented, he concludes by giving conferees some suggestions to qualify clinical child psychology as a specialty area, should that be found desirable.

ABPP has been established as a credentialing body to enable psychology to achieve designation as an independent profession. With ABPP certification, individuals could easily be identified by the public and the profession. Its establishment was stimulated by the proliferation of psychologists offering services following World War II. Psychologists in all specialty areas recognized by APA can achieve a designated diploma from ABPP. Recently, more circumscribed areas of psychology (clinical neuropsychology and forensic psychology) are gaining recognition by ABPP and are awarding diplomas to those submitting to the ABPP examination. If clinical child psychology should wish to become a specialty area, then perhaps ABPP could be approached to offer diplomas designating those with the the necessary qualifications.

Jacqueline Goldman, a psychologist active in the ABPP credentialing process, presented her views about the desirability of clinical child psychology seeking specialty status and, in so doing, seeking ABPP credentialing. In her presentation, she cogently relates the history of ABPP, some pitfalls and advantages of its activities. She then points out the implications for clinical child psychology, the procedures required, and gives us some of her perceptions about the desirability of clinical child psychology attempting to become a specialty area. .

The issues presented in this plenary session have broad reaching implications for training in clinical child psychology. These issues permeate our concern whether or not clinical child psychology is ever designated a specialty area of psychology.

[1]Although Dr. Aletky presented two separate papers at the Conference, her presentations are combined in the *Proceedings* (her paper appears in the first section).

The Relationship Between Licensing and Training Standards in Clinical Child Psychology

S. Joseph Weaver
University of Kansas Medical Center

Licensing for the practice of psychology, including clinical child psychology, is regulated in the United States and Canada by the state and provincial boards of examiners in psychology. These boards are themselves organized into the American Association of State Psychology Boards (AASPB).

The Growth of Licensing

The growth of the AASPB over the last 40 years is one of the most interesting phenomena of professional psychology. Connecticut began the process in 1945 and three more states (Virginia, Kentucky, and Ohio) did likewise by 1950. By 1960, there were 32 state boards of examiners of psychology (Carlson, 1978). Problems of different standards and consequent restriction of mobility of psychologists between states led to a meeting in Chicago in November, 1959, which was sponsored by the Board of Professional Affairs of the American Psychological Association (APA) and attended by representatives of 16 state boards. The members of the meeting decided two things. A national examination in psychology was badly needed as well as some structure to construct and administer the test. Also, an organization for the various state boards to communicate and act jointly in matters concerning the regulation of psychology was considered necessary. The organization had to be constituted by the state boards themselves. A constitution was drawn up at a constitutional convention in 1960, sent out to the boards for approval, and quickly drew a positive response. The formal organization of AASPB came into being in August, 1961, in New York City at the time of the APA convention. Annual meetings of AASPB have continued to be held in conjunction with the APA meetings ever since for obvious professional and financial reasons.

Shortly thereafter, a "National Examination" in psychology was constructed, which is now entitled *The Examination for Professional Practice in Psychology* (EPPP). This was made possible by the volunteered services of psychologists well experienced in test planning, item writing, and test editing, and the assistance of the Professional Examination Service (PES). The growth in the number of applications for licensure has been phenomenal in the last 20 years. The number of applicants for licensure taking the national examination in psychology has grown from 27 in 1965 to 2110 in 1975 to 5201 in 1983 (Professional Examination Service, 1984). Obviously, the numbers of psychologists seeking licensure for the practice of psychology have made licensure itself an important force in the profession. Therefore, the relationship between licensing and training standards has just as obviously become a major factor.

Basic Educational Standards in Licensing

What is the interaction between licensing and training standards in psychology . . . and therefore, clinical child psychology? Actually, there are many interactions between the activities of the AASPB and any efforts to define a program in professional psychology. The term *professional psychology* is used in the sense that the APA uses it to delineate that part of the profession that sells its services to the public (i.e., a practitioner). For example, the AASPB was instrumental, along with APA and the National Register of Health Service Providers, in stimulating, organizing, and carrying through to completion efforts to develop nationally agreed upon standards for defining a doctoral education in psychology. Two national meetings were held in 1976 and 1977 and criteria for the designation of doctoral programs in psychology were agreed upon and subsequently adopted by AASPB, the National Register, and APA (Wellner, 1978). Those standards for training are the most basic interaction between licensing and training standards. They *must* be the basis for planning for any new training standards in psychology, including clinical child psychology.

The requirement that those core or generic standards be the base of any new training standards is predicated upon the assumption that planners of new programs would wish their graduates to be able to sell their psychological services to the general public (i.e., practice their profession and receive renumeration for such services). Graduates of programs that do not meet the standards established by the profession and public licensing bodies are routinely denied licenses by such examining boards. This may sound very elementary and a "given" in any serious discussions of new training standards but it is the most fundamental relationship of all between the licensing bodies and the standards for training psychologists in any specialty.

Lack of Psychological Foundations in "Special" Programs

The lack of psychological foundations in special programs is an especially relevant point since one of the major bones of contention between licensing boards and graduates of special training programs is the frequent failure of special programs in psychology to provide their graduates with the basic foundations in psychology required by licensing boards. The specialty training itself is typically not questioned. The special program usually has some idiosyncratic theoretical or technological theme such as *humanistic training* and that special training may be very well provided for in the curriculum. Unfortunately, for various reasons the basic foundations in psychology may have been slighted so that the graduate cannot demonstrate to the satisfaction of the licensing boards that the degree is truly a *degree in psychology*. It may be an excellent degree in humanism or education, or counseling, or counselor education or pupil personnel services but it does not meet the standards for a doctoral degree in psychology agreed upon by the licensing boards and the national professional organization. Failure of any new training standards to incorporate the accepted generic standards would result in disaster for its graduates as well as acrimonious conflicts between the graduates and faculty of such training programs and the licensing boards.

At present, clinical child psychology seems unlikely to build new training standards that would violate the established generic educational standards. Presumably, one might, therefore, safely pass over this issue. Unfortunately, the issue has been complicated by the rise of another phenomenon in the field of licensing . . . that is specialty licensing.

Specialty Licensing

AASPB and the licensing boards adhere to codes of ethics requiring licensees to practice in specialty areas only when their training and experience would qualify them in that specialty. AASPB and the state boards do *not* usually license psychologists in specialties. They license *generic* psychologists and depend upon referencing a code of ethics to control any psychologist who might attempt to diagnose and treat patients outside of his fields of competence (Wiens & Menne, 1981). Some do adopt guidelines more clearly specifying the relevant education, training, and experience necessary to call oneself a specialist but these are generally a restatement of the criteria in the APA *Specialty Guidelines for the Delivery for the Services* (APA, 1981) and various internship requirements. There are some states, such as Virginia, in which particular political considerations have dictated specialty licensing, but they are a small minority. Unfortunately, the campaign for specialty licensing by some organizations speaking for special groups has grown in recent years.

The Problem with Specialty Licensing

The problems involved in specialty licensing are currently being exaccerbated by the demands of many individuals and special organizations who are interested in circumventing the national standards in psychology. Many individuals and some organizations speaking for special interests such as school psychology, marriage and family therapy, and counseling and guidance, have been licensed, are attempting, or are thinking of attempting to secure licensure on a basis of what is essentially specialty licensing. Furthermore, some specialty interests inside psychology in fields such as neuropsychology, forensic psychology, applied developmental psychology, and behavioral psychology are also considering specialty approaches to licensing.

The major problem with specialty licensing from the licensing boards' point of view is that there is almost no chance that the public consumer of psychological services could accuratley ascertain the competence (or lack thereof) of school psychologists, pupil personnel psychologists, guidance psychologists, humanistic psychologists, neuropsychologists, behavioral psychologists, and so forth. The average person does not even know the difference between a psychiatrist and a psychologist. How naive it is to think the average citizen will understand the esoteric terminology of specialty distinctions when educated state legislators cannot appreciate the significance of the distinction between doctoral psychologists and non-doctoral psychologists.

The only practical solution to this dilemma is to follow the lead of the other professions such as medicine and law, which have had to deal with the same problem for a much longer time than psychology. The definition of the term psychologists must first be standardized so the public knows what kind of a professional is meant by it. The public will want to be certain that a person officially using such a title possesses a common body of knowledge and experience relevant to the practice of psychology. The question of whether or not some specialist in psychology could provide more effective or efficient service could be more knowledgeably answered by a qualified psychologist than by a lay person. Arthur Wiens and John Menne (1918) stated this very well in their article in the *American Psychologist,* "On Disposing of Straw People," when they wrote. "Society assumes that a licensed psychologist will have sufficient breadth of education to recognize the parameters of a variety of problem situations and provide safe, effective, and appropriate consultation or make referral to another psychologist who can provide such help" (p. 390).

The push for specialty licensing by a variety of groups strikes at the heart of this position and, therefore, at the view of psychology as a unitary profession like law and medicine. Already the average citizen's understanding of what a psychologist is has been eroded by the passage of state laws recognizing non-doctoral psychologists as independent providers of psychological services. This has happened in several states such as Connecticut, Florida, Illinois, and Missouri. A major force behind many of these efforts within the profession is school psychology under the leadership of the National Association of School Psychologists. Another is the backlash efforts of clinical and counseling psychologists to maintain themselves as the health service providers against a flood of *backdoor* clinicians. The addition in the future of other psychological specialties to the groups already mentioned could swing the balance of power by fragmenting the voice of psychology in state legislative halls. This could toll the end of any generic profession of psychology and probably relegate the bits and pieces of the profession to a third class role in the health and mental health systems of the country. Do not think this could not happen. The business "buy-up" of hospitals, clinics, and the entire health care system of America is well under way. The new cost containment policies in government and business and the proliferation of HMOs, PPOs, and PPGs is already driving practicing psychologists out of the field. These organizations are dominated by business considerations and their closed panels of providers, restrictions on third party payments to psychologists, ablility to hire non-licensed people as psychologists under the exemptions provided by state laws, and general prejudice against paying for mental health services are already making it difficult for young psychologists to earn a living.

Detailed descriptions of the evolution of specialization in psychology (Judy Hall), lessons in specialization from other professions (Laura J. Schnaps and Bruce Sales), a multi-organizational survey of specialty licensing (Toni Alterman, Bruce Sales, and Richard Kilburg), and the legal implications of specialty recognition (Bruce Sales) can be found in the *Manual for the Identification and Continued Recognition of Proficiencies and New Specialties in Psychology* (APA, 1983). This is probably the best single resource on the topic.

Relevance of Specialty Training to Licensing

In addition to adopting a policy that basic doctoral education in psychology must be generic, the APA has also adopted policy statements that call for *broad* psychological education and training in specialty doctoral programs. This is most clearly seen in accreditation criteria in sentences such as the following:

> Training must provide skills which encompass several types of assessment and intervention procedures, rather than being restricted to a single type. Every student must become familiar with major assessment and intervention techniques and their theoretical bases. (APA, 1979, p. 7)

Similarly, organizations such as the Association of Psychology Internship Centers (APIC) and the National Register of Health Service Providers have adopted almost identical membership criteria as follows:

> The internship provides training in a range of assessment and treatment activities conducted directly with patients seeking psychological services. (APIC, 1984, p. 5)

The major implications of these criteria for any licensing board that is faced with evaluating whether or not an applicant from a new clinical child psychology training program has completed an acceptable education and internship is that the education and internship must be reasonably broad in its provision of training. Presumably, one problem might ensue if the curriculum and internship is concerned exclusively with children. The graduate of such a program might find the licensing board would restrict his area of practice to children. If the training did provide for some work with adolescents and adults, such a restriction might not be applied.

Most licensing boards typically do *not* overly concern themselves with questions of specialty competence unless the applicant claims such competencies (i.e., clinical, counseling, school, and industrial organizational), but blatantly fails to demonstrate appropriate education and specialty training. In such cases, the board might doubt the candidate's knowledge of psychology, its specialties and ethics, and investigate him in greater depth.

Is Clinical Child Psychology a Specialty?

A serious issue may be uncovered in the question of whether or not clinical child psychology is a specialty in its own right. There have been two approaches to the delineation of specialties, one by APA and the other by AASPB.

APA Recognition of Specialties

The APA has approached the question of specialties through the creation of various committees to study the general problem of defining a specialty. The major one was the Task Force on Specialty Criteria founded in 1979. This committee surveyed the members of APA boards, chairs of state boards of psychological examiners, presidents of state associations and APA divisions, and the various councils of training directors. It then developed a draft set of criteria. These were reviewed and revised and worked their way through the APA Governance. This process was aided by a formal pilot study involving a draft application for recognition by clinical child psychology. The end result was considerable revision and a *Manual for the Identification and Continued Recognition of Proficiencies and Specialties in Psychology* (APA, 1983). Operating on the assumption that the requirements set forth in this manual represent the will of the APA, one might assume they indicate what will be acceptable as a definition of any specialty. Clinical child psychology may then seem to be in the forefront of special fields seeking recognition. Its experience in meeting the demands of the pilot study probably means it ought to be able to satisfy virtually all of the APA requirements. Of course "virtually all" really means "not quite all" and it remains to be seen whether or not the APA method will result in the recognition of clinical child psychology or any other additional specialty group as a specialty. The sticking point may prove to be the final requirement, Criterion F, which demands that "The pattern of practice in the aggregate must be discriminably different from the pattern in other areas" (APA, 1983, p. 38).

Let us play Devil's Advocate and assume for the purposes of discussion that the APA, the AASPB, and perhaps some other influential organizations in psychology perceive that the interests of psychology as a whole lie in emphasizing the *unitary* aspects of the profession. This is not an unreasonable assumption, given the vast amounts of money, time, and effort the groups have expended to justify public and legal recognition of psychology as an estimable profession demonstrably coherent although separate from others of a somewhat similar nature. One logical argument for them to pursue would be that clinical child psychology is a subspecialty until it proves clearly that it is demonstrably different from the pattern of practice of the recognized specialties in psychology. This would mean demonstrably different from clinical psychology . . . or counseling psychology . . . or possibly also different from school psychology.

One way clinical child psychology may deal with their position may seem fairly clear, since APA has definitely outlined a methodology for establishing a different specialty. Furthermore, as was stated in the preceding discussion, clinical child psychology appears to have already jumped over virtually all of the hurdles.

Unfortunately, there is still the phrase, "a pattern of practice . . . discriminably different from the pattern in other areas." Given the fact that the APA governance has delayed accepting any new specialties for some years, one may reasonalby conclude that it is by no means certain that clinical child psychology will find a way to meet the requirements of Criteria F and win recognition as a bona fide specialty in the forseeable future.

How does one go about proving a "pattern of practice" is different from other patterns of practice? Fortunately, there is another approach to defining specialties that enjoys the great advantage of being the method preferred by the legal institutions of the country. It is a job analysis. Unfortunately, job analyses are quite complex, expensive, and time-consuming operations. Nevertheless, if clinical child psychology finds it cannot surmount the last obstacle, Criterion F, placed in its way by APA, it does have another alternative. Since it seems unlikely that any clinical child psychology organization will be able to raise sufficient funds to pay for a job analysis of this complexity, only two possibilities appear feasible. The first possibility would be for a small, self-constituted group such as the present training conference to organize itself so as to persuade a regular organization such as Section 1 of Division 12 (the Section on Clinical Child Psychology), to take on the task. Such an organization as Section 1 could then issue a call for volunteers to carry out a job analysis, perhaps with the help of a limited consultation from experts in the field. The second possibility might be to try to utilize the data bank from the only existing national job analysis of psychologists to see if differences between clinical child psychologists and the other recognized specialties could be clearly demonstrated. A brief review of that job analysis and its results might put the scope of the task in proper perspective as well as offer guidance on the feasibility of the proposal.

AASPB Job Analysis and Recognition of Specialties

In 1980, the AASPB was involved in a research program to demonstrate the validity of its national examination. It was strongly advised by psychological and legal experts to conduct such research and it started with a role delineation study carried out by the Professional Examination Service (Richman, 1981). Following that, AASPB also commissioned the Educational Testing Service (ETS) to carry out a multi-method job analysis of licensed psychologists in the United States and Canada.

Job Analysis of Licensed Psychologists. The goals of the job analysis were to identify the major job responsibilities of licensed psychologists and the knowledges and techniques considered important and used by the practitioners in the field. The results of such a job analysis would describe scientifically for the first time what practicing psychologists actually do, which would, in turn, provide a justification for delineating the content of the field and also the examination.

Originally, the study planned to develop separate surveys for the four psychological specialties that compromise the overwhelming proportion of licensees; clinical, counseling, school, and industrial/organizational psychology. Accordingly, the project staff carried out an extensive review of the literature, investigated the previous role delineation studies, and reviewed job descriptions from state and federal agencies. Four draft job analysis questionnaires (one for each specialty) were then tried out on limited samples in the United States and Canada. An unexpected finding was that there was so much overlap among the four specialties in the reported work functioning that it made more sense to combine the four drafts into one composite instrument that would cover all areas (Rosenfeld, Thornton, & Shimberg, 1983). The final survey instrument was entitled *Inventory of Responsibilities of Licensed Psychologists* and asked over 1,500 practitioners to rate 59 responsibilities and 111 knowledge areas and techniques.

The failure of the four recognized specialties to produce quite different descriptions of their practices does not augue well for any proposed new specialty. If clinical, counseling, school, and industrial/organizational psychology could not demonstrate different patterns of practice among themselves, how could a newcomer hope to do so? On the other hand, the finding of a great deal of overlap among the initial specialty questionnaires does not rule out the presence of some differentiation. Presumably, if a focus upon differences rather than commonalities were emphasized, significantly different aspects of the practices of psychologists in the differnt specialties might also be ascertained.

The authors of the job analysis themselves offer hope for such a possibility as follows:

> Those who would like to see some type of specialty credential instituted will find some support for their views in the results of the present job analysis study. Because of the decision rules adopted for the selection of knowledges and techniques used and considered important by a majority of licensed psychologists, and because of the rigor of the linking process, only 38 of the original 111 knowledges and techniques survived as possible topics for inclusion in a generic licensure exam.
>
> If one examines the knowledges and techniques separately for each specialty, a larger number of knowledges and techniques can be identified as (1) used, (2) important, and (3) linked to one or more of the job dimensions of a specialty's unique factor structure. (Rosenfeld, Shimberg, & Thornton, 1984, p. 19)

Although there may be many difficulties involved in attempting to milk the data in the *Job Analysis of Licensed Psychologists in the United States and Canada,* a reworking of the results should at least point the way to a worthwhile investigation focused upon the differences rather than the commonalities between specialties. Such an effort might prove very fruitful for clinical child psychologists desirous of demonstrating they really do have a pattern of practice different from that of the other specialties.

References

American Psychological Association, Committee on Accreditation. (1979). *Criteria for accreditation of doctoral training programs and internships in professional psychology.* Washington, DC: Author.

American Psychological Association. (1981). Specialty guidelines for the delivery of services. *American Psychologist. 36.* 640-681.

American Psychological Association. (1983). *Second Draft: Manual for the Identification and Continued Recognition of Proficiencies and New Specialties in Psychology.* Washington, DC: Author.

Association of Psychology Internship Centers. (1984). *Internship Programs in Professional Psychology Including Post-Doctoral Training Programs* (13th Ed.). Washington, DC: Author.

Carlson, H.S. (1978). The AASPB Story: The beginnings and first 16 years of the American Association of State Psychology Boards, 1961-1977. *American Psychologist, 33,* 486-495.

Professional Examination Service. (1984). *Annual report on the licensing examination program of the American Association of State Psychology Boards.* New York, NY: Author.

Richman, S. (1981). *Final Report to the American Association of State Psychology Boards on the role delineation study for the Examination for Professional Practice in Psychology.* New York, NY: Professional Examination Service.

Rosenfeld, M., Thornton, R., & Shimberg, B. (1983). Job analysis of licensed psychologists: Part 1 - Methodology. *Professional Practice of Psychology, 4,* 17-24.

Rosenfeld, M., Shimberg, B., & Thornton, R. (1984). Job analysis of licensed psychologists: Part 2 - Analysis and conclusions. *Professional Practice of Psychology, 5,* 1-20.

Wellner, A.M. (Ed.) (1978). *Education and credentialing in psychology.* Washington, DC: American Psychological Association.

Wiens, A.N., & Menne, J.W. (1981). On disposing of "straw people" or an attempt to clarify statutory recognition and educational requirements for psychologists. *American Psychologist, 36,* 390-395.

Should Clinical Child Psychology be Designated a Special Practice Area by The American Board of Professional Psychology

Jacquelin Goldman
University of Florida

Which do we favor: clinical child psychology or child clinical psychology or pediatric psychology or applied child developmental (hyphen) clinical psychology? Is there any difference in the training you would expect among these designations? Are they different specialities? Should they be licensed differently? Should we try to establish diplomate standing for one of these or all of them? What purposes would be served by the different alternatives that we might choose? Would our choices benefit the profession? the public?

In this paper I will discuss some historical issues in professional psychology, some proposals for designation of specialty training, and credentialing issues at the level of the diplomate in professional psychology.

Historical Issues in Child Clinical Psychology Training

Elsewhere (Goldman, 1982), I have reviewed the relationship between clinical child psychology and its historic roots, both within psychology and within allied areas. In that article, I ended with a prediction that clinical child training would probably fare better with a postdoctoral training model than with speciality training at the predoctoral level, particularly because of the problems with predoctoral funding. I think I was dead wrong. While I do not have current data on the number of predoctoral versus postdoctoral programs currently on the books, I am aware that quite a few predoctoral programs have approached clinical child psychology training by differentiating their clinical programs into tracks, one of which is likely to be a child oriented track.

Perhaps you are disenchanted by my lack of success in predictions. If my crystal ball was murky, I nonetheless believe that the alternative turn of events was fortunate. The move to the inclusion of clinical child tracks at the predoctoral level of training, if there is such a move, to keep clinical child psychology within the predoctoral level of training has several advantages, and I want to discuss these advantages with you, because they will be important in some of the later material that I will discuss with regard to a model for credentialing and the relationship of that model to the activities of the American Board of Professional Psychology (ABPP).

The American Psychologial Association (APA) accredits programs in clinical psychology. It does not accredit programs in clinical child psychology or in clinical adult psychology or even clinical gerontological psychology. The basis of accreditation, as almost all of you are surely aware, is that a basic science component is included in the curriculum. The basic science component includes, but is not restricted to (1) the *Biological Bases of Behavior* (physiological psychology, comparative psychology, neuropsychology, sensation and perception, psychopharmacology); (2) *Cognitive and Affective Bases of Behavior* (learning, thinking, motivation, and emotion); (3) *Social Bases of Behavior* (social psychology, group processes, organizational and systems theory); and (4) *Individual Differences* (personality theory, human development, abnormal psychology). In addition, instruction in *Ethics and Standards, Research Design and Methodology, Statistics,* and *Psychometrics* are required.

This basis science component is part of every clinical psychology program, regardless of the tracks that the program may include. It insures that the basic knowledge and identity as a psychologist are acquired by the student.

It is at this point that the various curricula in psychology and even within clinical psychology begin to branch out. Every clinical program will include an internship, but the predoctoral core of professional programs is not specified as such. If you look at the courses required beyond the basic science core, you will find a wide variety of "core professional courses" among clinical programs. In some programs assessment is stressed, some courses include both literature and clinical involvement with children and adults. In some programs, the Rorschach is taught systemtically, while in others, it is considered an interesting historical note.

The Issue of Specialization and its Value

While the idea of specialization has been an issue

for a long time in psychology, it has become more salient in recent years. As applied psychology grew, and it did grow, doubling the number of psychologists almost every decade for the past 90 years, APA proliferated the number of its divisions, most of the ones since about 1950 being practitioner oriented divisions (SOS Report, Sales, Bricklen, & Hall 1984a, 1984b).

The problems of how to identify psychologists have now become complicated by the problem of how to identify particular kinds of psychologists, even kinds of clinical psychologists, and among them, those clinical psychologists who work with children. Now among us we are even getting quite situational in our approach and wondering if pediatric psychologists aren't really different from clinical child psychologists. It is just the settings we work in, or are there basic and substantive issues here?

As we have become more self-conscious about matters relating to practice, we have developed formal standards for providers of psychological services. Now that we are larger and more visible, there has been a rush of groups, some of them devoted to working with particular populations, some devoted to particular work settings, and all of them interested in being designated in some way as specialties. Is this a group of many tails all trying to wag the same dog?

In response, APA has, though the Board of Professional Affairs, appointed a subcommittee on specialization (SOS). That subcommittee has produced a draft statement on specialization which includes both a statement of principles and a statement of possible procedures (Sales, Bricklin, & Hall 1984a, 1984b).

The general idea proposed by the SOS is that designtion of an area as a specialty will depend upon a scientific core (probably the same as outlined above), and an applied generic core, which reflects the fact that there are shared combinations of knowledge and skills within various areas of applied psychology. There actually may be a number of applied generic cores which overlap, some more appropriate for one specialization, others less appropriate. Then, finally, there would be a specific core unique to that specialty.

From a somewhat more empirical conceptualization, a speciality might be considered with regard to the client populations served, problems addressed, techniques employed, and service settings used. Moreover, a proficiency (defined as a more narrow scope than a specialty) could be more defined in similar terms. Boundaries of proficiencies could overlap specialities, and specialties could be separated from each other by virtue of their specific core components.

This general model is based upon the recognition that psychology, even in its broad applied enterprise, is constituted, not only of domains which overlap, but of domains which differ and that both aspects of similarity and difference will have to be taken into account when designating a speciality.

The whole notion of specialty is anathema to the souls of many psychologists, primarily academicians. Sechrest (1985) has gone so far as to suggest that clinical psychology renounce the idea that it is a specialty and lead the way for other groups to renounce the idea of specialization in psychology so that the whole question can be reexamined from scratch.

If Sechrest means what I think he means, he is implying that guild issues have become inextricably entwined with the definitional question. While I would agree that the issue is not a purely conceptual issue, I have come to the conclusion that politics is part of life and likely to invade academic issues as surely as it invades any other domain where humans strive not only for abstract virtues, but also for power and dominion. In my opinion, the idea of clinical psychology renouncing status as a specialty is only likely to intrude even more contaminating problems into the controversy. When the leader of the pack is killed, there is usually a fight for ascendancy and there is no guarantee that the surviving competitors will have any further wisdom or greater mercy that is presently the case.

Add to this the fact that applied psychology is contending in areas in which acronyms now abound, HMOs, PPOs, EAPs, to mention only a few. Guild issues, such as how to get third party payment agencies, while maintaining some sense of professional autonomy with regard to treatment issues, threaten to swamp applied psychology before it can even begin to get its definitions straight. In fact, we are even told that the private practitioner, the bulk of psychologists in this country, will be made obsolete by these organized health provider organizations.

In the midst of this, clinical child psychology occupies a track in a growing number of predoctoral programs, with a few additional predoctoral programs which define themselves as child oriented, and some programs at the postdoctoral level. Almost all states have generic licensing laws, and the public can't very well discriminate a pigeon-oriented psychologist from a child psychologist if university diplomas and state licenses are the criteria for discimination.

The American Board of Professional Psychology

The Council of Representatives of APA established the American Board of Examiners in Professional Psychology in 1946. The impetus for this action was the proliferation of psychologists as providers of direct client or patient work following World War II. Psychology had fought an uphill battle against medicine which claimed that psychologists who functioned as psychotherapists were practicing medicine without a license (Mayfield, 1978). In response, APA elected to establish a credentialing body so that psychology could gain a place as an independent profession and psychologists who were trained could be identified as such both by the public and by the profession. At that time clinical, counseling and guidance (later counseling) and industrial psychology were identified as specialty areas. School psychology was added in 1969, and last year (1984) the diploma in clinical neuropsychology was added as a fifth special practice area, and forensic psychology is slated to become the sixth special practice area.

Early in its history as an examining board, ABEPP developed examinations which dealt with diagnosis (or appraisal and evaluation), therapy (or counseling and constructive action) and ethical and professional attitudes and knowledge. These examinations, it may be added, are the only competency examinations which have ever been agreed upon among the profession at large as the basis of identifying competent practitioners with special skills and special practice areas.

Other groups have gotten into the credentialing business, but close examination of these groups reveals many of them to be vanity organizations, others to rest upon examination without curriculum requirements, without supervised experience criteria, and the like. Within psychology, the American Board of Professional Psychology has taken the lead and insisted upon standards of training and experience as the criteria for acceptance of its candidates. Recognizing its consideration for standards of competency and excellence, APA has continued to look to the American Board of Professional Psychology for leadership in identifying psychologists with competence in special practice areas.

This enterprise is not without its pitfalls. ABPP is subject to the same pressures as is APA. There are groups which clamor to gain recognition as special practice areas. There are threats that if ABPP doesn't develop these examinations within these special areas, the areas will take themselves elsewhere and develop their own examinations.

As you might imagine, this can lead to some interesting organizational stresses and problems. The American Board of Clinical Neuropsychology has a trial marriage with ABPP during a two year period when the diplomas are being awarded through a joint aegis. The American Board of Forensic Psychology has proposed a similar arrangement. The older special practice areas do not even have boards as such. There is no Board of Clinical Psychology, for example.

One issue within ABPP is whether to have a loose confederation of strong member boards or whether to have one strong Board of Professional Psyhology which has examination activities through committee structures. We have, in ABPP, a microcosm of the question of whether to have Federalism or States Rights. At the last Board of Trustees meeting of ABPP, this issue was discussed and debated. Here, at last, I think is where the efforts of the Subcommittee on Specialization, the doubts of academicians, and those of us who are interested in putting our own special interests on the map can begin to come together.

The mood seems to be for ONE American Board of Professional Psychology. The examination of specialists will probably (remember my success in my previous predictions) conform to some model like that proposed by the Subcommittee on Specialization. That is to say that there will be a basic science component, and an applied core, and then some speciality core. Whether that bodes well for any particular interest group is impossible to say. However the establishment of curriculum and accreditation procedures by APA would seem to be a reasonable basis upon which to develop specialty examinations. Only then can there be a logical basis for establishing competency examinations. Such examinations would presumably test the generic professional issues as well as the specialty core components. In the absence of curriculum and accreditation criteria, it would seem likely that the profession will bow to the biggest power groups and have specialities by fiat rather than by rational development. Inevitably power-derived specialities will wax and wane.

In the midst of the guild wars, we need to return to a self-conscious examination of curriculum issues, experience issues, and a means of identifying whether what we have is a group of clinical psychologist who have special proficiency, dealing with children with special techiques in special settings, or whether we have a special practice area which is so discriminably different that we must conceptualize the problems we approach and the processes with which we are concerned at a substantially different level of discourse that our brothers and sisters in the rest of clinical psychology.

In your own mind, given these questions, shorn of of the immediacy of political and power considerations, do we have a special proficiency or a special practice area? Do you believe that we should approach ABPP for the development of a special examination procedure in clinical child psychology, child clinical psychology, pediatric psychology, or applied child development (hyphen) clinical psychology? Should we be examined as clinical psychologists who have special interest in special populations, techiques, and settings?

For myself, I believe we should see whether we (clinical child psychologists) can identify a reasonable curriculum with which to push for APA accreditation. If so, perhaps we deserve designation as a special practice area. Otherwise, we are probably more of a special proficiency within clinical psychology. If we are a special proficiency and not a special practice area, we should not seek speciality designation. To do so would only politicize the issue and weaken all of clinical psychology as well as that part of clinical psychology which is devoted to the understanding and care of children.

While ABPP will continue to take a leading role in the development of examinations of competency, it seems to me that we all have the responsiblilty for not proliferating structures purely on the basis of guild and personally satisfying reasons. We can avoid the damage that over-ambition often produces by attending to our curriculum and our training. As we clarify the scope of our area, we will be able to develop reasonable means of identifying competent practitioners within that area. We are probably a little premature to push for such recognition at the present time.

References

Goldman, J. (1982). Clinical child psychology training and credentialing. *Journal of Clinical Child Psychology, 11,* 8-12.

Mayfield, P.N. (1978). ABPP — *Historical overview.* Unpublished manuscript.

Sales, B., Bricklin, P., & Hall, J. (1984a). *Specialization in psychology: Principles.* APA Board of Professional Affairs (Committee on Specialization). Unpublished manuscript.

Sales, B., Bricklin, P., & Hall, J. (1984b). *Specialization in psychology: Procedures.* APA Board of Professional Affairs (Committee on Specialization). Unpublished manuscript.

Sechrest, L.N. (1985). Specialization? Who needs it? *Clinical Psychologist, 38,* 1-3.

Summary of Concurrent Small Groups Discussions on Models of Training and Credentialing/Licensing Issues

Academic Level

Michael C. Roberts
University of Alabama

This group considered a broad range of issues related to training and saw as its primary goals to sum up the conference discussions to this point, develop the content for the final conference recommendations, and suggest ways to begin implementation. Several ideas and concepts were proposed for conference consideration:

1. In regard to the just completed presentations on credentialing, licensing, and designation by ABPP, and other regulatory actions regarding psychology specialties and practice, the group concluded that it would be premature at this point to consider any of these for the area of clinical child psychology. The group felt that the area, in general, and the training conference, in particular, should avoid being restrictive at such an early stage of defining the field of clinical child psychology and its necessary training components. Any attempts at credentialing or specialty licensing would be restrictive and exclusionary to other psychologists providing competent services for children, youth, and families. The area may choose to be restrictive at some later point, but certainly should not at this point.
2. The group requested that the conference consider proactive strategies for implementing the conference recommendations. This proactive pose included the need to influence, through both political and logical arguments, the following groups: The Council of University Directors of Clinical Training Programs, the APA Board of Education and Training, the Council of Chairs of Psychology Departments, the APA Accreditation Committee, and the Association of Psychology Internship Centers. Additionally, conferees should be urged to participate in training discussions, specialty designation procedures, and other relevant issues in meetings held in conjunction with various APA governance boards.
3. The group endorsed previous statements about influencing academic clinical psychology training programs through the Accreditation criteria to include *developmental bases of behavior* to the core list of the curriculum.

Additionally, the group wanted to push for much more substantial child experiences and coursework for *all* clinical psychology trainees. It is noted that generally trained psychologists *will* be providing *child* assessment and therapy services, regardless of their previous proclivities during their training careers. That is, service delivery to children is being offered by psychologists trained primarily or exclusively as adult oriented professionals. The ETS survey (Rosenfeld, Shimberg, & Thornton, 1984) indicates that psychologists report their practices involve substantial percentages of child work (viz, 10% are working with infants; 43% are working with children, and 64% are working with adolescents). Thus, most psychologists are serving children and youth in some ways to some degree. Therefore, the group recommends that the conference endorse the following resolution to the APA Accreditation Committee:

> In coursework and practica for assessment, psychopathology, and therapy, instruction and experience should include issues related to child and families for *all general clinical psychology training*.

In addition, this group recommends that the ethical issues course (as mandated currently under the Accreditaion Criteria) include specific instruction which includes having every student recognize and acknowledge the criteria on:

a. Knowing where one's professional competence ends
b. When a professional must refer the client to another specialist.

These ethical considerations should have special reference to the limits of child-related knowledge and practice of clinicians who work primarily with adults.

4. As suggested by other groups previously, the group endorsed the proposal for a Section 1 task force to extend the Division 37 Task Force report by developing specific recommendations for child experiences in internship training.
5. The group endorsed the *guiding principle* model (i.e., not courses, but topics and orientations needing coverage) of clinical child training, including work in:

A. Specialized child and family assessment.
B. Integration of therapeutic interventions and preventive interventions for specialized child work.
C. Specialized research methods.
D. Specialized clinical techniques and practica for child and family work.
E. Integration of specialized research and clinical practice with children to avoid bifurcation of these two essential elements of clinical child psychology.
F. Developmental orientation and specific knowledge of normal lifespan development as well as child and adult psychopathology.
G. Ethical and legal issues particular to child and family practice.
H. Interdisciplinary and intrapsychology specialty interaction.

6. The group urged the conference to recommend to the APA Accreditation Committee that the list of potential site visitors for APA programs include a designation of the specialty interests of the site visitors so that clinical child psychology programs can have inclusion of visitors with expertise and interest in the area. Additionally, it is suggested that clinical child specialists should be involved in site visiting panels when examining clinical child psychology programs.
7. The group recommends that inclusion of the specification that *all* specified clinical child psychology programs have faculty in the specialty.
8. The group recommends that more child-oriented psychologists be appointed to APA Boards (it is especially important that a child oriented person be on the Education and Training Board).
9. The group encouraged that the implementation committee of this clinical child psychology conference establish liaison and joint efforts to improve service delivery for children and families with other related doctoral level psychologists (e.g., Divisions 7, 16, 17, 29, 37, and Section 5 of Division 12, as well as with Division 12 itself).

The group urged that the Conference attempt to avoid divisiveness within the profession of psychology and promote the general concept of improving the provision of quality services for children, regardless of the label the professional uses in the provision of those services.

Reference

Rosenfeld, M., Shimberg, B., & Thornton, R. (1984). Job analysis of licensed psychologists: Part 2 — Analysis and conclusions. *Professional Practice of Psychology, 5,* 1-20.

Summary of Concurrent Small Group Discussion of Models of Training and Credentialing/Licensing Issues

Internship Level

Felicisima C. Serafica
The Ohio State University

The discussion started with an attempt to set goals for the group. Essentially the choice was between addressing issues of concern that have not been addressed thus far by the conference or formulating a set of summary statements and recommendations. The group opted to discuss issues, but in the course of discussing them, also arrived at a set of recommendations.

To provide a baseline, one of the participants gave a brief summary of the discussion of the internship level group following the plenary session on curriculum issues. Based on this report, our group decided to articulate the core experiences that define a child oriented setting. Prior to doing this, however, there was some discussion of models of internship training. The group concluded that, just as there are models of training in university programs, there are also models of internship training. The recommendations we are about to make acknowledge this heterogeneity. They are not directed toward making all internship settings homogeneous, but rather, to articulate the minimum defining characteristics of a child oriented internship setting.

1. A child oriented setting should be one where at least two thirds of the intern's experiences are in child related clinical activities. The remaining portion of experiences should be spent in working with adult clients whose presenting problems are not primarily child related.
2. A child oriented setting should provide to its interns didactic seminars on at least three topics: assessment, treatment, and case management, which should include consultation and how to deal with ethical, legal, and professional issues.
3. A child oriented setting should expose the intern to a broad range of ages, psychological problems, and techniques of assessment and treatment. Exposure to multiple settings would also be desirable, but it need not be required, since some settings might not have such diversity. For example, community mental health centers might have fewer different units than does a medical center.
4. A child oriented setting should have faculty who are broadly trained to deal with various types of psychological disorders.
5. A child oriented setting should provide exposure to multiple supervisors with different theoretical orientations.
6. The internship program should be an integral part of the clinical child psychology training program. To facilitate this integration, there should be better communication between the university training program and the internship setting. More specifically, the graduate program should provide the internship setting with a description of the intern's strengths and weaknesses. Based on this description, the internship setting would then formulate an individualized educational program (IEP) for the intern, including whatever additional experiences it deems important, over and above those related to the specific objectives of the university training program. The plan would be implemented following discussion and agreement between the appropriate representatives of the university and the internship. Written communication about the student's progress should occur at least twice a year, (i.e., around midyear and at the end of the internship year). It is important that university training programs acknowledge any reports from the internship setting, particularly in the use of feedback about the student.
7. Finally, a child oriented internship setting should acknowledge the need for flexibility and give the interns some opportunity to pursue their special clinical and research interests.

It should be noted that the group also considered whether or not interns should receive training in supervision. The conclusion reached was that, although it would be desirable, training in supervision would not be recommended as part of the core experiences. It would be more realistic to incorporate the training in a second year of internship experiences (if the internship duration is ever increased to two years). If a two-year internship is not possible, training in supervision should be part of a postdoctoral program.

Summary of Concurrent Small Group Discussions on Models of Training and Licensing/Accreditation Issues

Postdoctoral/Continuing Education Level

Rochelle L. Robbins
Harvard Medical School, Massachusetts Mental Health Center

The task of our group was to look at postdoctoral (PD) and continuing education (CE) issues related to this afternoon's sessions on models of training, credentialing and licensing. We took as our mission the examination of how to work within the model of a generic psychological approach *and* how to increase clinical psychological pratitioners' skills in working with children, youth, and families.

Our group outlined several types of PD/CE training needs:

1. PD/CE training and skill development for working with children, youth, and families for the generic professional psychologist. Our focus was on increasing the quality of work with the population.
2. PD/CE training to increase opportunities for the child trained clinicians to learn about what is new, special, and related to their current work. We were aware of comments related to the *half-life* of our training and the feeling that professionals working with children, youth, and families, needed to know about a very broad range of topics, populations, and settings. This range of topics might be effectively addressed through the CE format.
3. PD/CE experiences as contributing to continued excitement, interest, and vitality of practitioners in the field.
4. PD/CE training as a necessary part of our own identification as clinical child psychologists.

Our group also addressed issues specific to continuing education and postdoctoral training of clinical skills for service delivery to children, youth, and families by the generally trained clinical psychologist. We discussed the specifics of producing and assuring quality continuing education presentations. It was suggested that we look into what Section 1 may be considering in this area. Our discussions focused on a range of pragmatic issues from CE requirements by licensing boards to real world needs by front-line practitioners for specific skills. The group was concerned with qualifications of leaders of continuing education programs that address clinical skills with children, youth, and families, as well as the problem with continuing education programs that are too brief to develop skills. A model involving more than a single workshop or seminar experience was seen as desirable.

With regard to postdoctoral training at the programmatic level, we briefly touched on the respecialization requirements of APA and the suggested standards for postdoctoral clinical training programs presented in the 1985 APIC newsletter.

We summarized by noting that, while children, youth, and families remain underserved populations, and while many of the pratitioners working in this field were not *formally* trained, continuing education/postdoctoral programs, in particular, might effectively enlarge the number of qualified providers in this field.

Recommendations, Guidelines, and Conclusions

Introduction: Recommendations, Guidelines, and Conclusions

June M. Tuma
Louisiana State University

Conferences have been viewed as serving the function of a mediation agent for forces at work both within and without the profession. Earlier, I have said that the Hilton Head Conference on the Training of Clinical Child Psychologists has been stimulated from within by concerns with the present status of training programs, manpower shortages, as well as the inadequate manner in which conferences in the past have dealt with issues relevant to training clinical child psychologists. Impetus from without includes the pressing demand for services to children in need as well as the recent NIMH funding priorities of clinical child psychology training.

I have also earlier stated that the *best* we can hope from this conference is a momentum which will serve to make constructive changes in training programs for clinical child psychologists. Conversely, the *least* we can hope for is that the conference will make *all* psychologists more conscious of the multitude of issues important to serving children, youth, and families. It is important to note that *some* important impact is expected. However, implied in both of these extremes is that the conferees will make appropriate recommendations and plans for implememtation of these recommendations.

To serve as a stimulus for simultaneously considering implementation strategies as conferees deliberated over the many resolutions brought to their attention, Honore Hughes presented one model, a consultation model, of guiding programs in adapting their training programs to be consistent with the considerations of this conference. Her proposal focused on the implementation of programmatic changes within individual institutions. There are other considerations concerning implementation at the organizational level, as well. Very important examples of this concerns the dissemination of conference resolutions to the various committees and boards of the APA and the Association of Programs of Internship Centers (APIC). In addition, implementations should ideally reach individuals, professional psychologists and students, as well as students-to-be. Important as well, and it turned out that the conferees wisely incorporated resolutions to accomplish it, is to impact clinical psychologists other than clinical *child* psychologists.

Following the presentation by Hughes, the format of this final half-day session was one whereby the spokesperson for each level of training (Academic, Internship and Postdoctoral/Continuing Education) presented a final summary of the two-day deliberations by small groups assigned to each level of training and then to present resolutions which came from the conclusions of those deliberations. After presentation of each resolution, the entire plenary group discussed the resolution, ammendments were made, and vote was taken on the final form of each resolution.

The material presented in this section reflects the summary of the spokesperson for each level of training. Incorporated into the summary, the resolutions adopted by the conferees are interspersed (presented in italics) (see also Appendix F for a complete listing of conference recommendations). It should be noted that issues in addition to those which reached concensus are presented in the discussion of spokespersons. Issues which were deemed important by the conferees, but for various reasons were not adopted, are incorporated here as well as those that were adopted.

The intent of incorporation of the summaries of the concurrent small group discussions throughout these *Proceedings* is an attempt to present the entire context and flavor of the conference. As with any convening of large numbers of individuals, a lot more gets said than can possibly be included in a set of resolutions. Perhaps we could say the same thing about the summaries; that is, it is impossible to capture all of the important issues that were discussed, deliberated over, *discarded,* changed, eliminated, and so forth. However, the conference committee sincerely hopes that we have been able to capture the major essence of what occurred at the Hilton Head Conference on Training Clinical Child Psychologists.

Consultation and Transfer of Expertise Regarding the Professional Preparation of Clinical Child Psychologists: A Proposed Strategy for Effecting Change in Training Programs

Honore M. Hughes
University of Arkansas

It is clear from a number of recent articles and presentations that children and adolescents are an underserved and often neglected population with respect to mental health care (Denham, 1979; Tuma, 1982; Wohlford, 1979), and that the number of adequately trained clinical child psychologists in this country is disturbingly insufficient (Goggins & Goggins, 1979; Tuma, 1980). The inadequate training [for working with children] of clinical psychologists who have been prepared for intervention with adults (Johnson & Robbins, 1982; Tuma & Pratt, 1982) must also be addressed, since these professionals may find themselves serving children and families through sheer demand for services. It is apparent that more clinical psychologists must be sufficiently well trained to provide quality services to children; this more satisfactory preparation is important for both the clinical child psychologist and the "generalist" clinician who serves children and youth infrequently. These training issues need to be addressed in two ways: (a) by increasing the number of clinical child psychologists trained, and (b) by making the child-oriented aspect of general (i.e., adult-focused) training programs more adequate.

The following proposal outlines a method for consultation and transfer of expertise to professionals involved in training students in psychology to provide services to children and families. It is predicated upon the assumption that a number of training issues which are currently unresolved will have been resolved at the conference on professional preparation, or at least partially so (e.g., whether school and developmental psychology programs will be included in providing clinical child training). The proposal presented will be revised in light of the decisions made at the upcoming conference on training, since the current methods proposed represent the opinions of the author. Programs targated for consultation will be those at the pre-internship, internship, and postdoctoral levels which acknowledge the need to broaden or strenghten the clinical child content and practica in their general or specialized programs (e.g., track or subspecialty). The consultation will consist of designated experts in the field of clinical child psychology visiting target programs and making recommendations in relation to specific areas of training which need to be modified in order to improve the preparation of students for providing clinical services to children and youth. The proposal will be presented in three major sections: (1) the initial planning steps for the provision of consultation, (2) the form and logistics of the transfer of expertise, and (3) possible funding sources for the consultation.

Initial Planning Steps

Two important steps in developing a consultation process are: (1) to establish the criteria for adequate training in general and specialized programs, and (2) to create a procedure for the transfer of expertise in the area. It is anticipated that both of these steps will be addressed at the proposed conference. Areas for which guidelines likely will be developed include curricula, practica, opportunities for community contacts related to children, youth, and families and qualifications of faculty identified as clinical child psychologists. I would argue that separate criteria be established for training programs with three different types of goals: (1) those general programs in which students are primarily trained to work with adults; (2) specialized general programs which through informal tracks or areas of concentration prepare clinical child psychologists; and (3) programs which utilize the formalized subspeciality approach to training clinical child psychologists.

The second major step in the development of the consultation is to establish a procedure for the transfer of expertise. This process would include aspects such as: (1) establishing the content to be transmitted during the consultation; (2) identifying potential core persons with expertise in the chosen content areas who would be interested in participating in the consultations; and (3) establishing the consultation/transfer teams.

The first two of the three aspects would likely be

addressed at the conference on training. I would anticipate that the content of the consultation would emerge out of discussions regarding criteria for adequate preparation and that the specific standards delineated would vary according to whether the training program is a general or specialized one at the predoctoral level, an internship site, or a postdoctoral "retread" or advanced child training program. Additional practical concerns to be included in the content of the consultation could consist of suggestions regarding methods of presenting proposals to administrators which would enhance the chances of a positive reception, both within the academic department and at higher levels, as well as strategies related to ways to incorporate training program changes into proposals for training grants.

The identification of core trainers with expertise in the established content areas could be accomplished at the training conference, as well as through questionnaires sent to clinical child psychologists. Experts in the various areas could be self-nominated, and/or invited from among the members of Section One, Section Five, Division 37, Division 7, and the American Orthopsychiatric Association, the National Association of School Psychologists, or other organizations whose members serve children.

After the content areas and the core training people are identified, a central training committee would appoint three-person consultation teams on an "as needed" basis. The teams would be selected for each consultation partially on the basis of the expertise needed at the requesting training site, plus would include people who represent areas of expertise which are common to and necessary for all training programs in clinical child psychology.

Progress/Logistics of Consultation

After the content and personnel for the consultation teams have been established, the actual form and logistics of the transfer of expertise must be addressed. My conceptualization of the form that this process might take includes four phases: (1) the identification of consultee programs, (2) visits to the requesting sites, (3) mutual feedback and follow-up, and (4) final evaluation of the requesting program by the consultation team after a 2- or 3-year period.

In order for directors of training programs to be aware of the consultation services, the availability of this source of expertise must be communicated to potential consultee sites at all levels. This information could be disseminated through notices in APA publications, as well as by sending letters of information and explanation to directors of training in graduate and professional schools, internships, and postdoctoral programs. I am assuming that an APA body such as the Education and Training Board would make quite clear the necessity for enhancing the quality of child-oriented preparation as a requirement of accreditation.

The first phase would take place when personnel from the individual training programs who wish to receive consultation services contact the central executive committee. Questionnaires would be sent to the requesting program for the purpose of first identifying the persons most involved in the clinical child area of the training program, then having those people specify areas of need and interest for the consultation and describe the functional operation of their training program. In response to this information, the organizational committee would assign an appropriate consultation team. Based upon the acquired information, the team members would study the identified needs, and establish a tentative plan for training. The suggestions made regarding preparation of clinicians to work with children and families would be provided within the context of the program's current operation and be as realistic and feasible as possible.

After the establishment of a tentative plan for transfer of expertise, the consultation team would make a two-day visit to the recipient site. The basic agenda for this second phase could consist of information-gathering the first day and information-sharing the the second day. The consultation team would talk with the faculty members who have clinical child interests, as well as with students and other support faculty. Topics that might be addressed would include current courses taught, the clinical training sites, the major clinical research interests of faculty members, support for clinical research, and the type and methods of supervision provided. Students might be queried regarding their background, interests, and future plans. Major purposes of the first day would be for the consultants to obtain a clear picture of the way the program currently functions, and to become cognizant of potential additional resources, both in the academic and larger community.

The second day of the visit would emphasize collaborative efforts on the parts of all involved and would be spent in the actual transfer of expertise, with the consultants making suggestions and providing direction based on their experience, modified to meet the consultee program's structure and needs. Persons attending this meeting might include, as an example, in an academic department of psychology, the Director of Clinical Training, the Director of the Psychological Clinic, the Department Chairperson, and a student representative, as well as the faculty primarily concerned with clinical child interests and responsibilities. The suggestions would be presented in a 2- or 3-year time frame, and substantial portions of the meeting would involve discussion of the logistics of implementation. Recommendations would be made regarding the necessity for additional faculty, for developing new courses, or for utilizing courses taught in other departments (e.g., special education, speech pathology, or home economics). Advice could also be provided in relation to utilizing community resources for possible additional training sites (e.g., Head Start, shelters for battered women, or adolescent treatment centers) and establishing contacts with community agencies in order to increase the number of child referrals to the program's Psychological Clinic. Similar suggestions would be made at the internship and postdoctoral levels, as appropriate.

The consultants would also focus their recommendations on preventing difficulties in implementation. Based on their experience with other programs, a consultation team member might also accompany the Director of Clinical Training during a meeting with a higher administrative official in which issues such as hiring an additional faculty member and/or creating new courses might be discussed. Before the consultation team departs, tentative plans will be made for follow-up contact every six months for 2 or 3 years, as well as for contact on an as needed basis. Within one month of the consultation team's visit, a report detailing the information gathered and recommendations made will be sent to the individual program and the central training committee.

The third phase of the process of expertise transfer would consist of feedback and follow-up after the report is received. At this point, feedback from the consultee program, which had not been shared during the on-site visit, would be provided to the team members regarding their consultation. The purpose of this information would be to let the team know how well, in retropsect, their advice met the needs of the program, and to provide suggestions for modifications in the consultation process. At that time definite arrangements would be made for scheduled "check-in" phone contacts every six months. During these contacts progress attained in the past six months and plans for the upcoming time period would be discussed. Possible topics covered might include suggestions for writing a new training grant or dealing with a recalcitrant administrator. The consultant might also provide additional on-site contacts if the department is experiencing difficulties for which such a visit would be warranted. At the end of the designated 2 or 3 year consultation period, the consultation process will be evaluated from the point of view of both parties involved. The requesting programs would evaluate the recommendations made and the process of expertise transfer and provide detailed descriptions of both the positive and negative aspects of the process.

The fourth phase of the transfer would be another short visit to the consultee program in order to evaluate the modifications that have been implemented and to decide whether the program meets the established criteria. Discussions would be held with the personnel involved in the consultation regarding the changes that have been implemented, the difficulties that were experienced, and the structure and functioning of the newly modified training program. The consultant team will then make a decision regarding the status of the program in relation to accreditation. Feedback will be provided to the program stating whether the program meets the guidelines, either as a general clinical training program, or as a specialized training program which prepares clinical child psychologists. The same would apply to internships and postdoctoral programs. The categories of accreditation which would be communicated to the organizational committee could be *accredit, provisional,* or *no accreditation,* with the reasons for the decision outlined in detail and shared with the program. If a specialized program were fully or provisionally accreditated, then the organizational committee would list the name of the program in the publications that would be used for communicating the availability of track or subspecialty training at the pre-internship, internship, and postdoctoral levels.

Funding

The third major section contains ideas related to obtaining funding for the consultation teams and the transfer of expertise. The potential sources of funding range from external support (e.g., from NIMH) to the costs being met by each requesting program. It is anticipated that there would be a substantial number of requests for consultation as greater numbers of directors of programs which train clinicians are made aware that better quality child-oriented training must be available for students who wish to work (or may end up working) with children, in order (a) to provide for specialization, and (b) to more broadly train students who have a general (i.e., mostly adult) focus.

The organizational executive training committee or a designated subcommittee would be charged with obtaining financial support for the consultation. One potential external funding source might be NIMH, since it has been noted by that organization that training and service deficiencies exist in the area of children and youth (Denham, 1979). Other potential avenues to pursue might include financial arrangements made through APA in a manner similar to the way current APA accreditation site visits are funded, with some portion of the visit financed through departmental budgets. Some of the costs might be borne by several of the APA divisions, such as Section One and Division 37, or a fund might be established to which all organizations and individuals interested in training regarding services to children might contribute. Private foundations which have been sympathetic to the needs of children and families might also be cultivated as resources.

To summarize, in order to effect change in training programs, a strategy has been proposed which is in the form of consultation and transfer of expertise. It includes three major steps: (1) establishing guidelines for training and creating a procedure for consultation; (2) developing a four-stage process of consultation which includes identification of interested programs, site visits, feedback and follow-up, and evaluation; and (3) identifying funding sources for the proposed transfer of expertise. It is felt that this consultation process would promote the sharing of knowledge and experience between persons active in the field of clinical child psychology and personnel in training programs who wish to modify and strengthen the preparation of their graduates for work with children, youth, and families.

References

Denham, W.H. (1979, August). *Training for child mental health: An NIMH priority.* Paper presented at the annual meeting of the American Psychological Association, New York.

Goggins, J.E., & Goggins, E.B. (1979). When adult therapists work with children: Differential treatment considerations. *Professional Psychology, 10,* 330-337.

Johnson, J.H., & Robbins, R.L. (1982). On the need for clinical child psychology training within the context of general clinical training programs. *Journal of Clinical Child Psychology, 11,* 35-38.

Tuma, J.M. (1982). Proposal for a national conference on professional preparation of clinical child psychologists. *Journal of Clinical Child Psychology, 11,* 3-7.

Tuma, J.M. (1980, August). *Redirecting training efforts to provide services to children, youth, and families.* Paper presented at the annual meeting of the American Psychological Association, Montreal.

Tuma, J.M., & Pratt, J.M. (1982). Clinical child psychology practice and training: A survey. *Journal of Clinical Child Psychology, 11,* 27-34.

Wohlford, P. (1979). Clinical child psychology: The emerging speciality. *The Clinical Psychologist, 12,* 25-26.

Summary and Proposals for Recommendations for Academic Training in Clinical Child Psychology[1]

Annette M. La Greca
University of Miami

Over the past two days, we have discussed many issues relevant to academic training. Although a general consensus has been reached in some areas, others are in need of further discussion and deliberation. In addition, and most importantly, we must develop a plan for action so that this conference may have a lasting impact on the training of clinical child psychologists.

To summarize the many ideas that were discussed, I've organized the discussion around three main areas of focus. These are (1) the aspects of clinical child psychology training that are important for all clinical training programs, (2) recommendations for specialized training in the clinical child area, and (3) other general issues of importance.

Areas of Importance for All Clinical Psychology Training Programs

First, there has been considerable discussion of, and agreement upon, the importance of a *life-span developmental* approach in all clinical psychology training. More specifically, it was recommended that (a) a course on the (life-span) developmental basis of *normal* behavior be required in all graduate level clinical psychology training programs, and that this be made a part of the APA guidelines, and (b) that students be provided with some experiences with "normal" children in "normal settings" as a part of their graduate training (e.g., observations of children in day care).

The conference, therefore, unanimously voted on the following:

Resolution 1. *We recommend* ***all*** *APA approved programs providing professional training in clinical psychology* ***require*** *a course on the developmental bases of normal behavior (emphasizing a life-span developmental approach).*

Resolution 2. *It is desirable that all APA approved programs providing professional training in clinical psychology include experiences with* ***normal*** *children and youth, as well as with other age groups, in diverse,* ***normal*** *settings as a part of every student's graduate level training.*

Secondly, there was considerable sentiment that all graduate students in clinical psychology should receive *at least minimal training* in the areas of child assessment, child psychopathology, and child/family intervention (i.e., treatment, consultation, and prevention). This training should occur both on a didactic level, and in practicum settings. The amount or proportion of training that should be devoted to child issues was not specified or delineated, but it was felt that some of this training could occur within the context of more general courses or practicum experiences.

Third, there was discussion of the importance of providing graduate students with some experience in psychological consultation in all graduate psychology training programs. This could be accomplished in a variety of ways, such as through coursework or by integrating consultation into practicum experiences.

Fourth, it was emphasized that ethical guidelines on working with children, youth, and families should be presented and reinforced with all students in graduate psychology programs. In this manner, students may be able to make appropriate decisions regarding the limits of their competence when they function in a professional role. Moreover, some legal/ethical issues are particular to children, youth, and families, and given that many general clinical psychologists work with these individuals, they need to be cognizant of such special considerations.

Fifth, it was advocated that prevention attitudes and skills be integrated into clinical training at *all* levels (graduate, internship, and postdoctoral).

Sixth, the importance of facilitating students' awareness of the various *systems* within which the child functions (e.g., family, peer group, schools, etc.) was noted.

The following resolution concerning most of these recommendations is as follows:

Resolution 3. *We encourage that training suffi-*

[1]In each of the three final summaries, the final resolutions are interspersed (in italics). The reader will note that the resolution numbers are not here presented in order. The entire set of recommendations are presented in Appendix F (without comment).

cient to provide minimal competencies in assessment, psychopathology, and intervention (e.g., treatment, consultation, prevention) with children, youth and families, be included at the graduate level in all clinical training programs. Such training experiences should occur on both a didactic and practicum level.

Areas of Importance in Clinical Child Psychology Training

Numerous issues specific to clinical child psychology training emerged during our discussions of the past two days. Before getting into specifics, however, I'll describe some general trends.

There appeared to be much consensus that we continue with specialty training in the clinical child psychology area, but that we *not* seek *specialty status* in any organized manner at the present time. It was felt that specialty status was too premature. Many issues of concern were raised with respect to seeking specialty status, most notably (1) problems in educating the consumer as to differences between a clinical child specialist and a (general) clinical psychologist, and (2) difficulties in determining a uniform set of criteria that could currently be utilized to license or otherwise credential individuals in the clinical child area because of the diversity of current training programs.

Despite reluctance to pursue specialty status now, there appeared to be agreement over the importance of continuing and refining clinical child training programs at the graduate (and internship) level.

Areas that were mentioned as important for inclusion in *all* clinical child psychology programs were as follows:

(1) Life-span developmental coursework and practical experiences.
(2) Experience with children and families of different ethnic minorities.
(3) Training experiences in the systems that affect a child's functioning (e.g., family, school, community). A systems approach could be integrated into existing training programs.
(4) Emphasis on the special ethical and legal issues involved in work with children, youth, and families.
(5) Integration of prevention concepts and experiences into clinical child training.

In addition to the above, the areas of child assessment and child/family intervention were discussed at length. For the most part, conference participants shied away from delineating specific courses or content areas that should be covered, recognizing the impossibility of providing students with practical experience with every assessment instrument or method. Rather, it was advocated that assessment be viewed as a problem-solving, hypotheses-generating process that requires *psychological understanding* of the child and the systems affecting the child. Several guidelines were advocated for achieving this goal, as follows:

(a) Students should be familiarized with assessment instruments that exist for children of different ages (0-18 years).
(b) Students should be familiarized with multiple and varied methods of assessment (e.g., interviews, observations, standardized tests, etc.).
(c) An appreciation of the special considerations involved in assessing children of minority backgrounds should be provided.
(d) A thorough understanding and appreciation of psychometric theory should be provided, so that trainees can critically evaluate existing assessment instruments, as well as new measures as they are developed.
(e) The importance of integrating information obtained from various sources should be recognized.
(f) An awareness of the systems within which the child functions, and how these systems interact with the assessment process, should be provided (e.g., sensitivity in terms of what information to obtain on a child, and with whom the information may be shared). Related to this is an appreciation of the special ethical considerations one faces in the child assessment area.

These considerations were unanimously supported by the conferees.

In addition to the first two resolutions, which apply to clinical *child* programs as well as other programs, conferees endorsed the following three resolutions:

Resolution 4. *Similarly, we encourage that training, sufficient to provide minimal competencies in assessment, psychopathology, and intervention (e.g., treatment, consultation, prevention) with adults be included at the graduate level in all programs training clinical child psychologists. Such training experiences should occur on both a didactic and practicum level.*

Resolution 5. *We encourage that a knowledge base and experience with children from different minority backgrounds be provided at graduate and internship levels by all programs training psychologists in the clinical child area.*

Resolution 7. *We recommend that graduate programs offering training in the clinical child area foster an appreciation of the broad and diverse contexts within which children develop and within which psychologists working with children, youth, and families must function (e.g., family, school, etc.).*

A similar *critical* approach to intervention methods was advocated. In general, participants felt that the strength of clinical training within a scientist-practitioner model was that it provided a critical approach to clinical methods.

To express the strength of their convictions, conferees unanimously endorsed the following resolution:

Resolution 10. *We endorse the Boulder Scientist-Practitioner Model as the model for training in* clinical child psychology.

Another major topic of discussion has been the status of the Division 37 Task Force document (*Guidelines for Training Psychologists to Work with Children, Youth and Family,* see Appendix E). This document was the subject of much deliberation. On the positive side, adopting such a set of guidelines might facilitate the development of some uniformity among clinical child training programs and ensure that individuals receive adequate clinical preparation. However, serious drawbacks to adopting such guidelines as requirements for all clinical child programs were noted. One possible limitation is that many existing programs providing quality training could not meet each and every *requirement.* Rather than facilitating the growth of clinical child programs, the document may actually serve to hinder or undermine specialty training efforts. My personal view is that they may be extremely helpful as a set of guidelines for students (and others) who are interested in clinical child psychology training to enable them to develop their own IEPS (Individual Eduational Plans) for training, that can extend over the entire course of their training years (including graduate school, internship, postdoctoral, and continuing education). However, I have concerns about adopting them as requirements that we wish to enforce on any level at the present time. The issue of how we wish to approach these guidelines is one that remains for full group discussion.

Conferees expressed their sentiments by endorsing the following:

Resolution 9. *We endorse the Division 37 Task Force document (*Guidelines for Training Psychologists to Work With Children, Youth and Families,* Roberts, Erickson, & Tuma, 1985) as guiding principles for those implementing training programs in clinical child psychology. We further recommend that these guidelines be used flexibly and not in a restrictive manner.*

Finally, although most of the discussion centered on issues relevant to professional training, the importance of training clinical child psychology researchers was stressed. If we wish to advance knowledge in clinical child psychology, we must not lose sight of this very important goal.

Other Issues of Importance for Clinical Child Psychology Training

Several additional issues germane to the structure and review of clinical child training programs and the nature of affiliation between clinical child psychology and other groups of psychologists maintaining interests in children emerged.

Several of the plenary presentations addressed the issue of subspecialization within clinical child psychology (e.g., working within rural settings, with multiproblem children, or in pediatric settings). For the most part, the participants appeared to advocate viewing these specific areas as suitable for subspecialty training that extends beyond a *general* clinical child psychology preparation rather than developing expertise in these areas in all clinical child psychologists.

In terms of APA site reviews for existing programs that train clinical child psychologists, it was stressed that each site visiting team have at lease one member with expertise in the clinical child area.

The following resolution received unanimous endorsement:

Resolution 6. *We recommend that APA site visitor teams reviewing programs that claim to train clinical child psychologists ensure that a member of the visiting team has expertise in clinical child psychology.*

Regarding program structure, it was advocated (perhaps facetiously?) that each defined clinical child psychology training program have at least one clinical child faculty member. More importantly, the extensive difficulties of maintaining a clinical child psychology training program with only one clinical child faculty member available for implementation were recognized. The following resolution expresses the conviction:

Resolution 8. *We recommend that every graduate program providing training in clinical child psychology have at least one clinical child faculty member.*

Finally, in terms of boundary issues with other psychologists maintaining interests in children and families (e.g., school, community, and applied developmental psychologists), there appeared to be considerable consensus that we should work to join forces and establish successful liaisons with these other groups. The dangers of becoming too restrictive and too much of a "guild" were noted, with the high potential for alienating others who may best be viewed as allies rather than adversaries.

Summary and Proposals for Recommendations for Internship Training in Clinical Child Psychology

A.J. Finch, Jr.
Medical University of South Carolina

Rochelle L. Robbins
Harvard Medical School
Massachusetts Mental Health Center

The concurrent small group discussions on internship training in clinical child psychology during the Hilton Head Conference were truly developmental in nature. The internship discussions were born with a cry of protest regarding the Division 37 guidelines for training psychologists to work with children, youth, and families (Roberts, Erickson, & Tuma; see Appendix E). In this nine page article, one paragraph was devoted to the internship year. The group was in agreement that the internship year was of far more importance than the passing mention provided in the guidelines. The group viewed the internship as an essential component of clinical child psychology training that needed to be integrated more closely with the other predoctoral experiences and that the academic and internship programs shared the responsibility for providing the intern with at least minimal competence before the completion of the doctoral degree. However, as the discussions evolved, it was obvious that this document served a heuristic purpose in motivating the group. The group resolved that Section 1 develop a document (similar to the Division 37 guidelines) that focuses on internship training. Conferees endorsed the following resolution:

Resolution 17. *It is recommended that Section 1 create a standing committee on internship training with the purpose of rounding out the recommendations made at the conference. Section 1 should also expand upon these recommendations.*

Discussion focused on training as it applied to both general clinical psychology internships and clinical child psychology internships. With regard to general clinical psychology internship training, it was recommended that *all* interns be provided with supervised experience and training in working with a broad range of populations, including children, youth, families, and adults. Consequently, it was concluded that although internships and interns could choose to specialize with a particular population, a (unspecified) minimum amount of training with both child and adult populations was essential. In addition, it was felt that *all* interns should be provided supervision by supervisors from a variety of theoretical perspectives to provide the intern with broadbased experiences in working with clients. Although most of the remaining recommendations center mainly on clinical child psychology internship programs, many have direct application to general clinical psychology internship programs.

An internship in clinical child psychology is a post clerkship, post practicum, and post externship level training program designed to be an integral part of the training of clinical child psychologists. The exact number of hours of experience with children, youth, and families necessary prior to internship was not determined. The internship should provide experiences of a greater depth and variety than those provided by pre-internship training. An internship in clinical child psychology should include work with both adults and children. However, the internship should provide a *minimum* of two-thirds of time and experiences with children, families, and related systems to be considered a *clinical child psychology* internship. Conferees unanimously supported the following resolution:

Resolution 13. *Internships that call themselves child oriented should provide a minimum of two-thirds experience in child related activity.*

The group recognized that each internship program is partially determined by the nature of the facility, the staff, the particular populations served, as well as funding patterns of agencies supporting them. Consequently, each internship program will be unique in certain aspects; therefore, guidelines need to be flexible. However, certain core requirements were felt to be common to most internship programs in clinical child psychology.

Internship programs in clinical child psychology should be broadbased with regard to populations served, theoretical orientation, and experiences provided. In addition to the need for experiences with adults, the clinical child psychology intern should receive experiences with children from as broad an age range as possible, with experiences with infants through adolescents being the goal. Diversity in gender, in socioeconomic background, in ethnic origin and in presenting problems also should be the goal. The group felt that experiences with a wide variety of populations in different settings was necessary to insure that the intern would have a frame of reference from which to function during his/her future practice. Populations may include, but not be limited to, those with emotional problems, mental retardation, developmental problems, sensory impairment, and physical handicaps.

Throughout the discussions, certain themes continued to emerge. First, any understanding of the nature of the problems presented by the child must take into consideration the developmental level of the child. Certainly, some behaviors are normal at one age that may be seen as more pathological at another time. Only through an understanding of life span development can these behaviors be properly understood.

These issues are contained in the following resolution:

Resolution 14. *We recognize that the nature of each internship program is partially determined by the nature of the facility, the staff, the particular populations served, and the funding patterns of supporting agencies. Consequently, each internship program will be unique in certain aspects and guidelines will need to be flexible.*

Internship programs in clinical child psychology should be broadbased with regard to populations served, theoretical orientation, and experiences provided. In addition to the need for experiences with adults, the clinical child psychology intern should receive experiences with children from as broad an age range as possible with experiences with infants through adolescents being the goal.

Diversity in gender, in socioeconomic background, in ethnic origin, and in presenting problems of served clients is a desired goal. An understanding of the nature of the problem presented by the child must take into account the developmental level of the child.

As important as an understanding of the child's developmental level is, an understanding of the child's various systems, such as family, school, peers, community, and so forth, is also important. Internship programs in clinical child psychology should insure an understanding of these systems and their interactions through experiences in dealing with them. (Since these considerations were accounted for by resolution number 7 in the academic level, and thus would address this concern, it was not repeated for the internship level.)

A diversity of theoretical orientations for the supervisors of the clinical child psychology interns was felt to be essential to familiarize the intern with different frameworks for dealing with children and their families. The group felt that the intern needed training designed to provide the necessary skills to treat the child and his/her family from the theoretical approach most appropriate for the individual case.

Internship training in clinical child psychology should include didactic and supervised training in at least assessment, intervention strategies, and consultation skills. In addition, training and experience in prevention was seen as highly desirable. The nature of the didactic training and supervised experiences in each of these areas should be as broadbased and varied as possible. Case management conferences should be utilized to integrate assessment, treatment, and consultation with ethical considerations and increase awareness of evaluating the success of the chosen intervention. Thus, conferees unanimously endorsed the following resolution.

Resolution 16. *Internship training in clinical child psychology should include didactic and supervised training at least in assessment, intervention strategies, case management, and consultation skills. In addition, training and experience in prevention are highly desirable. The nature of the didactic training and supervised experiences in each of these areas should be as broadbased and varied as possible. Case management conferences should be utilized to integrate assessment, treatment, and consultation, with ethical considerations and an increased awareness of the need for evaluating the success of our chosen intervention also being considered.*

Due to the varied backgrounds of the interns coming to an internship program, internship experiences should be individually tailored to meet the specific needs of the particular intern while emphasizing the particular strengths of the program. It was recommended that the equivalent of an individual education plan (IEP) be developed for each intern at the beginning of the internship year. The internship, in collaboration with the academic program, should specify competencies, training experiences, and methods for evaluating performance. These sentiments were expressed in the following resolution:

Resolution 12. *The graduate program and internship site will engage in sufficient communication so that an individualized plan for each intern can be written by the internship site upon acceptance of the intern. This plan will be reviewed periodically with continued communication with the graduate program.*

Internships should be developmental in nature, in the sense that the intern increases his/her skills during the course of the internship year. Consequently, an intern's work should be more closely supervised initially, with increased freedom and responsibility given to the intern as skills develop. Since each clinical child psychology intern will have a different educational plan and develop differently, each intern probably should have a particular internship staff member to serve as the primary training supervisor and to monitor his/her program. Such a staff member would be responsible for insuring that the intern's educational needs were being met and that his/her experiences and responsibilities are developmentally appropriate.

To insure that each clinical child psychology intern has an individually tailored experience, the group felt that the intern's university based training program should provide the internship program with a description of the intern's strengths, weaknesses, and needs. The internship program would then develop the individual education plan and provide the university with information on how the intern was progressing. It was felt that a written evaluation of the intern's progress should be provided at midyear and at the end of the year. In addition, the university should react to each of these reports. The group felt that increased interaction between the university graduate program and the internship program was badly needed and should be an integral part of quality training. Conferees unanimously endorsed the following:

Resolution 11. *We reaffirm the Accreditional Guidelines presented in the APA* **Monitor** *(American Psychological Association, 1979), especially as it intends to increase collaboration to accomplish integration of the internship within the total doctoral training experience:*

> *VII.B.2c*
> *Close working relationship should be established between the internship program and the graduate program in professional psychology in order to facilitate advisement of students and matching of internship site characteristics with intern talents and interests. Doctoral programs and internship centers have a responsibility for mutual communication concerning evaluation of students' preparation for field experience, their progress in the field program, and their evaluation of the field experience. Specific procedures should be established for such communication; mutual visits are strongly encouraged. (p.16)*

Although the internship in clinical child psychology is primarily a clinical experience, the group felt that research should be integrated into the training program. Internship programs will vary greatly as to how research is integrated, but applied clinical research models should be provided and time made available for intern research. Frequently, an artificial distinction is made between clinical and research activities, when in actuality, the two can be combined through careful planning. Despite its problems, the Boulder model was felt to be the most desirable within clinical child psychology internship. The following resolution was unanimously supported:

Resolution 15. *It is encouraged that research be incorporated into the internship program, both by allowing time and providing role models.*

Requirements for entry into a clinical child psychology internship program were discussed, but not finalized. However, it was felt that clinical child psychology interns should be from regionally accredited coherent doctoral programs in psychology. Consideration was given to whether or not the intern should be from a specific professional program, such as clinical, counseling, or school psychology. However, consensus on this item was not reached. Internship programs in clinical child psychology may have different prerequistie experience requirements for admission. These prerequisites should be made explicit to prospective interns and their predoctoral programs. Similarly, internships should specify the clinical competencies which are expected to be achieved by the intern during the internship.

An internship program in clinical child psychology should have a faculty or staff skilled in providing services to the various populations served by the intern. In addition, internship staffs should be multidisciplinary with the intern receiving supervision from a variety of professionals. Experiences in interacting with professionals from other disciplines was felt to be an experience usually unavailable on a preinternship level.

Internship programs should have interns from a variety of programs so that the interns can learn from each other. An open noncompetitive exchange of ideas and skills among interns should be encouraged. In addition, internship programs should facilitate the development of a sense of cohesive group cooperation and support among the interns.

Some discussion was given as to whether the internship should be extended to two years. The additional year would allow for expanded direct service and consultation, as well as supervisory experiences and increased supervision. In addition, since most states require two years of supervised experience for licensure, this extra requirement could be met by expanding the internship. However, the group was divided on this matter, and no recommendations for change were made.

Funding for internship programs was of considerable concern to the group. Since service demands may be greater in programs where patient funds are used to support interns, there exists the possibility that training needs might suffer or be compromised by overly specialized funding services. There seemed to be no solution to the reality of funding problems and internship programs will need to exercise care to maintain their training focus.

Summary and Proposals for Recommendations for Postdoctoral/ Continuing Education in Clinical Child Psychology

Dennis Drotar
Case Western Reserve University School of Medicine

Postdoctoral training and continuing education have an important place in the development of clinical child psychologists in the following areas: (1) refinement and extension of skills; (2) learning of new developments in research and techniques; and (3) maintaining and stimulating interest in the field. One of the most impressive features of postdoctoral training is the variety of programs that are offered. As a consequence, it is difficult to make generalizations about postdoctoral training, especially in view of the absence of much-needed survey information concerning the goals of programs, their structure, the training experiences offered, and the impact on professional development. In further articulating the goals and structure of postdoctoral training in clinical child psychology, it is useful to think in terms of the two major kinds of postdoctoral training programs upon which postdoctoral training is based: (1) general training in clinical psychology and (2) specialized training in clinical child psychology. (A third possibility, formerly considered as postdoctoral training, respecialization for psychologists who were not trained in clinical psychology, is now fully considered under the APA guidelines and is actually more akin to predoctoral training in structure.)

Depending upon whether one has been trained in a general versus a specialized training program, the goals of postdoctoral training will be quite different. For example, for those trained in a more general clinical psychology program, postdoctoral (academic and internship) training can be the means for changing one's career directions toward a clinical child psychology focus. On the other hand, for those trained in a specialized clinical child psychology training program, the postdoctoral fellowship provides a means to extend the depth of one's clinical experience and/or to specialize with new populations.

There was uniform sentiment for the importance of postdoctoral training, especially postdoctoral training with a formalized structure in developing both the professional identity and skills of clinical child psychologists. The importance of the postdoctoral training experience accrues from a number of sources: (1) there is a great deal to learn in clinical child psychology, especially when one considers the new advances in knowledge that have been made in specialized assessments and interventions (e.g., behavioral and neuropsychological); (2) the professional maturity needed for skilled clinical work with children and their families takes a long time to develop; (3) postdoctoral training can offer unique training experiences, especially mentorship; (4) the development of the complex skills needed to be a scientist-practitioner is a continuous and ardous process which can be greatly facilitated by postdoctoral training; and (5) job opportunities can require additional specialized training to enhance marketability of skills.

The fact that many postdoctoral training experiences are best construed as a match between the interests, talents, and level of professional development, and the training setting makes it difficult to characterize programs. In fact, this reliance on personal motivation and individual tailoring of programs is one of the key ingredients of postdoctoral training. However, there are a number of different general program structures that can be mentioned: (1) a broad ranging program within clinical child psychology (often located in medical settings) in which trainees are exposed to a range of populations, techniques, and supervisions; and (2) more specialized programs that may concentrate on a specific age population (e.g., adolescence), experiences within a specific setting (e.g., pediatric psychology), or on a set of skills and/or orientation (e.g., training in family therapy). The great variability of postdoctoral training programs makes it difficult to characterize their content. However, programs can be differentiated on the dimension of breadth versus depth of exposure in broad areas of training in clinical child psychology, such as assessment, intervention, consultation, case management, and research. The postdoctoral fellowship provides a means of pursuing knowledge in more depth in any one of these areas as well as being exposed to new populations and areas of skill development. The postdoctoral fellowship can provide trainees with a particularly valuable experience in developing new areas of consultation and program development in a way that is not generally possible for predoctoral trainees via a close collaboration with a mentor-colleague. The professional maturity that is needed to develop important areas of skills (such as consultation and case management) means that postdoctoral training can be a particularly useful means of facilitating the development of such skills. Finally, a postdoctoral training program can be an important vehicle for extending skills in applied developmental research and, thus, in implementing the scientist-practitioner model. There was uniform agreement in the group about the importance of research experiences in postdoctoral training programs in clinical child psychology.

Because of the diversity of structure, goals, and breadth of postdoctoral training programs, no specific resolutions were posed for postdoctoral training. Rather, the following resolution directing more Section 1 effort toward developing guidelines was unanimously supported:

Resolution 20. *With Section 2, we recommend that Section 1 establish a task force to conduct a survey of current postgraduate programming in clinical child psychology and to establish guidelines for postdoctoral programming. These guidelines should include specification of levels and types of supervision.*

Continuing Education

The group recognized that psychologists who are working with children and their families experience a need for continuing education. As with postdoctoral training, it is useful to address the different groups for which continuing education may be needed. For example, one group of psychologists who may require continuing education are those with general training in clinical psychology. Another group are those trained in clinical child psychology. Each of these targeted groups may experience a need for continuing education to extend their skills, especially with new populations or techniques. One of the most compelling reasons for the necessity of continuing education programs is the empirical finding that there are many more psychologists who are now practicing with children than have been adequately training to do so. In some instances, such psychologists may be pressed into service because they are the only psychologists in a given area. However, one issue that concerned the group was the necessity for the clinicians to acknowledge the limits of one's knowledge and to utilize referrals more effectively. There was concern that some psychologists who work with children may not realize their limitations or their need for continuing education. In an attempt to encompass these sentiments in a recommendation, conferees endorsed the following:

Resolution 18. *Whereas preparation backgrounds for people functioning as clinical child psychologists range widely, and whereas knowledge of significant relevance to clinical child psychologists continues to burgeon, we recommend that continuing education be considered an ethical responsibility of all clinical child psychologists. In particular, assessment, intervention, consultation, and prevention are areas needing ongoing professional renewal.*

One of the most knotty dilemmas concerns the lack of quality control in continuing education programs. There was agreement that such programs vary considerably in quality and that most psychologists do not have the means to differentiate high versus low quality programs. To help rectify this dilemma, there was general agreement that clinical child psychologists should be more active in offering continuing education programs at national and especially at regional meetings. High quality continuing education programs offered by experienced psychologists would also have the advantage of enhancing the visibility of clinical child psychology within the profession of psychology at large.

The question of the most effective means of marketing programs in continuing education could not be easily decided. Some felt that formal marketing surveys would be useful. Others felt that interest would be stimulated by high quality offerings independent of documented need. It was also recognized that there were a number of options in format for continuing education, including workshops, videotaped presentations, books, and manuals. Programs that emphasized the continuity of a group educational experience were felt to be especially valuable. The strength of concern regarding continuing education was expressed by unanimous endorsement of the following resolution:

Resolution 19. *We recommend that Section 1 form a task force to establish and publish criteria for continuing education offerings in areas relevant to clinical child psychology.*

A final area of discussion concerned the needs and job satisfaction of psychologists who are practicing with children and families. There is a need for information to document the special educational and supportive needs of clinical child psychologists at various phases in their careers.

The resolutions that were recommended and passed by the group reflected an interest in greater activity on the part of Section 1, greater involvement in continuing education efforts of Section 1 within APA programs for continuing education, and a need to generate better continuing education in the field at large. The following resolution was, thus, endorsed:

Resolution 21. *We recommend that the Section 1 Executive Committee attempt to gain representation on appropriate governance structures of APA, including the Education and Training Committee of APA, and subcommittees dealing with continuing education.*

Appendices

Appendix A

Members of the Conference

Richard Abidin, Ph.D., *Chair, Institute of Clinical Psychology*
University of Virginia
Charlottesville, VA 22903

Patricia J. Aletky, Ph.D., *Office of Professional Affairs*
American Psychological Association
1200 Seventeenth Street NW
Washington, DC 20036

Debra Bendell, Ph.D., *Assistant Professor*
Mailman Center for Child Development
University of Miami School of Medicine
P.O. Box 160820
Miami, FL 33101

Andrew Bradlyn, Ph.D., *Assistant Professor*
Department of Clinical Psychology
Box J-165, JHMHC
University of Florida
Gainesville, FL 32610

Diana Cunningham, Ph.D., *Chief Psychologist and Director of Training*
Dallas Child Guidance Center
2101 Welborn
Dallas, TX 75219

Lynne D. Doran, Ph.D.
Department of Psychology
Yale Child Study Center
230 Frontage Road, Box 3333
New Haven, CT 06510

Paul L. Doerring, Ph.D., *Private Practice*
Psychological Institute of Hilton Head Island
P.O. Box 5547
Hilton Head Island, SC 29938

Dennis Drotar, Ph.D., *Associate Professor*
Department of Pediatrics
Rainbow Babies & Children's Hospital
Cleveland, OH 44106

Jean Elbert, Ph.D., *Assistant Professor*
Child Study Center
1100 N.E. 13th Street
Oklahoma City, OK 73117

Marilyn Erickson, Ph.D., *Professor*
Department of Psychology
VA Commonwealth University
Richmond, VA 23284

Sheila Eyberg, Ph.D., *Professor*
Department of Clinical Psychology
Box J-165, JHMHC
University of Florida
Gainesville, FL 32610

Robert Felner, Ph.D., *Director of Clinical Training*
Department of Psychology
Auburn University — 4090 Haley Center
Auburn, AL 36849

A.J. Finch, Jr., Ph.D.,*Professor*
Medical University of South Carolina
Department of Psychiatry & Behavioral Sciences
Charleston, SC 29425

Frank Fincham, Ph.D., *Assistant Professor*
Department of Psychology
University of Illinois — Urbana
Champaign, IL 61820

David Glenwick, Ph.D., *Associate Professor*
Department of Psychology
Fordham University
Bronx, NY 10458

Jacqueline Goldman, Ph.D., *Professor*
Department of Clinical Psychology
Box J165 — JHMHC
University of Florida
Gainesville, FL 32610

Jeanne E. Hamilton, Ph.D., *Assistant Professor*
Saint Albans Psychiatric Hospital
P.O. Box 3608
Radford, VA 24143

Jerome H. Hanley, Ph.D., *Executive Director to the Commissioner for Children's Services*
Office of Executive Policy & Programs
1205 Pendleton Street, Room 422
Columbia, SC 29201

Honore Hughes, Ph.D., *Associate Professor*
Department of Psychology
University of Arkansas
Fayetteville, AR 72701

James H. Johnson, Ph.D., *Associate Professor*
Department of Clinical Psychology
Box J-165 JHMHC
University of Florida
Gainesville, FL 32610

Norine Johnson, Ph.D., *Director of Psychology and Training*
Department of Psychology
Kennedy Hospital
50 Warren Avenue
Brighton, MA 02135

Freda A. Jones, Ph.D., *Assistant Professor*
Child Study Center
1100 N.E. 13th Street
Oklahoma City, OK 73117

Kathy S. Katz, Ph.D., *Director of Psychological Training*
Georgetown Child Development Center
3800 Reservoir Road NW
Washington, DC 20007

Paul Kettlewell, Ph.D., *Pediatric Psychologist*
Department of Pediatrics
Kaisenger Medical Center
Danville, PA 17821

Thomas R. Kraft, Ph.D., *Private Practice*
1010 Wisconsin Avenue, Suite 415
Washington, DC 20007

Annette LaGreca, Ph.D., *Associate Professor, Coordinator of Clinical Child/Pediatric Psychology Training*
Department of Psychology
University of Miami — Box 248185
Coral Gables, FL 33124

Carol R. Lewis, Psy.D., *Assistant Clinical Professor*
Elizabeth General Hospital
50 Northfield Avenue
West Orange, NJ 07052

Anita K.F. Li, Ph.D., *Professor*
Department of Educational Psychology
University of Calgary
2500 University Drive, N.W.
Calgary, Alberta, Canada T2N IN4

Raymond P. Lorion, Ph.D., *Professor*
Department of Psychology
University of Maryland
College, Park, MD 20742

Anthony Mannarino, Ph.D., *Assistant Professor and Associate Director of Child & Adolescent Services*
Department of Psychiatry
University of Pittsburgh School of Medicine
3811 O'Hara Street
Pittsburgh, PA 15213

Gary Melton, Ph.D., *Professor and Director of Law Psychology Program*
Department of Psychology
University of Nebraska
Lincoln, NE 68588

Thomas H. Ollendick, Ph.D., *Professor and Director of Clinical Training*
Department of Psychology
Virginia Polytechnic Institute & State University
Blacksberg, VA 24061

Martha Perry, Ph.D., *Private Practice*
Northwest Psychological Services
10518 NE 68th Street
Kirkland, WA 98033

Sheila Ribordy, Ph.D., *Associate Professor*
Department of Psychology
DePaul University
2323 North Seminary Avenue
Chicago, IL 60614

Rochelle L. Robbins, Ph.D., *Chief Psychologist and Director of Outpatient Services*
Department of Child Psychiatry
Harvard Medical School
74 Fenwood Road
Boston, MA 02115

Michael C. Roberts, Ph.D., *Associate Professor*
Department of Psychology
University of Alabama
University, AL 35486

Alan O. Ross, Ph.D., *Professor and Director of Clinical Training*
Department of Psychology
State University of New York
Stony Brook, NY 11794

Donald K. Routh, Ph.D., *Professor*
Department of Psychology
Box 248185
University of Miami
Coral Gables, FL 33124

Sandra Russ, Ph.D., *Associate Professor and Director of Clinical Training*
Department of Psychology
Case Western Reserve University
Cleveland, OH 44106

Stanley Schneider, Ph.D., *Special Assistant Director*
Division of Human Resources
National Institute of Mental Health
5600 Fishers Lane, Room 7-103
Rockville, MD 20857

Carolyn Schroeder, Ph.D., *Private Practice*
Chapel Hill Pediatrics, P.A.
Doctor's Building, 901 Willow Drive
Chapel Hill, NC 27514

Felicisima Serafica, Ph.D., *Associate Professor, Director of Clinical Training*
Department of Psychology
Ohio State University
214 Townshend
Columbus, OH 43210-1224

Steven N. Sparta, Ph.D., *Chief Psychologist*
Child Guidance Clinic
Children's Hospital Health Center
8001 Frost Street
San Diego, CA 92123

June M. Tuma, Ph.D., *Professor*
Department of Psychology
Louisiana State University
Baton Rouge, LA 70808

Douglas Ullman, Ph.D., *Professor*
Department of Psychology
Bowling Green State University
Bowling Green, OH 43403

C. Eugene Walker, Ph.D., *Professor and Director of Clinical Training*
Department of Psychiatry
University of Oklahoma Health Services Center
P.O. Box 26307
Oklahoma City, OK 73126

S. Joseph Weaver, Ph.D., *Associate Professor and Director of Psychology*
Children's Rehabilitation Unit
University of Kansas Medical Center
Rainbow Boulevard at 39th Street
Kansas City, KS 66103

Donald Wertlieb, Ph.D., *Assistant Professor*
Community Health Plan
Tufts University
One Fenway Plaza
Boston, MA 02215

Diane J. Willis, Ph.D., *Director of Psychological Services*
Child Study Center
1100 NE 13th Street
Oklahoma City, OK 73117

Appendix B

Demographic Data on Conference Participants

As pointed out earlier in these *Proceedings,* the Conference Committee selected participants on the basis of position papers that were submitted. Thus, the first round of invitations went to (1) those individuals who were selected to present at the Conference and (2) those selected to participate without presentation (the rest of those submitting position papers). The remaining participants were selected from those who let the Committee know they were interested in attending.

A total of 75 invitations were issued with only 50 accepting due to various reasons. One individual was not able to attend, however, so the total number of participants was 49, one short of our goal.

The following tabulations are presented to indicate demographic and training experience of those assembled. It should be stressed again here, however, that the Conference Committee was under no constraint to compose a representative sample of clinical child psychologists. We were from the very beginning interested in bringing together those who had a pointed interest in the conference (and thereby training) and this we judged on the basis of their efforts in preparing a coherent position paper and/or indicating interest in training issues.

In compiling the information presented in the tables, those individuals from NIMH and APA were included. Thus, it should be stated here that two of those indicating that they held administrative posts were representatives from APA and NIMH. Also, one of the most experienced persons in attending previous conferences was from NIMH.

The entire list of participants and their affiliations and title appear in Appendix B.

Table 1: *Year of Birth*

Year of Birth	Number
1921-1925	4
1926-1930	2
1931-1935	3
1936-1940	9
1941-1945	8
1946-1950	12
1951-1955	8
No Information	3
Total	49

Table 2: *Year of Earned Degree*

Year	Number
1951-1955	2
1956-1960	0
1961-1965	6
1966-1970	9
1971-1975	11
1976-1980	18
1981-1985	2
No Information	1
Total	49

Table 3: *Locus of Professional Activity*

Geographical Area	Number
East	15
Midwest	8
South	17
Southwest	6
West	2
Canada	1
Total	49

Table 4: *Diplomate Status (ABPP)*

Area	Number
Clinical	7
Counseling	0
Industrial /Organizational	0
School	0
Total	7

Table 5: *School Granting Highest Degree*

School	Number
University of Pittsburgh	4
Purdue University	4
University of Rochester	3
Rutgers University	3
University of Iowa	2
University of Kansas	2
University of Washington	2
University of Alabama	1
Boston University	1
Bowling Green State University	1
University of California, Los Angeles	1
Catholic University of America	1
Clark University	1
University of Hong Kong	1
University of Illinois	1
Louisiana State University	1
University of Michigan	1
University of Mississippi	1
University of Nebraska	1
University of Northern Illinois	1
North Texas State University	1
Northwestern University	1
The Ohio State University	1
Oklahoma State University	1
University of Oklahoma	1
University of Oregon	1
Oxford University, England	1
George Peabody University	1
Saint Louis University	1
University of South Carolina	1
Stanford University	1
Syracuse University	1
Wayne State University	1
University of West Virginia	1
Yale University	1
No Information	1
Total	49

Table 6: *Year of Joining APA*

Year	Number
1946-1950	1
1951-1955	1
1956-1960	0
1961-1965	6
1966-1970	7
1971-1975	12
1976-1980	15
1981-1985	4
No Information	2
Total	49

Table 7: *Number of Divisional Memberships*

Number of Divisions	Number
0	3
1	7
2	7
3	10
4	8
5	9
6	3
7	1
No Information	1
Total	49

Table 8: *Divisional Membership*

	Class of Membership	
Division	Member	Fellow
2	1	
7	8	1
8	4	
9	5	1
12	29	10
13	1	
16	2	
18	2	2
22	1	
25	4	1
27	4	4
29	4	1
30	1	
31		1
33	7	1
34	1	
35	6	
36	1	
37	16	10
38	13	1
39	2	
41		1
42	2	
43	5	
Total	109	34

[a]Totals reflect multiple divisonal membership. APA members without divisional affiliation: 3. No Information: 1.

Table 9: *Principal Organizational Affiliation*

Affiliation	Number	Total
University Setting		23
Department Chair	1	
Progam Head	1	
Director of Clinical Training	5	
Coordinator of Child Training	2	
Faculty	14	
Internship Setting		
Medical School		13
Director of Clinical Training	2	
Director of Child Services	4	
Faculty	7	
Service Agency		
Child Clinic	1	2
Chief Psychologist	1	
Private Hospital		1
Director of Training	1	
Private or Group Practice		6
Administration, Federal, or State Programs		3
No Information		1
Total		49

Table 10: *Participation in Earlier Conferences*

Conference	Number
West Virginia	1
Chicago and Vail	1
Boulder, Chicago, and Vail	1
Menninger Postdoctoral	2
Primary Health Care Providers	1
UAF	1
Total	7

Table 11: *Specialty Training Obtained by Participants*

Specialty Training	Number	
Number Receiving Specialty Training		41
Doctoral Level	4	
Internship Level	12	
Postdoctoral Level	8	
Doctoral and Intership	8	
Internship and Postdoctoral	5	
All three levels	3	
Other	1	
Number with no Specialty Training		4
No Information		4

Appendix C

Conference Committee

Jean C. Elbert
James H. Johnson
Annette LaGreca
Thomas H. Ollendick
Carolyn Schroeder
June M. Tuma, *Conference Coordinator*

Concurrent Small Group Leaders

Richard Abidin
Dennis Drotar
Jean C. Elbert
Marilyn Erickson
Jacqueline Goldman
Norine Johnson
Gary Melton
Donald K. Routh
Carolyn Schroeder
C. Eugene Walker
S. Joseph Weaver
Donald Wertlieb

Concurrent Small Group Reporters

Andrew Bradlyn
Dennis Drotar
Lynne Doran
A.J. Finch, Jr.
Sheila Eyberg
Honore Hughes
Annette LaGreca
Anthony Mannarino
Thomas H. Ollendick
Felicisima Serafica
Rochelle L. Robbins
Michael C. Roberts
Diane J. Willis

Appendix D

Preconference Planning, Conference Procedures, and Postconference Activities

June M. Tuma
Louisiana State University

Planning for the Conference began at the initiation of the Society of Pediatric Psychology (now Section 5, Division 12, American Psychological Association) as early as February, 1977. Representatives of different components of child psychology, including various segments of the American Psychological Association (APA), in particular, the Section on Clinical Child Psychology (Section 1, Division 12), the newly formed Division on Children, Youth, and Families (Division 37), and the Society of Pediatric Psychology, began to explore the amount of interest in, and the possibility of, a conference on training psychologists to provide services to children. Much concern has been voiced by these different groups and individuals about manpower shortages, underservice to children, lack of concensus on the training requisites for providing services to children, lack of clear definitions of these child oriented psychologists' roles and functions, lack of response of graduate departments of psychology to adequately provide training in this specialty area, resulting in unavailable training for child work and the problem of inadequately trained psychologists offering services to children and their families.

Discussions were held at regional and national conferences and during executive committee meetings of the above-mentioned organizations. A number of individuals were identified who would serve on the committee in other ways to promote the conference. The first task in getting the conference underway was posed as approaching the APA goverance for support and sponsorship. Accordingly, a brief draft of a conference proposal was prepared in 1977 by June Tuma in consultation with Allan Barclay and other interested individuals. The proposal was presented to the APA Education and Training (E&T) Board on October 27, 1978, with the support of the Interdivisional Coalition which recommended to the E&T Board to form a task force on the conference. The E&T Board designated June Tuma and Allan Barclay cochairpersons of an ad hoc committee for promoting such a conference under E&T sponsorship. The task force's charge was to prepare a final proposal for a conference on training clinical child psychologists to submit to NIMH for funding. Three additional persons were recruited to this committee: Theodore Blau, Alan Ross and Diane Willis.

In 1978, the proposal was routed to the Board of Professional Affairs, the Board of Social and Ethical Responsibility for Psychology, the Board of Scientific Affairs, and, finally, to the APA Board of Directors for their action in the fall of 1978. Favorable responses were obtained from all boards; thus, the conference had the full support of all major APA boards and the APA Board of Directors.

The proposal was additionally routed to interested individuals in the psychological community and to representatives of the Psychology Manpower Branch of NIMH for their reaction. Copies of the proposal were sent to the executive committee members of Section 1, Division 37, Society of Pediatric Psychology, Divisions 7, 12, 16, 33, 37, 38, 39, and members of the Interdivisional Coalition for Children, Youth, and Families. The comments and suggestions from all of these sources were integrated into the second draft.

On November 22, 1978, the ad hoc committee requested funding from the American Psychological Foundation (APF), then chaired by George Albee. The Foundation awarded the ad hoc committee a grant for the purpose of funding planning meetings during 1979. With funds from the APF, the ad hoc committee for the proposed conference met at the APA Central Office four times in 1979. Deliberations included the rationale, the issues, the format, participant selection, the site, the length, and the proceedings of the conference, as well as proposals for a viable followup and evaluation of conference effectiveness.

A third revised draft of the conference proposal was then presented to a more general psychologist audience at the 1979 APA Annual Meeting held in New York, both in an open meeting sponsored by the E&T Board (Tuma & Barclay, 1979) and in a separate symposium on training clinical child psychologists (Tuma, 1979). These meetings were well attended and indicated to the committee that there was considerable support for a conference.

To further assess the support for the conference, calls for position papers were published in the December 1979 issue of the *Monitor* as well as in the *Journal of Clinical Child Psychology, American Psychologist, The Clinical Psychologist, Professional Psychologist, Journal of Pediatric Psychology,* and newsletters of Division 37 and Section 5. In addition, the committee placed an advertisement in the *Monitor* for information about programs in clinical child psychology as well as information about individuals' training in the area.

Several other activities were approved by the ad hoc committee in preparation for the conference. Noting that there was no data base for the present status of training clinical child psychologists (or those who worked with children without formal training), funds were approved for a survey of the membership of Section 1, Society of Pediatric Psychology and Division 37 (Tuma, 1983a; Tuma & Pratt, 1982; Tuma & Cawunder, 1983; Tuma & Cohen, 1983; Tuma & Salcedo, 1983) concerning their training and for a survey of the teaching assessment techniques in clinical psychology training programs (Elbert, 1983, 1984). To obtain further data about training, another advertisement was placed in the April *Monitor* asking for information from psychologists.

The proposal for the conference was perfected, with Gary VanderBos of APA and June Tuma, co-principal investigators (Tuma & VanderBos, 1979). This was submitted to the National Institute of Mental Health on January 29, 1980 (see Tuma, 1982a, for brief version). A site visit was held at APA Central Office on May 9, 1980. Feedback was obtained from NIMH in June, 1980. The proposal was disapproved because of the review committee's opinion that the proposal was too narrow.

Even though the funding was not received, the APF renewed the grant for planning meetings during 1980 and the committee decided to continue to meet to determine if the proposal should be altered to address the reviewers' concerns or to pursue the conference along different lines. Four more planning meetings were held in Washington, D.C. during 1980. At the meetings, resolutions to pursue private and participant funding for the conference were made. Another open forum was held at the APA annual meeting in Montreal (Tuma & Barclay, 1980).

In 1981, two more planning meetings were held to receive reports on results of attempts to get private foundation funding. Since the conference was delayed (the new projected date for the conference was 1983), on November 23, 1981, a letter was sent to those who submitted position papers and/or expressed interest in participating in the conference. The letter reviewed the status of the grant and outlined the plans to seek private and/or participant funding.

The spring issue of *Journal of Clinical Child Psychology* published the papers from the symposium presented at 1979 APA annual meeting (plus some additional submissions related to training) as a Special Issue on Training (Brady & Friedrich, 1982; Goldman, 1982; Johnson & Robbins, 1982; Mannarino & Fischer, 1982; Tuma, 1982a; Roberts, 1982; Tuma & Pratt, 1982).

During 1982, there were no funds for planning meetings and all planning for the conference ceased. There was, however, a rebirth of interest in the conference in June of 1983 during an Emerald Isle, North Carolina, meeting of the training committee of Section 1 (the committee was appointed by Diane Willis, President of Section 1) (Section 1, 1983a). The training committee (composed of Jean C. Elbert, James H. Johnson, Tom H. Ollendick, Carolyn S. Schroeder, and June M. Tuma, as chair) dispensed with the training committee charge to make recommendations for training in assessment, intervention, and consultation at Emerald Isle (Elbert, 1983; Johnson, 1983a, 1983b; Ollendick, 1983; Section 1, 1983b; Tuma, 1983b). In addition to rather specific recommendations in those areas, the committee recommended to Section 1 that a training conference was the only way to make impact on training in clinical child psychology and asked that Section 1 consider sponsorship of such a conference (Section 1, 1983b; 1984a). The executive committee of Section 1, meeting at APA's annual meeting in the fall of 1983, approved the conference, and at the midyear meeting of 1984, allocated money for publication and distribution of conference proceedings (Section 1, 1984b). Plans were then made to hold the conference in May, 1985, at Hilton Head Island. Finalization of the program and specific funds were allocated at the executive committee meeting of Section 1 in January, 1985 (Section 1, 1985).

Summary of Events

Preconference Acitivities

1977

February 10-11, 1977	Initial conception of holding a conference, Society of Pediatric Psychology Executive Committee Meeting, Oklahoma City.
1977 Activities	Contacted Section 1, Division 12, Division 37, others, in regard to interest in a conference; composed initial conference committee.

1978

October 27, 1978	Proposal for a conference (with support from Interdivisional Coalition on Children, Youth, and Families) was presented to the Education and Training Board of APA.
November 22, 1978	Letter to American Psychological Foundation for funding of conference planning meetings (funding approved for 1979).
1978 Activities	Proposal routed to other APA Boards and Board of Directors and widely circulated to receive index of support of conference and feedback about the conference format. Copies sent to Section 1 and 5 (Division 12), Divisions 7, 12, 16, 17, 33, 37, 38, 39, Interdivisional Coalition of Children, Youth, and Families, as well as individuals expressing interest, other organizations (e.g., ABPP, American Orthopsychiatric Association, APIC, AASPB, AAPSC).

1979

February 9-10, 1979	Planning Meeting, Washington, DC.
March 16-17, 1979	Planning Meeting, Washington, DC.
May 15-17, 1979	Planning Meeting, Washington, DC.
August 2-3, 1979	Planning Meeting, Washington, DC.
September 3, 1979	Symposium, Mapping a future: Clinical Child Psychology Training, Annual Meeting of the American Psychological Association, Montreal.
September 4, 1979	Open Meeting on Conference plans, sponsored by the E&T Board, APA Annual Meeting, Montreal.

1980

January 29, 1980	Grant proposal submitted to NIMH.
March 29-April 3, 1980	Planning Meeting, Washington, DC.
May 9, 1980	NIMH site visit, National Conference, Washington, DC.
June, 1980	Feedback from NIMH.
August 2-3, 1980	Planning Meeting, Washington, DC.
September 4, 1980	Open Forum: Planning for a Conference on Professional Training of Clinical Child Psychologists, APA annual meeting.
September 19-20, 1980	Planning Meeting, Washington, DC.
December 6-7, 1980	Planning Meeting, Washington, DC.

1981

March 27-28, 1981	Planning Meeting, Washington, DC.
March 27-28, 1981	Section 1 Executive Committee Meeting, New York.
August 26, 1981	Interdivisional Coalition meeting at APA annual meeting.
December 11-12, 1981	Planning Meeting, Washington, DC. Authorization of data base studies (Tuma) and assessment surveys (Elbert).

1982

March 5-6, 1982	Mini-Conference on Training, Division 37 Executive Committee Meeting, APA, Washington, DC. Task Force Report (Roberts, Erickson, & Tuma, 1985).
March, 1982	Publication of Special Issue on Training, *Journal of Clinical Child Psychology*.
August 23, 1982	Diane Willis, President of Section 1, appointed the Section 1 Training Committee (identical with the Conference Committee).

1983

June 10-12, 1983	Section 1 Training Committee meeting, Emerald Isle, North Carolina.
August 26-30, 1983	Conference recommended by the training committee to be held in 1985 approved by Section 1, Executive Committee Meeting, at the annual meeting of the APA, Annaheim APA.

1984

February 4, 1984	Training Committee Meeting, Washington, DC. (immediately after the Section 1 Executive Committee meeting).
February 4, 1984	Section 1 appropriated funds for the conference. Section 1 Executive Committee Meeting, Washington, DC.
August 26, 1984	Section 1 Executive Committee Meeting, update on conference, annual meeting of APA, Toronto, Canada.
1984 (3 issues)	*Journal of Clinical Child Psychology* announced conference to be held Hilton Head, SC, May 15-18, 1985.
1984	Announcements about conference in other newsletters and publications (Society of Pediatric Psychology, Division 37, *Monitor, American Psychologist*).

1985

January 26-27, 1985	Finalization of program for Conference, allocation of funds for the conference. Mid-year meeting of Executive Committee, Section 1, Miami, Florida.

Conference

May 15-18, 1985	Conference on Training Clinical Child Psychologists was held at Hilton Head Island, South Carolina.

Details of the Conference

The format of this conference was based on the assumption that new and constructive ideas are best generated if highly motivated people are permitted to put forth proposals in an atmosphere that is freed as much as possible from premature considerations of the realities that may restrain the implementation of these proposals. To this end, the conference was first planned to be held in two overlapping phases devoted to (1) generation of proposals and (2) implementation planning. The first phase was to be composed only of people who generated ideas without being constrained by the influence of people who would respond negatively to the feasibility of the proposals. Thus, there was no need (and actually an argument against) having persons in positions of influence for implementation present during the first phase. In theory, those of influence would only come to the second phase of the conference, with some overlap of the two phases. This second phase would wrestle with the manner in which the recommendations could be accomplished. However, since the funds dictated against having a more extended conference, the second phase was deleted from the plan. Instead, the generational phase was kept to two days, while the implementation phase took place over only a one-half day period with the same conferees.

The conference participants for this conference were selected differently from the way that most conferences proceed with this task. The Committee was entirely free from the constraints of having to select individuals who were in positions of influence, who represented particular interfacing organizations, who wanted to observe, who lived in certain geographical locations, who had certain demographic characteristics and so forth. The only criteria for selection was that a clearly articulated position paper which addressed an area deemed important to training clinical child psychologists was submitted.

The conference planners believed that motivation was assured if those who were selected to attend were drawn from a pool of individuals who responded to a *Call for Position Papers* (published in the *Journal of Clinical Child Psychology, American Psychologist, The Clinical Psychologist, Journal of Pediatric Psychology, Monitor,* and *Professional Psychologist*). The requirement was a brief (2,000 word) statement addressed to one of a series of suggested topics dealing with the professional preparation of clinical child psychologists. Suggested topics were:

1. The need for specialty training in clinical child psychology.
2. The boundaries of specialty practices in clinical child psychology.
3. Strategies for effecting change in training programs in clinical child psychology.
4. Information dissemination relative to training resources and/or practicum and intern training resources.
5. Career changes relative to opportunities for re-training in clinical child psychology.
6. The personal and social requirements for clinical child psychology training programs.
7. Evaluation of quality control in clinical child psychology training programs.
8. The interface of specialty training with issues of generic licensing and/or other credentialling procedures.

A number of individuals responded to the original call for papers. Since the original call occurred very early, and it appeared for a time that the plans for the conference would have to be aborted, a second call for papers was issued in 1983 and published during 1984 in the same publications noted above. In addition, the original group of individuals who submitted papers were contacted and asked to update their submissions. Once received, five members of the Conference Committee (excluding the Conference Coordinator who knew the identity of authors of the papers) read the manuscripts (devoid of all identification) and rated them on a one to five scale reflecting a judgment of relevance, coherence, quality of exposition, and persuasiveness. Reviewers also made notes on each manuscript for suggested alterations, should they be accepted for presentation. Twenty-four papers were selected as being articulate statements of positions important for conferees to consider. Those individuals who submitted papers that were not accepted were issued the first round of invitations to attend the conference without presentation. In addition, a number of individuals responding to a call for individuals who wanted only to attend without presentation (published in the 1984 issues of the *Journal of Clinical Child Psychology*) were also issued invitations. To cover the needed topics, several individuals were invited to give their perspective of more specialized issues (i.e., Stanley Schneider from NIMH, Patricia Aletky from APA, S. Joseph Weaver from the AASPB).

In all, seventy-five invitations were issued, with forty-nine people able to accept the invitation to attend. A listing and the characteristics of the participants are presented in Appendix A and B, respectively.

Prior to the conference, participants were divided up into three small discussion groups (representing academic, internship and postdoctoral/continuing education) which were to follow each morning and afternoon plenary sessions. The goal was to change the composition of each group to insure maximal contact of Conferees and cross-fertilization of ideas. There were four groups in which everyone would participate. Although unevenly divided, three groups of individuals were identified as the constituency: those teaching in (a) graduate programs, (b) internship programs, and (c) those involved in postdoctoral training. An attempt was made to match the individual's primary work setting level to the assignment of the first and third groups. The second and fourth groups were assigned to consider implications for the other two levels of training. (In actuality, this assignment was not possible for all groups.) Those participants who did not represent teaching settings were shifted to various groups, also in rotating fashion.

Conference Format

Participants arrived at Hilton Head Island during the afternoon of Wednesday, May 15, 1985. Participants registered in the afternoon and were received at a reception honoring the conference participants. Each of the two following days started with an early morning plenary session followed by a short break and reconvention in small group rooms for three concurrent small group discussions until noon. Position papers presented in the plenary sessions followed the order presented in the conference *Proceedings* (see Table of Contents). After an hour lunch break, two afternoon plenary sessions separated by a short break, were presented. Concurrent small groups convened again in the late afternoon. Two conference participants (pre-selected) in each small group served as small group discussion leader and reporter. After a brief break, the total group was again convened for an hour at late day to receive feedback from reporters of the six concurrent small group meetings for the day.

The last day of the conference was devoted to recommendations and implementation suggestions. Only one paper was presented during the plenary group meeting that day. Then, the recommendations from each level of training were received from a spokesperson chosen from the concurrent group reporters of the previous two days. Discussion of the reports were followed by resolutions by level of training (academic, internship, postdoctoral/continuing education).

In addition to reporting to the total group after each day, each reporter also dictated a summary of the small group deliberations. Likewise, spokespersons for the levels of training dictated a report of their summaries and resolutions. All of this written material was submitted to the conference coordinator prior to the end of the conference. The conference adjourned at 12:30 p.m. Saturday.

Postconference Activities

Reporting Activities.

August 24, 1985	Report on conference to Executive Committe of Section 1, at the 93rd annual meeting of the American Psychological Association, Los Angeles, CA.
August 25, 1985	*Clinical Child Psychology Training: Report on the Hilton Head Conference,* symposium presented at the 93rd annual meeting of the American Psychological Association, Los Angeles, CA (Elbert, 1985; Johnson, 1985; LaGreca, 1985; Ollendick, 1985; Schroeder, 1985. Tuma, 1985a).
August 25, 1985	Presentation on conference recommendations in relationship to pediatric psychology training issues (Tuma, 1985b), presented at the 93rd annual meeting of the American Psychological Association, Los Angeles, CA.
Fall, 1985	Publication of report on conference in *Division 37 Newsletter* (Willis, 1985).
Fall, 1985	Publication of report on conference in *Society of Pediatric Psychology Newsletter* (Tuma, 1985c).
Fall, 1985	Publication of *Proceedings: Conference on Training Clinical Child Psychologists* (Tuma, 1985d).
Winter, 1985	Publication of Conference Recommendations, *Journal of Clinical Child Psychology* (Tuma, 1985e).
Spring, 1986	Publication of mini-proceedings, *Journal of Clinical Child Psychology* (Tuma, 1986a).
Spring, 1986	Publication of report on conference in *The Clinical Psychologist* (Abidin, 1986; Chan, 1986; Johnson, 1986; Johnson & Tuma, 1986; Roberts, 1986; Routh, 1986; Sparta, 1986; Tuma, 1986b).

Implementation Activities.

August 25, 1985	Formation of committees on development of guidelines for internship training (Jean C. Elbert, Chair) and postdoctoral/continuing education (Thomas H. Ollendick, Chair).
Fall, 1985	Nomination by Division 37, Section 1 and Section 5, Division 12, of several child psychologists to the Standing Committee on Children, Youth, and Families of the Board of Social and Ethical Responsibility of Psychologists, American Psychological Association.

References

Abidin, R. (1986). Commentary on the Hilton Head Conference. *The Clinical Psychologist, 39,* 15.

Brady, C.A., & Friedrich, W.N. (1982). Levels of Intervention: A model for training in play therapy. *Journal of Clinical Child Psychology, 11,* 39-43.

Chan, D.A. (1986). Clinical child psychology: When to specialize? *The Clinical Psychologist, 39,* 16-17.

Denham, W.H. (1979, August). NIMH policy in relation to training for service delivery to children and youth: Implication for psychology education. In *Clinical child psychology: Mapping a future.* Symposium presented at the annual meeting of the American Psychological Association, New York.

Elbert, J.C. (1983). Report of the subcommittee on assessment issues. *Journal of Clinical Child Psychology, 12,* 373-374.

Elbert, J.C. (1984). Training in child diagnostic assessment: A survey of clinical psychology graduate programs. *Journal of Clinical Child Psychology, 13,* 122-133.

Elbert, J.C. (1985, August). Recommendations for internship level training. In J.M. Tuma (Chair), *Clinical Child Psychology Training: Report on the Hilton Head Conference.* Symposium presented at the 93rd annual meeting of the American Psychological Association, Los Angeles, CA.

Goldman, J. (1982). Clinical child psychology training and credentialing. *Journal of Clinical Child Psychology, 11,* 8-12.

Johnson, J.H. (1983a). Report of the subcommittee on child treatment. *Journal of Clinical Child Psychology, 12,* 373.

Johnson, J.H. (1983b). Preliminary report of the Section 1 clinical child training questionnaire. *Journal of Clinical Child Psychology, 12,* 372-373.

Johnson, J.H. (1985, August). Resolutions of the Hilton Head Conference on the Training of Clinical Child Psychologists. In J.M. Tuma (Chair), *Clinical Child Psychology Training: Report on the Hilton Head Conference.* Symposium presented at the 93rd annual meeting of the American Psycological Association, Los Angeles, CA.

Johnson, J.H., & Robbins, R.L. (1982). On the need for clinical child psychology training within the context of general clinical training programs. *Journal of Clinical Child Psychology, 11,* 27-34.

Johnson, J.H., & Tuma, J.M. (1983). Editorial: Training in clinical child psychology: A brief overview of selected issues, *Journal of Clinical Child Psychology, 12,* 365-368.

Johnson, J.H., & Tuma, J.M. (1986). The Hilton Head Conference: Recommendations for clinical child psychology training. *The Clinical Psychologist, 39,* 9-11.

Johnson, N.G. (1986). A director of an APA-approved internship speaks on the Hilton Head Conference. *The Clinical Psychologist, 39,* 13.

LaGreca, A. (1985, August). Recommendations for academic level training. In J.M. Tuma (Chair), *Clinical Child Psychology Training: Report on the Hilton Head Conference.* Symposium presented at the 93rd annual meeting of the American Psychological Association, Los Angeles, CA.

Mannarino, A.P., & Fischer, C. (1982). Survey of graduate training in clinical child psychology, *Journal of Clinical Child Psychology, 11,* 22-26.

Ollendick, T.H. (1983). Report of the subcommittee on continuing education. *Journal of Clinical Child Psychology, 12,* 374.

Ollendick, T.H. (1985, August). Recommendations for postdoctoral/continuing education. In J.M. Tuma (Chair), *Clinical Child Psychology Training: Report on the Hilton Head Conference.* Symposium presented at the 93rd annual meeting of the American Psychological Association, Los Angeles, CA.

Roberts, M.C. (1982). Clinical child psychology programs: Where and what are they? *Journal of Clinical Child Psychology, 11,* 13-21.

Roberts, M.C. (1986). The Clinical Child Psychology Training Conference at Hilton Head: No sun or sand, just good hard work. *The Clinical Psychologist, 39,* 11-12.

Roberts, M.C., Erickson, M.T., & Tuma, J.M. (1985). Addressing the needs: Guidelines for training psychologists to work with children, youth, and families. *Journal of Clinical Child Psychology, 14,* 70-79.

Routh, D.K. (1986). What they said at Hilton Head: All psychologists need to know more about children. *The Clinical Psychologist, 39,* 7-9.

Schroeder, C.S. (1985, August). Process notes on the Hilton Head Conference. In J.M. Tuma (Chair), *Clinical Child Psychology Training: Report on the Hilton Head Conference.* Symposium presented at the 93rd annual meeting of the American Psychological Association, Los Angeles, CA.

Section 1. (1983a). Minutes of the meeting of the executive committee, February 25 and 26, 1983. *Journal of Clinical Child Psychology, 12,* 314-317.

Section 1. (1983b). Minutes of the meeting of the executive committee, August 25, 1983. *Journal of Clinical Child Psychology, 12,* 369-374.

Section 1. (1984a). Minutes of the meeting of the executive committee, February 4 and 5, 1984. *Journal of Clinical Child Psychology, 13,* 103-107.

Section 1. (1984b). Minutes of the meeting of the executive committee, August 26 and 27, 1984. *Journal of Clinical Child Psychology, 13,* 326-329.

Section 1. (1985). Minutes of the executive committee, January 26 and 27, 1985. *Journal of Clinical Child Psychology, 14,* 264-267.

Sparta, S.N. (1986). Comments on the Hilton Head Conference: Let's get down to basics. *The Clinical Psychologist, 39,* 14-15.

Tuma, J.M. (1979). Projected conference on professional preparation of clinical child psychologists. In A. Barclay (Chair), *Clinical child psychology: Mapping a Future.* Symposium presented at the annual meeting of the American Psychological Association, New York, NY.

Tuma, J.M. (1982). Proposal for a national conference on professional preparation of clinical child psychologists. *Journal of Clinical Child Psychology, 11,* 3-7.

Tuma, J.M. (1983a). Specialty training for psychologist service providers to children. *American Psychologist, 38,* 340-342.

Tuma, J.M. (1983b). Report of the Section 1 committee on training clinical child psychologists. *Journal of Clinical Child Psychology, 12,* 372-374.

Tuma, J.M. (1984). National Conference on the training of clinical child psychologists. *Journal of Clinical Child Psychology, 14,* 223-234.

Tuma, J.M. (Chair). (1985a). *Discussion Session: Clinical Child Psychology Training: Report on the Hilton Head Conference.* Symposium presented at the 93rd annual meeting of the American Psychological Association, Los Angeles, CA.

Tuma, J.M. (1985b). Training issues in pediatric and clinical child psychology. In A. LaGreca (Chair), *Discussion session: Training issues in pediatric psychology.* Symposium presented at the 93rd annual meeting of the American Psychological Association, Los Angeles, CA.

Tuma, J.M. (1985c). Highlights of the 1985 conference on training clinical child psychologists. *Newsletter of the Society of Pediatric Psychology, 9*(3).

Tuma, J.M. (Ed.). (1985d). *Proceedings: Conference on training clinical child psychologists.* Baton Rouge, LA: Section on Clinical Child Psychology.

Tuma, J.M. (1985e). Recommendation: Conference on training clinical child psychologists. *Journal of Clinical Child Psychology, 14,* 282-284.

Tuma, J.M. (1986a). Clinical child psychology training: Report on the Hilton Head conference. *Journal of Clinical Child Psychology, 15.*

Tuma, J.M. (1986b). The Hilton Head Conference on Training Clinical Child Psychologists: History and background. *The Clinical Psychologist, 39,* 4-7.

Tuma, J.M., & Barclay, A. (Co-Chairs). (1979). *Planning for a professional training in clinical child psychology.* Open meeting of the annual meeting of the American Psychological Association, New York, NY.

Tuma, J.M., & Barclay, A. (1980). *Planning for a conference on professional training in clinical child psychology.* Open forum at the annual meeting of the American Psychological Association, Montreal, Canada.

Tuma, J.M., & Cawunder, P. (1983). Orientation and practice patterns of members of professional child psychology societies and divisions. *The Clinical Psychologist, 36,* 72-75.

Tuma, J.M., & Cohen, R. (1981). *An investigation of factors relating to practice and training in pediatric psychology: A survey.* Unpublished manuscript.

Tuma, J.M., & Pratt, J.M. (1982). Clinical child psychology practice and training: A survey. *Journal of Clinical Child Psychology 11,* 27-34.

Tuma, J.M., & Salcedo, R. (1981). *Training and practice of Division 37 members: A survey.* Unpublished manuscript.

Tuma, J.M., & VanderBos, G.R. (1979). *Proposal for a conference on the professional preparation of clinical child psychologists.* Grant submitted to the National Institute of Mental Health.

Willis, D.J. (1985). President's message: On Hilton Head. *Division of Child, Youth, and Family Services Newsletter, 8,* 1,4.

Appendix E

Guidelines for Training Psychologists to Work with Children, Youth, and Families[1]

Marilyn T. Erickson, Michael C. Roberts and **June M. Tuma**

The Division of Child, Youth, and Family Services (Division 37 of the American Psychological Association) has been concerned by the lack of standards regarding training for psychologists working with children, youth, and families. The lack of standards for training has negative implications for the quality of services for children, youth, and families. A continuum of services is necessary for meeting the variety of needs presented by children, youth, and families. Outlined in the following sections are guidelines that are considered necessary for training specialists in the delivery of services to children, youth, and families. The following recommendations should be considered "guiding principles" for training, not as a set of procedures and standards for program accreditation.

Competence in psychology for working with children, youth, and families is directly linked to training for that competence. Consequently, these recommendations attempt to outline training experiences and coursework necessary (but not sufficient) to be a competent psychologist working with children, youth, and families and the systems affecting them.

A number of psychological specialties and subspecialties are currently active in providing services to children, youth, and families. Groups of professionals utilizing specific titles or labels associated with these interests may adopt additional standards within the broad category of psychology for children, youth, and families. The primary purpose of this statement is to provide a basic or minimal set of criteria for the training of psychologists working with children, youth, and families, regardless of setting and population characteristics.

Goals of Training

The following goals of training doctoral-level psychologists working with children, youth, and families are recommended:

1. Training should provide at least minimal entry level skills for providing professional psychological services to children, youth, and families. Child-specialty professional psychologists should be capable of assessing and diagnosing children's psychological problems, understanding the broad range of their etiologies, and treating/intervening/preventing on behalf of children, adolescents, and their mentors (e.g., parents, teachers) in a range of settings (e.g., home, schools, institutions, medical clinics). Thus, training for the provision of services should provide exposure to and experience with different child populations, disorders, and settings for professional functioning.

2. Training should provide the scientific basis for professional psychological applications.

3. Training should include specialized research contributing to an understanding of children, families, and psychological development, as well as in the evaluation of therapeutic interventions.

4. Child, youth, and family related issues should be integrated into psychology-based courses at all levels, regardless of specialty designation. For example, child therapy issues should be discussed in a course on principles of psychotherapy and behavior change; child research should be covered in the course on general research methods; child psychopathology should be covered in a general psychopathology course.

Specialized coursework and experiences are necessary for training in psychology for working with children, youth, and families. They may be obtained through a general curriculum, but, more often, they may necessitate a specialty curriculum. Regardless of curriculum designation, specialized work should be fundamental to training as well as relevant to the type of functioning or specialty for which training is provided. The following topic areas may be combined or integrated in various ways to form courses and/or practica, in order to accomplish the general goals listed above:

- Child Development and Lifespan Developmental Psychology
- Psychopathology: Child and Adult
- Mental Retardation and Developmental Disabilities
- Specialized Child Assessment Techniques
- Child Psychotherapy and Behavior Change
- Parent, Family, and School Intervention Techniques
- Specialized Clinical Practica in Child, Parent, and Family Therapy
- Research Methods in Child Psychology
- Ethics and Legal Issues Related to Children, Youth, and Families
- Subspecialties within Psychology for Children, Youth, and Families

Each of these topics is considered in more detail in the next section with a rationale for their inclusion in training programs for psychologists working with children, youth, and families.

Topics and Rationale

Child Development and Lifespan Developmental Psychology. Child Development should cover theoretical and practical aspects of physical and psychological development of the child. Developmental milestones and transitions should be taught the child specialty trainee. Topics should include perceptual, physical, cognitive, social, language, personality, and emotional development across the human lifespan. Lifespan developmental psychology should include the prenatal, neonatal, infant, toddler, nursery school, middle childhood, adolescent, young adulthood, middle adulthood, and late adulthood periods. Knowledge of normal development and behavior is essential for determining the presence of abnormal development and behavior. Child, youth, and family practice requires knowledge of the developmental process and its impact on the child as well as the eventual adult.

Psychopathology: Child and Adult. Abnormal development should be examined with a particular emphasis on childhood.

[1]Report of the Division 37 Task Force on Training. Approved by Executive Committee of Division on Child, Youth, and Family Services (Division 37 of the American Psychological Association), August 1983.

Different theoretical viewpoints on deviant behavior need to be presented. A basis for understanding the etiology of disorders, conducting assessment, and developing a diagnosis should be provided for a range of childhood emotional, behavioral, learning, and cognitive disorders. Exposure to physical disorders with psychological concomitants (e.g., medical illness) as well as to those of a primarily psychological nature should be included.

Mental Retardation and Developmental Disabilities. These areas should include coverage of etiology, assessment/diagnosis, and intervention/prevention of mental retardation and other developmental disabilities. This coverage should involve exposure to (a) significant research, (b) experiences working with developmentally delayed persons and their families, and (c) consultation for programming involving these clients. Developmentally disabled child clients and their families represent a significant population for settings in which psychologists practice. Specialty training should be oriented to meeting the special needs of this population.

Specialized Child Assessment Techniques. Accurate assessment of children and families requires special training experiences. Didactic coursework *and* practical experiences should be provided in the psychological assessment of children, youth, and family functioning. Such coverage should go beyond the training of general intelligence testing (e.g., WISC-R, Stanford-Binet) to include advanced and specialized instruments (e.g., Leiter International Performance Test, Illinois Test of Psycholinguistic Abilities, AAMD Adaptive Behavior Rating Scale). Other assessment and diagnostic skills should include infant and developmental testing (e.g., Bayley Scales of Infant Development), personality (e.g., Personality Inventory for Children, Children's Apperception Test), achievement (e.g., Peabody Individual Achievement Test), hyperactivity (e.g., Connors' Teacher Rating Scale), learning disabilities (e.g., Hiskey-Nebraska), behavioral and ecological methods. Training in testing should also be provided for special populations of speech and hearing impaired children, physically handicapped children, disadvantaged and minority children, mentally retarded children, and neuropsychologically-impaired children. Training should be provided to aid in deciding which assessment tools are most appropriate for specific different disorders. If actual experience cannot be provided with the numerous diagnostic instruments, then information should at least be provided on the uses and availability of these tests.

Child Psychotherapy and Behavior Change. This area should include the various theoretical approaches to treating children, youth, and families, including (but not restricted to) behavioral, cognitive, educational, eclectic, play, and traditional therapies. While a basic approach might be identified, unbiased exposure to alternative therapies is requisite. This topic should involve an examination of those therapies which are empirically-based and those that have not been subjected to experimental validation. In addition, instruction should be given in strategies for determining the relevance of particular interventions for specific disorders and conditions. Prognosis following various therapies should be considered.

Parents, Family, and School Intervention Techniques. Since the child does not live in a vacuum, didactic coursework should involve the foundations of therapeutic interventions with parents, siblings, and other family members, as well as teachers and other school personnel. Treatment modalities should include family therapy, parent training, consultation, and classroom intervention.

Specialized Clinical Practica in Child, Parent, and Family Therapy. Clinical practica should be designed to complement the didactic courses in assessment/diagnosis and treatment/intervention. They should provide a variety of clinical problems and a broad spectrum of client demographic characteristics. This practicum experience would be in addition to a child and adult practicum. The practica could be conducted in a number of different settings such as schools, child inpatient units, psychological services centers and child guidance clinics, residential treatment centers, community mental health centers, pediatric/medical hospitals, and office practices. Close supervision by qualified specialty psychologists must be guaranteed in these settings. Additionally, interaction with professionals from a variety of disciplines should be encouraged (e.g., social work, psychiatry, education, pediatrics, etc.).

Research Methods in Child Psychology. In addition to a general understanding of research methodology, the student should become conversant with the various topics and techniques extant in psychology that are oriented toward child and family research. The assumption of a downward extension of adult techniques in research is not adequate. Individual case studies and group techniques should be covered with program and clinical evaluation procedures.

Ethics and Legal Issues Related to Children, Youth, and Families. Special attention should be given to the ethical and legal rights of children and youth as related to psychological activities in different domains (courts, therapy, schools). Sensitivity to protecting children's rights should be instilled in the student in such areas as child custody hearings, psychological testing, school placement, confidentiality in therapy, and informed consent/assent for treatment and research participation. Sensitivity to the rights of the family and society in these areas is also of importance.

Subspecialties within Psychology for Children, Youth, and Families. Given the diversity of child research and practice, subspecialty areas have emerged and more are likely to develop. Exposure is needed to professional subareas such as clinical child psychology, school psychology, pediatric psychology, applied developmental psychology, forensic child psychology, and child neuropsychology, for example. This exposure may come within courses devoted to the clinical phenomena of these subspecialties or as part of a course on professional issues and topics.

Additional Considerations of Training

Faculty and Students in Specialty. There should be a recognizable set of faculty and students in programs offering training for psychologists offering services to children, youth, and families. The faculty members should have a primary identity and responsibility for the area. Additional faculty may also have related interests to bolster the program. Area faculty should have relevant training and experiences in psychological research and practice for children, youth, and families. Particular attention should be given to guaranteeing optimal faculty models of professional functioning in this area of psychology. Students should be selected specifically for the specialty program. Students entering other areas should be allowed to transfer to the specialty training provided standards and quality of training are maintained. Too small a number of specialty students does not encourage development of identity or interaction conducive to skills acquisition. Too large a number may also interfere with these features, but is related to the number of available faculty. A coordinator of the specialty training should be responsible for ensuring the implementation of these guidelines.

Clinical or School Internship. Related to the predoctoral training standards at the university level is the necessary component of the intensive predoctoral training experience for those students. Attention should be given by the training program to the nature and quality of the training the specialty student receives on his or her internship. A child-oriented internship should be completed. Rotation to different child and family settings should maximally provide exposure and training. Additionally, where internships (e.g., a consortium) provide training through adult and child rotations, the student should avail him or herself of critical training opportunities, but in all likelihood would find it optimal to devote no less than two-thirds time to child-related work.

Letter of Specialization. The coordinator of the training area should provide a formal letter detailing how each student has completed the minimal requirements of training to provide psychological services to children, youth, and families.

Limitations on Psychologists Working with Children, Youth, and Families. A final critical consideration in defining training requirements as well as placing limits for psychologists providing specialty services derives from the American Psychological Association Ethical Standards. The Principle of Competence states: "Psychologists recognize the boundaries of their competence . . ." (p. 2). In addition, for those choosing to practice professional psychology in the area of children, youth, and families, the Standard for Providers of Psychological Services 1.6 similarly applies: "Psychologists shall limit their practice to their demonstrated areas of professional competence." Since competence is directly linked to training for that competence, the Guidelines for Training outlined here provide guidance in defining necessary training to provide competent psychological services to children, youth, and families.

Examples of Existing Training Programs Fulfilling the Training Recommendations

This section describes three existing training programs that fulfill the training recommendations for psychologists working with children, youth, and families. These doctoral-level, university-based programs offer training in clinical child psychology, applied developmental psychology, and school psychology. (These areas were selected for illustration; other specialty training areas might also be related.) Each program described here takes a different specific professional orientation, yet all three provide extensive and quality training for the psychologist working with children, youth, and families. These program descriptions demonstrate that the training recommendations can be fulfilled regardless of specialty orientation. These descriptions also illustrate the various combinations of coursework, practica, and experiences a training program can formulate, while still subscribing to the training recommendations outlined here. (The names of the particular programs presented here are withheld in fairness to other programs also found to fulfill the training recommendations, but for which space limitations do not allow description here.)

Clinical Child Psychology Training Program

Program A offers a Ph.D. in clinical psychology with a specialty concentration in clinical child psychology within an APA-approved clinical psychology training program. A core curriculum is required of all students in the clinical program with additional requirements placed on the specialty student in clinical child psychology. Requirements relevant to specific Training Recommendations:

Mental Retardation
Clinical Practicum (Basic: 2 semesters)
Psychological Assessment I & II (2 semesters)
Child Development, Psychopathology and Treatment I & II (2 semesters)
Advanced Child Practicum I & II (2 semesters)
Professional Specialty Seminar (4 semesters)

Specialty students also gain additional relevant experiences in a department-based Psychological Clinic, a residential and day-treatment center for children, an early childhood day care center, and a treatment program for child abusing parents. The training recommendations are fulfilled in the following way.

Child Development and Lifespan Developmental Psychology. Normal lifespan development is covered in one-half of the first semester in a two semester sequence of Child Development, Psychopathology and Treatment, required of all specialty students.

Psychopathology: Child and Adult. This topic is covered in the equivalent of one semester across the two-semester sequence required of all specialty students in Child Development, Psychopathology and Treatment.

Mental Retardation and Developmental Disabilities. This topic is covered in a one semester course required of all clinical students, including clinical child specialties.

Specialized Child Assessment Techniques. Child assessment is covered in several courses and practica:

1. Intellectual, personality, and educational testing for children is taught in the basic psychological assessment courses (2 semesters) required of all clinical students in the first year (including specialty students).
2. Specialized child techniques are taught in the Professional Specialty Seminar on a continuing basis (4 semesters are required of all specialty students) and in the Advanced Child Practicum (2 semesters required of specialty students).

Child Psychotherapy and Behavior Change. Didactic and applied clinical work is covered in several courses and practica provided in the general core curriculum and specialty concentration.

1. Coursework includes a Modification of Behavior course required of all clinical students, the Child Development, Psychopathology and Treatment sequence (2 semesters) required of specialty students, and the continuing Professional Specialty Seminar.
2. Two semesters of basic clinical practicum (I & II) required of all clinical students involve treatment of child and family problems using different modalities.
3. Two semesters of Advanced Child Practicum are required of all specialty students in addition to #2.
4. Clinical child specialty students are typically placed in a 12-month paid position at a residential and day-treatment center for children run by the university as a training facility. Position involves therapy, case management, and consultation to teachers, counselors, and social workers.

Parent, Family, and School Intervention Techniques. Specialty students gain experience with intervention with parents and families through Basic Practicum (2 semesters), Advanced Child Practicum (2 semesters), and the residential treatment center positions. Didactic courses which cover this topic include the Child Development, Psychopathology, and Treatment sequence (2 semesters) and the Professional Specialty Seminar.

Specialized Clinical Practica in Child, Parent, and Family Therapy. The Advanced Child Practicum (2 semesters required of all specialty students) is set in a family practice medical center (a branch of the university's medical school). The students also observe and consult with private pediatricians. Specialty faculty supervise this experience on a rotating semester basis. Additional clinical experiences are available in the department's psychological clinic and the community mental health center.

Research Methods in Child Psychology. A course in basic research methodology is required of all clinical students, including specialty students. An optional one-semester course is available in experimental child psychology. The Professional Specialty Seminar contains a "research journal club" (once a month) for review of relevant articles and topics. A master's thesis and doctoral dissertation are required of the specialty student with encouragement to do the projects on a child-related topic.

Ethics and Legal Issues Related to Children and Families. Ethical issues regarding research are covered in the basic research methods class; issues regarding therapy are covered in a course on Principles of Psychotherapy, and in the Basic Clinical Practicum. All three courses are required of all clinical students regardless of specialty. An optional course on psychological ethics is regularly available, but not required. This topic is also covered more specifically to children and families in the Professional Specialty Seminar and the Advanced Child Practicum.

Subspecialties within Psychology for Children, Youth, and Families. Exposure to and discussion of various subspecialties in addition to the clinical child specialty training is primarily handled through the Professional Specialty Seminar. Recent topics include discussion of the roles of the pediatric psychologist, the diagnostic techniques of child neuropsychology, and the child psychologist in the courtroom for child custody decisions.

Applied Developmental Psychology Training Program

Program B is an applied developmental training program housed in the developmental area of a department of psychology. Both applied and theoretical training is provided the specialty student through required and elective courses. Required courses and experience include:

Human Development
Family Interaction
Lifespan Studies
Psychotherapy
Research Methodology in Developmental Psychology
Child Psychological Assessment (2 courses)
Clinical Practicum (2 years)
Child Psychopathology (2 courses)
Professional Issues and Problems
Psychopathology

The following describes how the Training Recommendations are fulfilled.

Child Development and Lifespan Developmental Psychology. This topic is covered in a required one-quarter course in Human Development in the first year of training and a later required seminar in Lifespan Studies. Optional courses are available on various life stages including infancy, childhood, and adolescence.

Psychopathology: Child and Adult. Two courses on Child Psychopathology are required of the specialty student as is Psychopathology (Adult).

Mental Retardation and Developmental Disabilities. This topic is covered in the courses on Child Psychopathology required of all specialty students. Additionally, an independent course on this topic is available, but not required.

Specialized Child Assessment Techniques. Two semesters are required on basic child and family assessment in the first year through the course on Child Assessment. Specialized techniques are acquired in the second year of Clinical Practicum.

Child Psychotherapy and Behavior Change. The student gains experience in therapeutic interventions in two ways:

1. A required didactic course covers child psychotherapy, in particular (one quarter).

2. The second year of a required two years of child practicum involves psychotherapy and consultation.

Parent, Family, and School Intervention Techniques. The second year of Clinical Practicum required of specialty students involves direct intervention with families. Additionally, didactic material is gained through a required course in Family Interaction and a specialized seminar in Psychopathological Families.

Specialized Clinical Practica in Child, Parent, and Family Therapy. The second year of the required two-year clinical sequence involves specialized work with children and families through therapy and consultation.

Research Methods in Child Psychology. Research methodology is covered in two courses required of the specialty students: Research with Normal Children and Research with Psychopathological Populations.

Ethics and Legal Issues Related to Children and Families. A required course on Professional Issues and Problems covers this topic.

Subspecialties within Psychology for Children, Youth, and Families. The Professional Issues and Problems course exposes the student to various allied child-oriented subspecialties in addition to the Developmental and Applied Developmental focus. Students interact with a variety of disciplines in a children's hospital, a psychological clinic, and a mental retardation center.

School Psychology Training Program

Program C offers an Ed.D. in school psychology through the department of educational psychology in the college of education. Specialty students are required to take a set sequence of courses with additional electives. Specialty courses include:

Child Psychology
Seminar in Developmental Psychology
Consultation in the Helping Professions
Seminar-Practicum in School Psychology (2 semesters)
Marital and Family Systems
Marital and Family Therapy

The topics outlined in the training recommendations are handled in the following way.

Child Development and Lifespan Developmental Psychology. Specialty students are required to take a one-semester course in Child Psychology ranging from the prenatal period through adolescence. A required advanced Seminar in Developmental Psychology covers human development across the lifespan.

Psychopathology: Child and Adult. A joint seminar-practicum sequence for two semesters is required of all specialty students and covers developmental deviations and child psychopathology.

Mental Retardation and Developmental Disabilities. A course is available to students covering this topic, but it is not required. Aspects are covered in a section of the Seminar Practicum in School Psychology. Applied field work in special education frequently involves this topic.

Specialized Child Assessment Techniques. The joint Seminar-Practicum requires students to undertake diagnostic procedures in a range of techniques and for differing areas of child and family functioning.

Child Psychotherapy and Behavior Change. This topic is covered didactically and clinically in the joint Seminar-Practicum (2 semesters) and in field placements (1 day a week) in a school system with practicing school psychologists and classroom teachers.

Parent, Family, and School Intervention Techniques. Two didactic courses are required on Marital and Family Systems and Marital and Family Therapy. These cover different theories and interventions as well as allow applied experiences in parent and family therapy through school system referrals.

Specialized Clinical Practica in Child, Parent, and Family Therapy. Clinical experience is gained in two ways with supervision by university faculty and qualified field placement supervisors.

1. The joint Seminar-Practicum requires clinical work of the student as child therapist and consultant for interventions with schools. This field work typically takes place within a school system or a child abuse intervention center.

2. Two courses in Marital and Family Systems/Therapy contain experiential components.

Research Methods in Child Psychology. This topic is covered primarily in the advanced Seminar in Developmental Psychology required of all specialty students.

Ethics and Legal Issues Related to Children and Families. The joint Seminar-Practicum sequence covers ethical standards and the interaction of law and professional psychology with special consideration given to children's rights. Ethical issues in consultation are also discussed in a seminar on consultation in the Helping Professions.

Subspecialties within Psychology for Children, Youth, and Families. The seminar-practicum provides some exposure to subspecialties as alternative roles in areas such as forensic practice and clinical child psychology in addition to the program's training in school psychology.

Appendix F

Recommendations: Conference on Training Clinical Child Psychologists

Academic Training

1. We recommend that *all* APA approved programs providing professional training in clinical psychology *require* a course on the developmental bases of normal behavior (emphasizing a life-span developmental approach).

2. It is desirable that all APA approved programs providing professional training in clinical psychology include experiences with "normal" children and youth, as well as with other age groups, in diverse, "normal" settings as a part of every student's graduate level training.

3. We encourage that training sufficient to provide minimal competencies in assessment, psychopathology, and intervention (e.g., treatment, consultation, prevention) with children, youth and families be included at the graduate level in all clinical training programs. Such training experiences should occur on both a didactic and a practicum level.

4. Similarly, we encourage that training, sufficient to provide minimal competencies in assessment, psychopathology, and intervention (e.g., treatment, consultation, prevention) with adults be included at the graduate level in all programs training clinical child psychologists. Such training experiences should occur on both a didactic and practicum level.

5. We encourage that a knowledge base and experience with children from different minority backgrounds be provided at graduate and internship levels by all programs training psychologists in the clinical child area.

6. We recommend that APA site visitor teams reviewing programs that claim to train clinical child psychologists ensure that a member of the visiting team has expertise in clinical child psychology.

7. We recommend that graduate programs offering training in the clinical child area foster an appreciation of the broad and diverse contexts within which children develop and within which psychologists working with children, youth, and families must function (e.g., family, school, etc.).

8. We recommend that every graduate program providing training in clinical child psychology have at least one clinical child faculty member.

9. We endorse the Division 37 Task Force document (*Guidelines for Training Psychologists to Work With Children, Youth, and Families,* Roberts, Erickson, & Tuma, 1985), as guiding principles for those implementing training programs in clinical child psychology. We further recommend that these guidelines be used flexibly, and not in a restrictive manner.

10. We endorse the Boulder Scientist-Practitioner Model as the model for training in clinical child psychology.

Internship Level Training

11. We reaffirm the Accreditation Guidelines presented in the APA *Monitor* (American Psychological Association, 1979), especially as it intends to increase collaboration to accomplish integration of the internship within the total doctoral training experience:

VII.B.2c.
Close working relationships should be established between the internship program and the graduate program in professional psychology in order to facilitate advisement of students and matching of internship site characteristics with intern talents and interests. Doctoral programs and internship centers have a responsibility for mutual communication concerning evaluation of students' preparation for field experience, their progress in the field program, and their evaluation of the field experience. Specific procedures should be established for such communication; mutual visits are strongly encouraged. (p.16)

12. The graduate program and internship site will engage in sufficient communication so that an individualized plan for each intern can be written by the internship site upon acceptance of the intern. This plan will be reviewed periodically with continued communication with the graduate program.

13. Internships that call themselves child oriented should have a minimum of two-thirds of the training experience in child-related activity.

14. We recognize that the nature of each internship program is partially determined by the nature of the facility, the staff, the particular populations served, and the funding patterns of supporting agencies. Consequently, each internship program will be unique in certain aspects and guidelines will need to be flexible.

Internship programs in clinical child psychology should be broad based with regard to populations served, theoretical orientation, and experiences provided. In addition to the need for experiences with adults, the clinical child psychology intern should receive experiences with children from as broad an age range as possible with experiences with infants through adolescents being the goal.

Diversity in gender, in SES background, in ethnic origin, and in presenting problems of served clients is a desired goal. An understanding of the nature of the problem presented by the child must take into account the developmental level of the child.

15. It was encouraged that research be incorporated into the internship program, both by allowing time and providing role models.

16. Internship training in clinical child psychology should include didactic and supervised training at least in assessment, intervention strategies, case management, and consultation skills. In addition, training and experience in prevention are highly desirable. The nature of the didactic training and supervised experiences in each of these areas should be as broad based and varied as possible. Case management conferences should be utilized to integrate assessment, treatment, and consultation, with ethical considerations and an increased awareness of the need for evaluating the success of our chosen interventions also being considered.

17. It is recommended that Section 1 create a standing committee on internship training with the purpose of rounding out

the recommendations made at the conference. Section 1 should also expand upon these recommendations.

Note: The general thrust of this motion seemed to be that it is desirable that a document similar to the Division 37 report be developed. This document should focus specifically on guidelines for internship training.

Postdoctoral/Continuing Education

18. Whereas preparation backgrounds for people functioning as child psychologists range widely, and whereas knowledge of significant relevance to clinical child psychologists continues to burgeon, we recommend that continuing education be considered an ethical responsibility of all clinical child psychologists. In particular, assessment, intervention, consultation, and prevention are areas needing ongoing professional renewal.

19. We recommend that Section 1 form a task force to establish and publish criteria for continuing education offerings in areas relevant to clinical child psychology.

20. With Section 2, we recommend that Section 1 establish a task force to conduct a survey of current postgraduate programming in clinical child psychology and to establish guidelines for postdoctoral programming. These guidelines should include specification of levels and types of supervision.

21. We recommend that the Section 1 Executive Committee attempt to gain representation on appropriate goverance structures of APA, including the Education and Training Committee of APA, and subcommittees dealing with continuing education.

References

American Psychological Association. (1979). Criteria for accreditation of doctoral training programs in psychology. *APA Monitor, 10,* 16.

Roberts, M.C., Erickson, M.T., & Tuma, J.M. (1985). Addressing the needs: Guidelines for training psychologists to work with children, youth, and families. *Journal of Clinical Child Psychology, 14,* 70-79 (see Appendix E).